MAJOR GEN. SIR E. W. C. CHAYTOR, K.C.M.G., K.C.V.O., C.B., A.D.C.

The New Zealanders
in
Sinai and Palestine

BY

LIEUT.-COLONEL C. GUY POWLES, C.M.G., D.S.O.

Brigade Major N.Z.M.R. Brigade 1914-1916
A.A. & Q.M.G Anzac Mounted Division 1916-1918

From material compiled by
MAJOR A. WILKIE, W.M.R.

1922

This book is dedicated in all humility by one of those who "came through" to the memory of our Glorious Dead. It was they who made the name of the Brigade to be feared by the enemy; and to be honoured above all others by those with whom it went into battle; and to be loved by all those friends at home and in the many countries through which it journeyed and in which it fought. And it was they who by their supreme sacrifice bestowed an inspiration upon their comrades, both those with whom they served and those who came after.

> *These laid the world away; poured out the red*
> *Sweet wine of youth; gave up the years to be*
> *Of work and joy, and that unhoped serene,*
> *That men call age; and those who would have been*
> *Their sons, they gave, their immortality.*
>   —*Rupert Brooke.*

INDEX.

	PAGE
Introduction by General Sir John Maxwell	vii.
Introduction by General Sir Archibald Murray	xii.
Introductioin by General Sir Edmund Allenby	xiii.
Introduction by Lieut.-General Sir Harry Chauvel	xv.

I. How the Brigade returned to their horses after Gallipoli 1
   How the Brigade marched through the Land of Goshen 6
   Formation of the Anzac Mounted Division 12
II. How the Brigade took the Way of the Land of the Philistines 14
   The Battle of Romani 26
III. The Advance through the Desert 42
   The Capture of El Arish 49
   The Battle of Magdhaba 50
   The Battle of Rafa 65
IV. How the Brigade entered Palestine and went up against Gaza 82
   The First Battle of Gaza 84
   The Second Battle of Gaza 97
   The Occupation of the Line of the Wadi Ghuzzeh .. 106
   The destruction of the Turkish railway at Asluj 110
   The Shellel Mosaic 114
V. How the Turkish line was broken at Beersheba 128
   How the Brigade rode through to Jaffa 142
   The Action of Ayun Kara 145
   The Occupation of Jaffa 155
VI. The Capture of Jerusalem 160
   The Action at the River Auja 161
   The Action at Khirbet Hadrah 162
   How the Brigade went down to Jericho 172
VII. How the Brigade crossed the Jordan and entered Moab 190
   The crossing of the Jordan 194
   The Attack upon Amman 197
VIII. Down by Jericho 216
   The King's Birthday Parade at Bethlehem 225
   The Action at Abu Tellul 231
   Formation of Chaytor's Force 236
IX. How the Brigade crossed the Jordan for the last time. .. 238
   The Advance of the N.Z.M.R. Brigade for the Final Operations 245
   The Capture of Amman 250
   The Surrender of the remnants of the Turkish IV. Army 253
   Antimalarial Work 258
X. The Return to the Plains 263
   The Departure of the C.M.R. to Gallipoli 263
   The March to Rafa 267
   The Return to Egypt 268
   Patrolling—The Delta 269
   Aotea Home 273
Appendices:
   Abbreviations 277
   Glossary 277
   Commanding Officers 278
   A Brigade Diary 282
   Notes 284

REFERENCE
TO CONVENTIONAL SIGNS

Railways	—+—+—+—+—
Main Roads	
Other Roads	
Good Tracks	
Telegraph Lines	
Jewish Colonies	✡
Heights in feet above Sea Level	5020
„ „ „ below „ „	-1254

BRITISH

Infantry	Division	7
	Brigade	161
Cavalry		
Arab Army		
Army H.Q.		
Corps H.Q.		XX
Arab Army H.Q.		
Divisional H.Q.		60
Patrols, Cav. & Inf.		
Heavy or Siege Artillery		
Armoured Car		
Motor Transport Columns		

AERIAL

Aerodrome and Advanced Landing Ground	
Areas bombed	

TURKISH

Infantry	Division	53
	Regiment	72
German Infantry		
Cavalry		
Army H.Q.		VII
Corps H.Q.		II
Divisional H.Q.		26
Heavy Artillery		
Disorganised retreating Columns		
Motor Transport Columns		
Horse Transport Columns		
Lines of Retreat		

AERIAL

Aerodrome	
Areas bombed	

FORMATIONS ARE SHOWN THUS:

Concentrated

in Line

in Column of Route

Front Line 18-9-18 — — — —

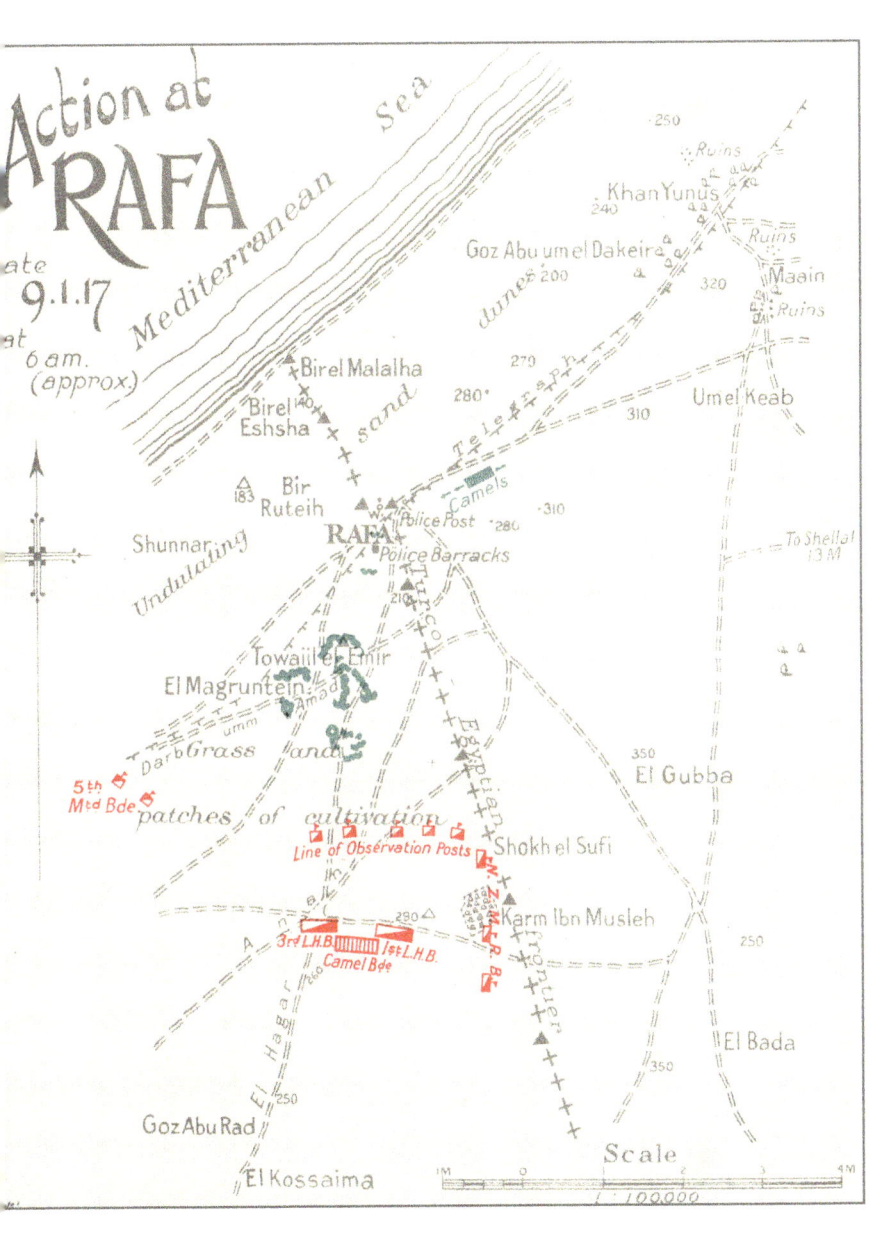

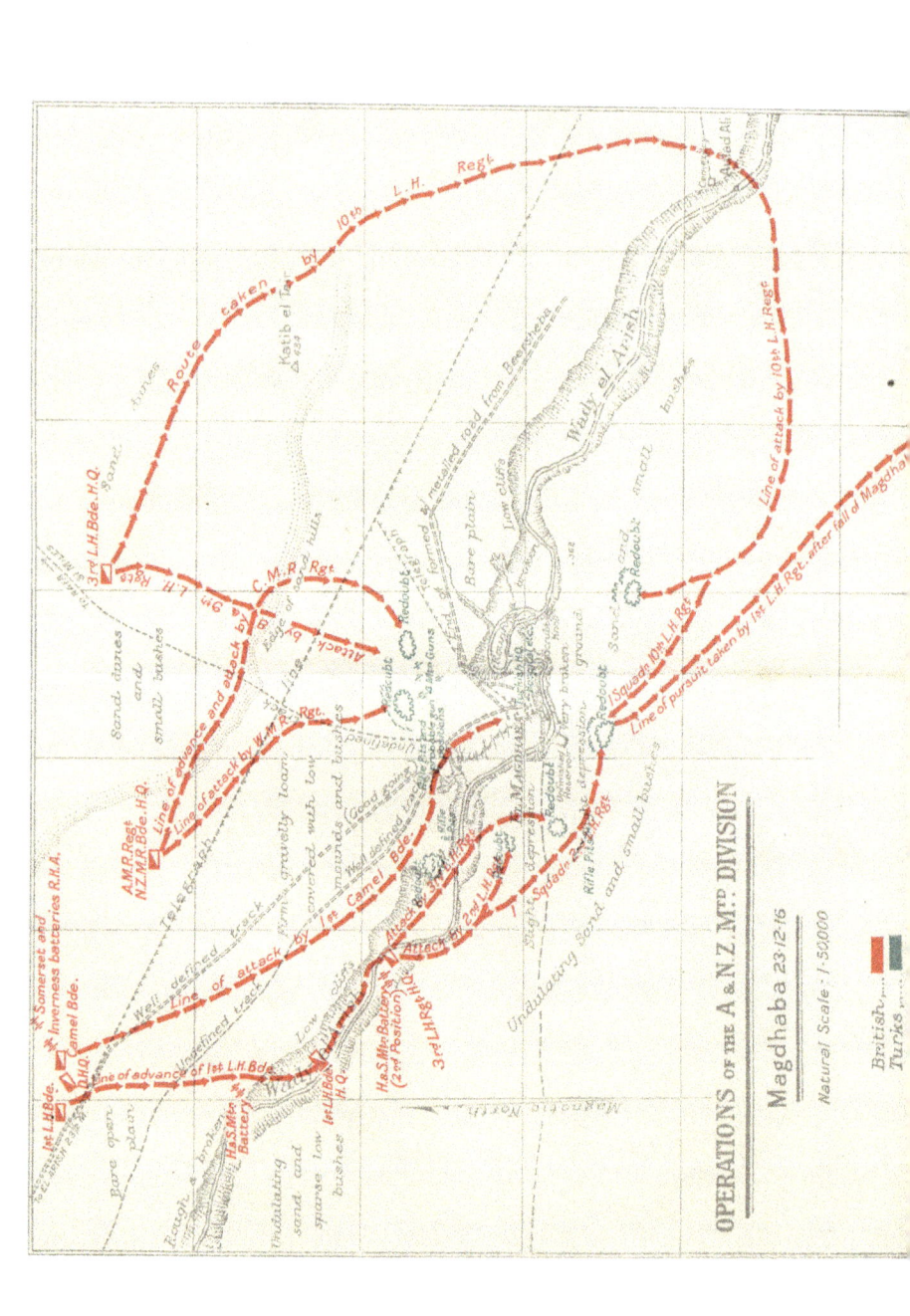

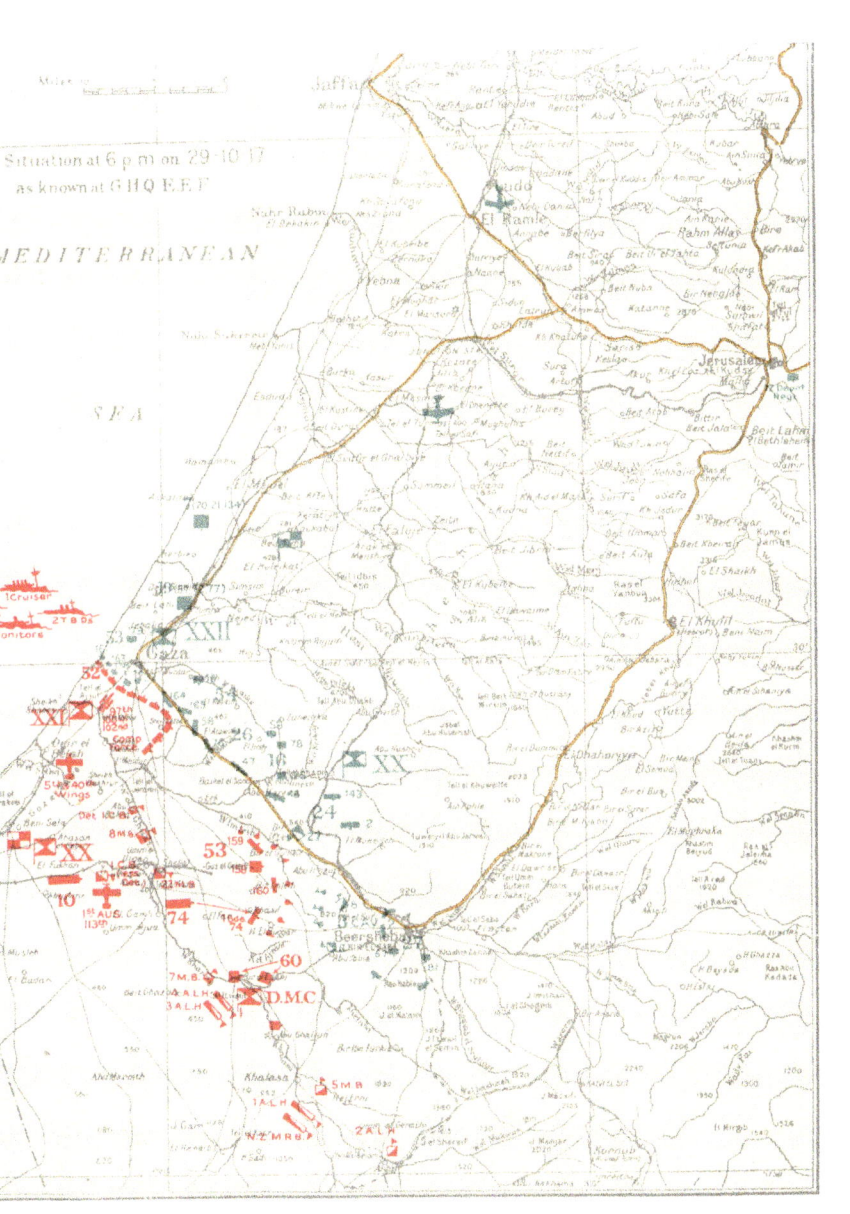

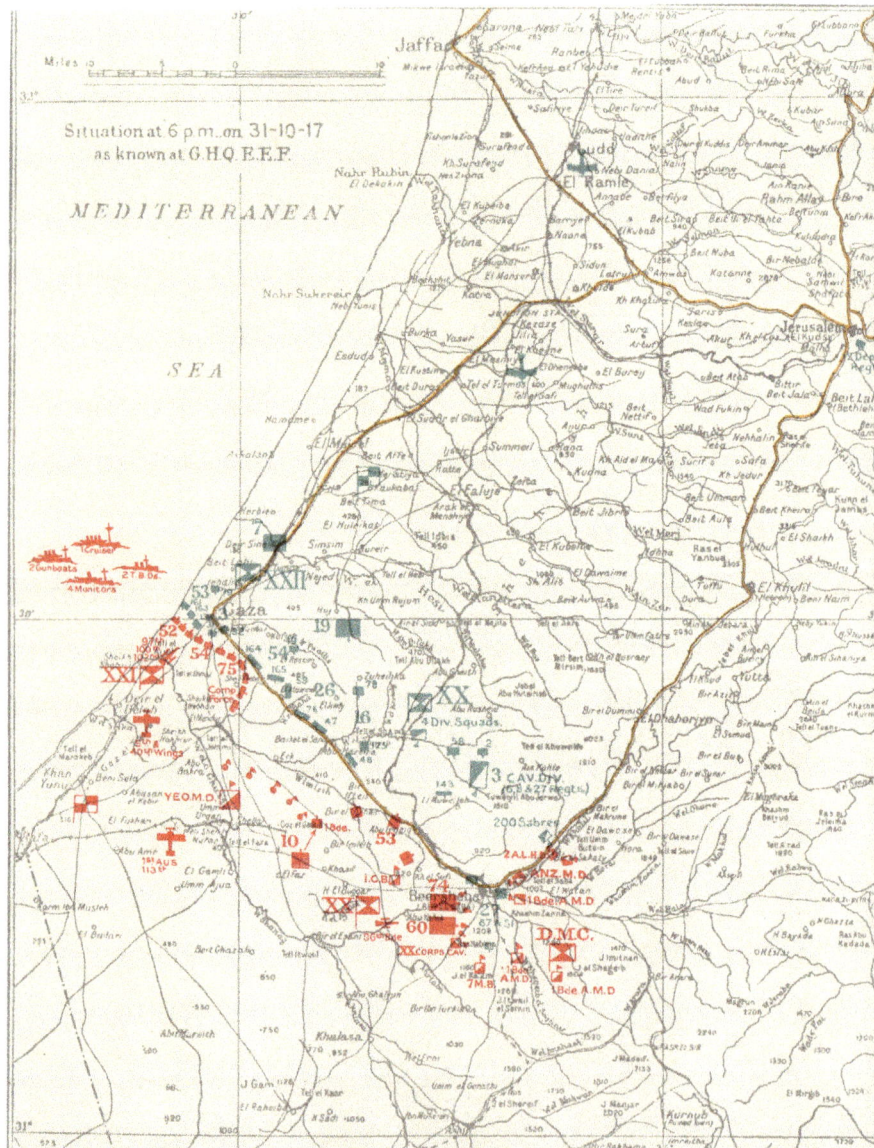

ADVANCE THROUGH PHILISTIA.

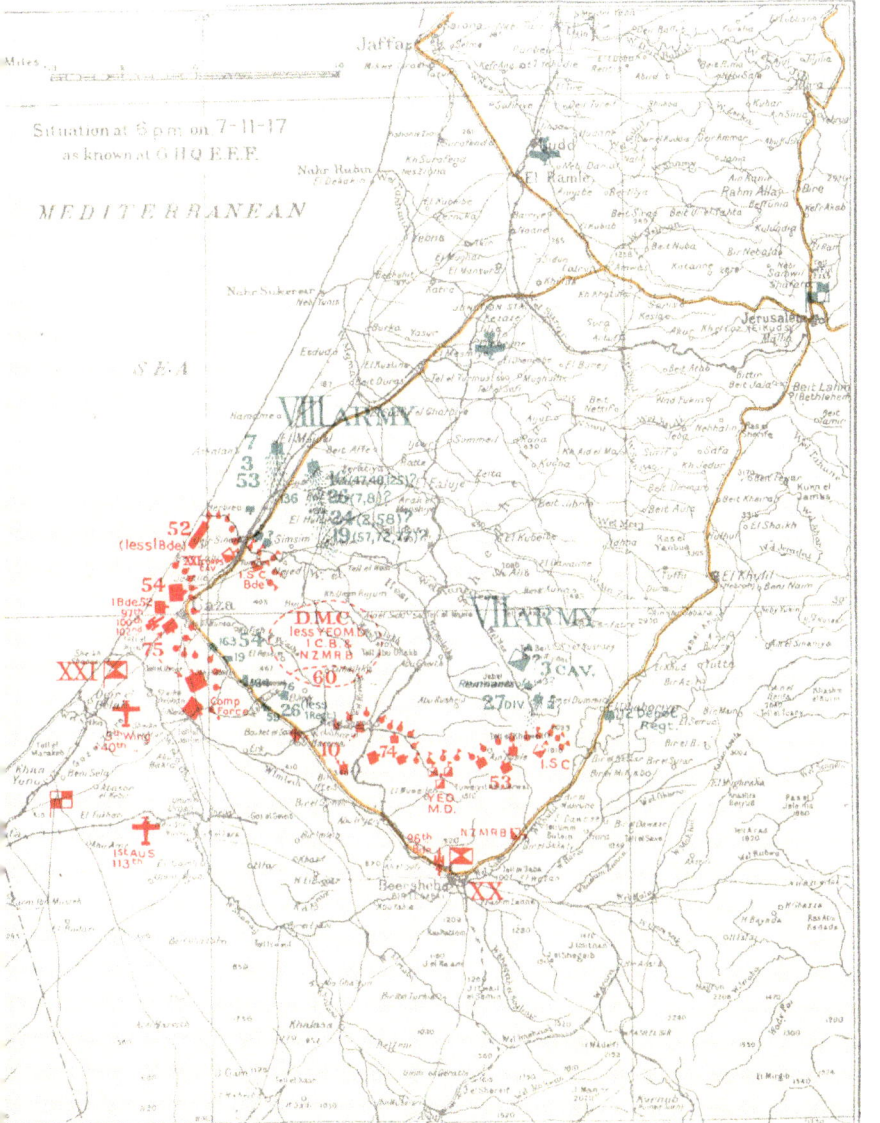

ADVANCE THROUGH PHILISTIA.

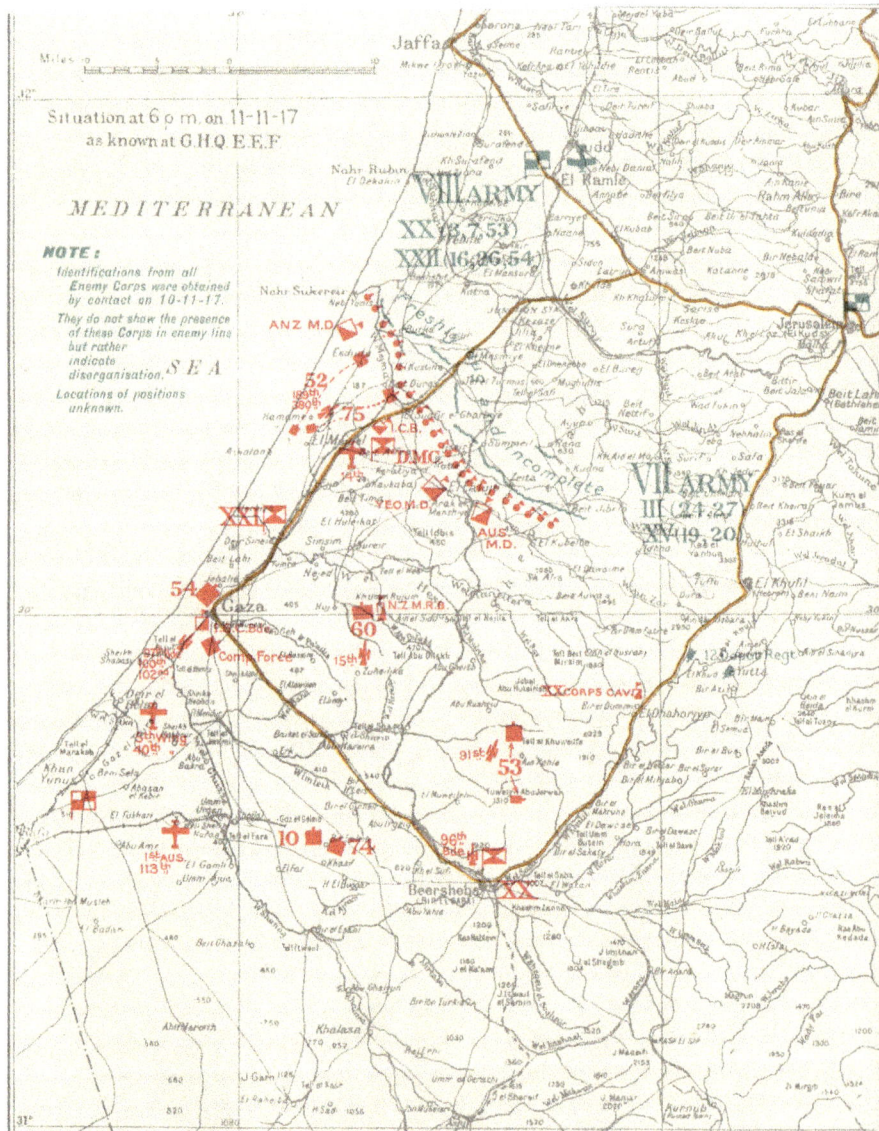

ADVANCE THROUGH PHILISTIA.

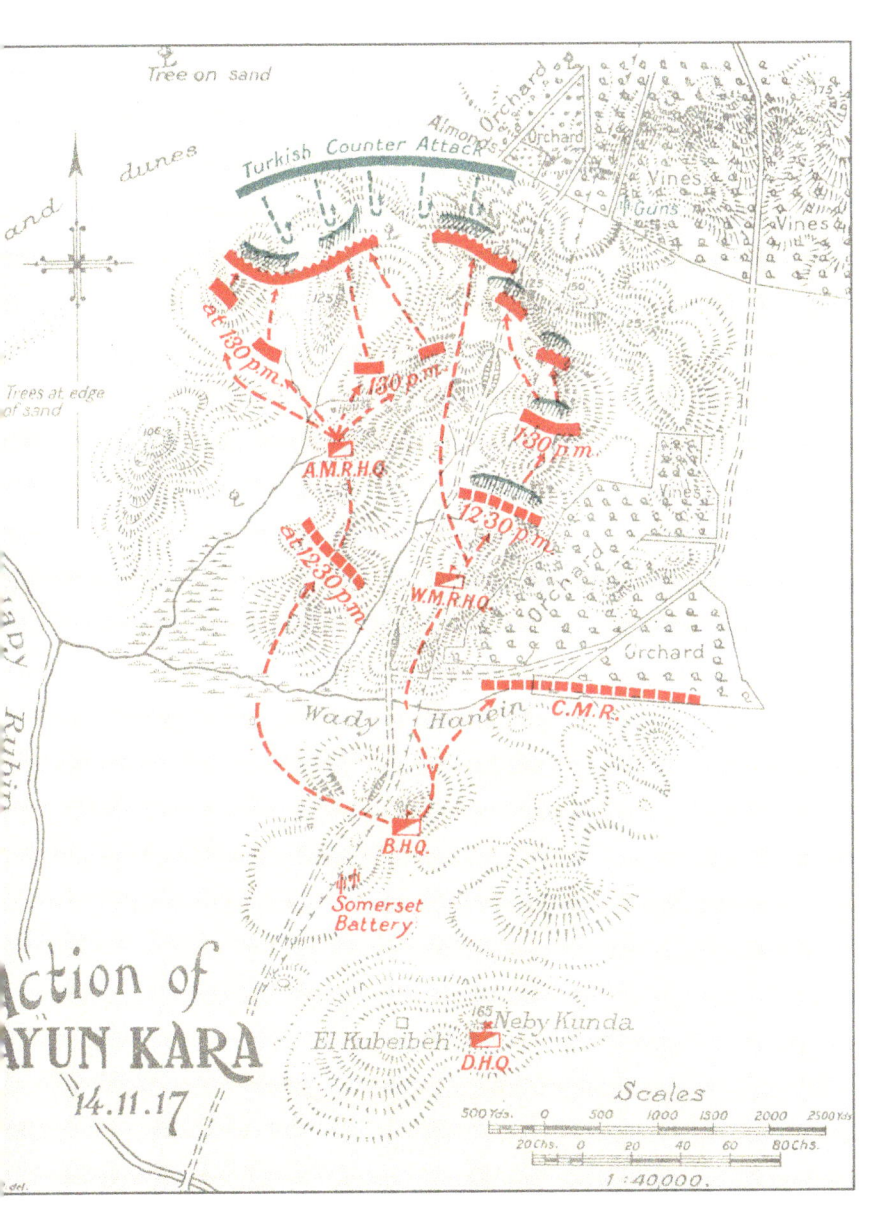

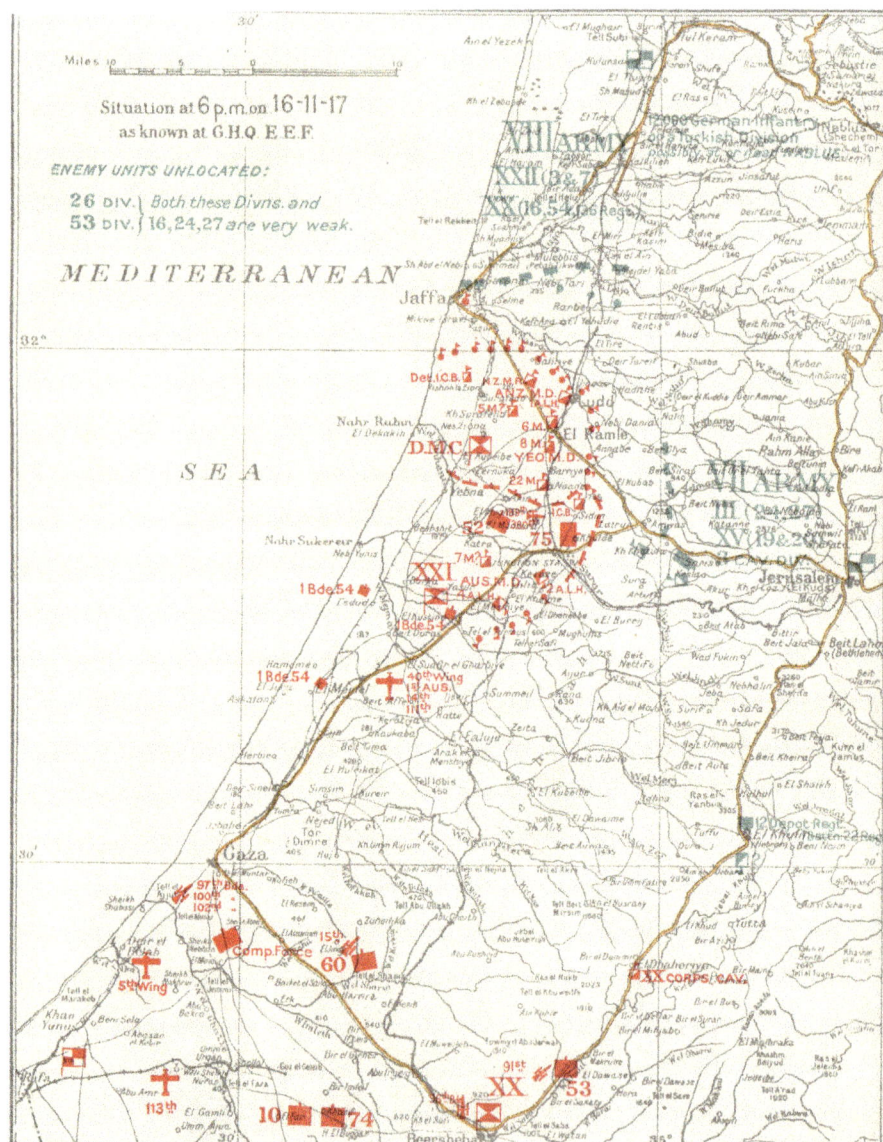

ADVANCE INTO JUDÆA.

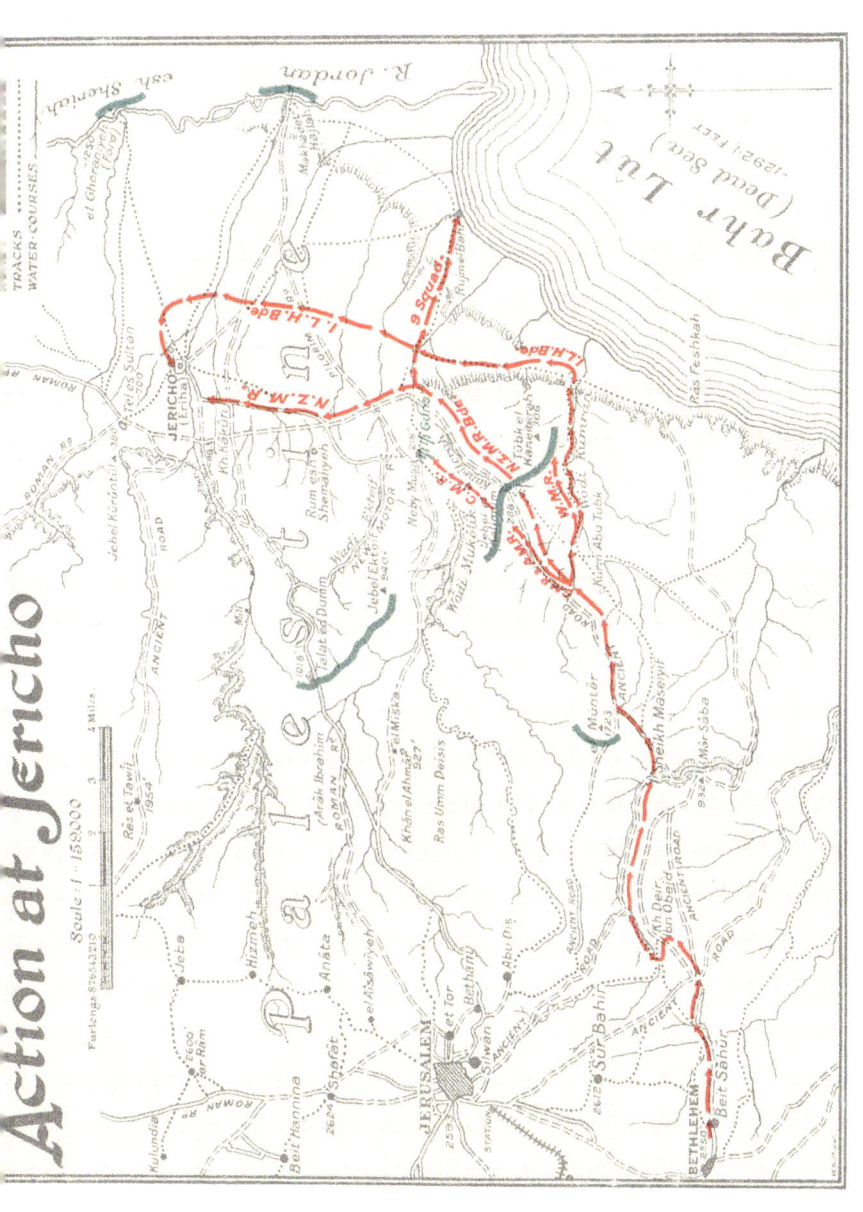

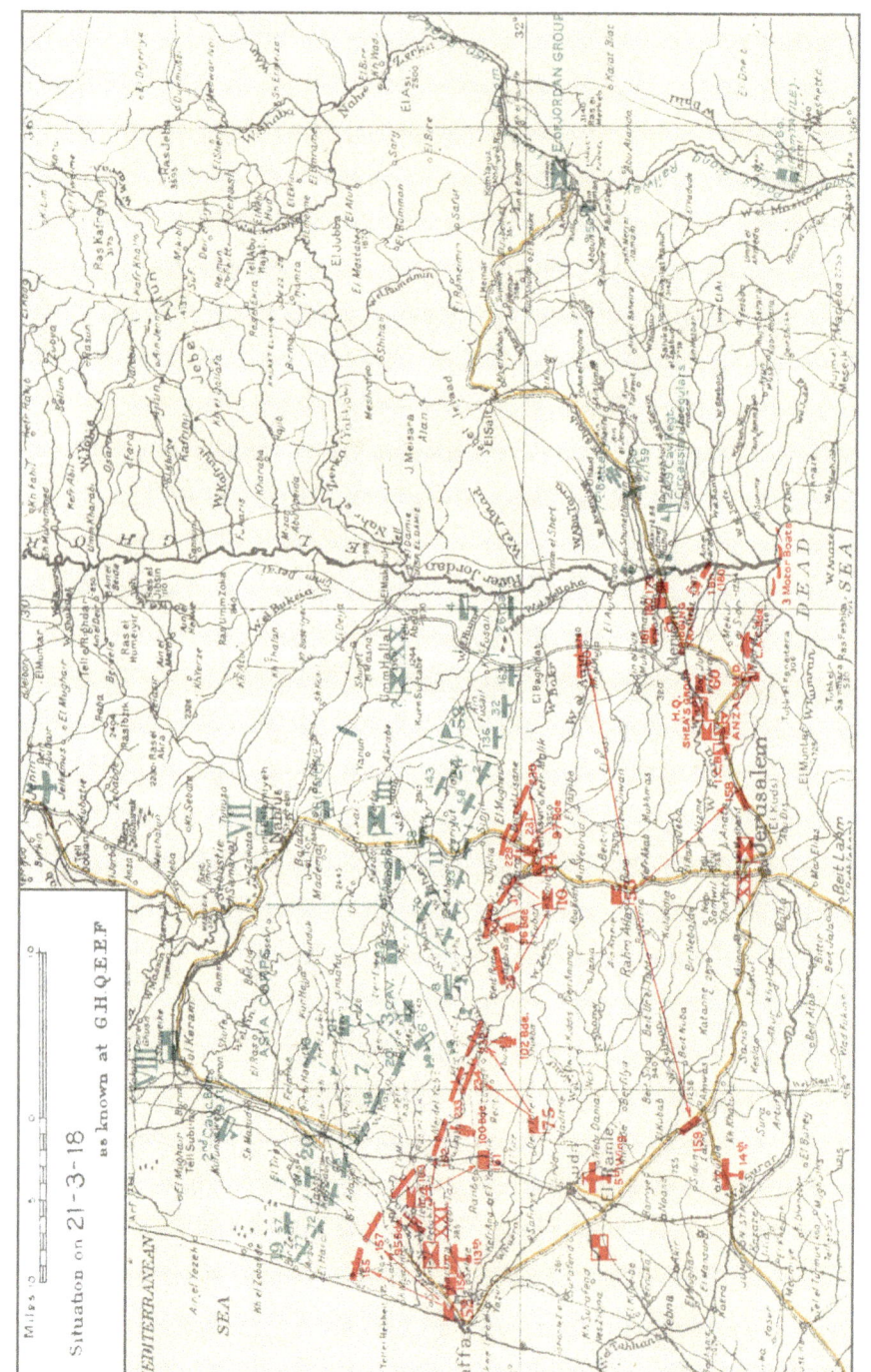

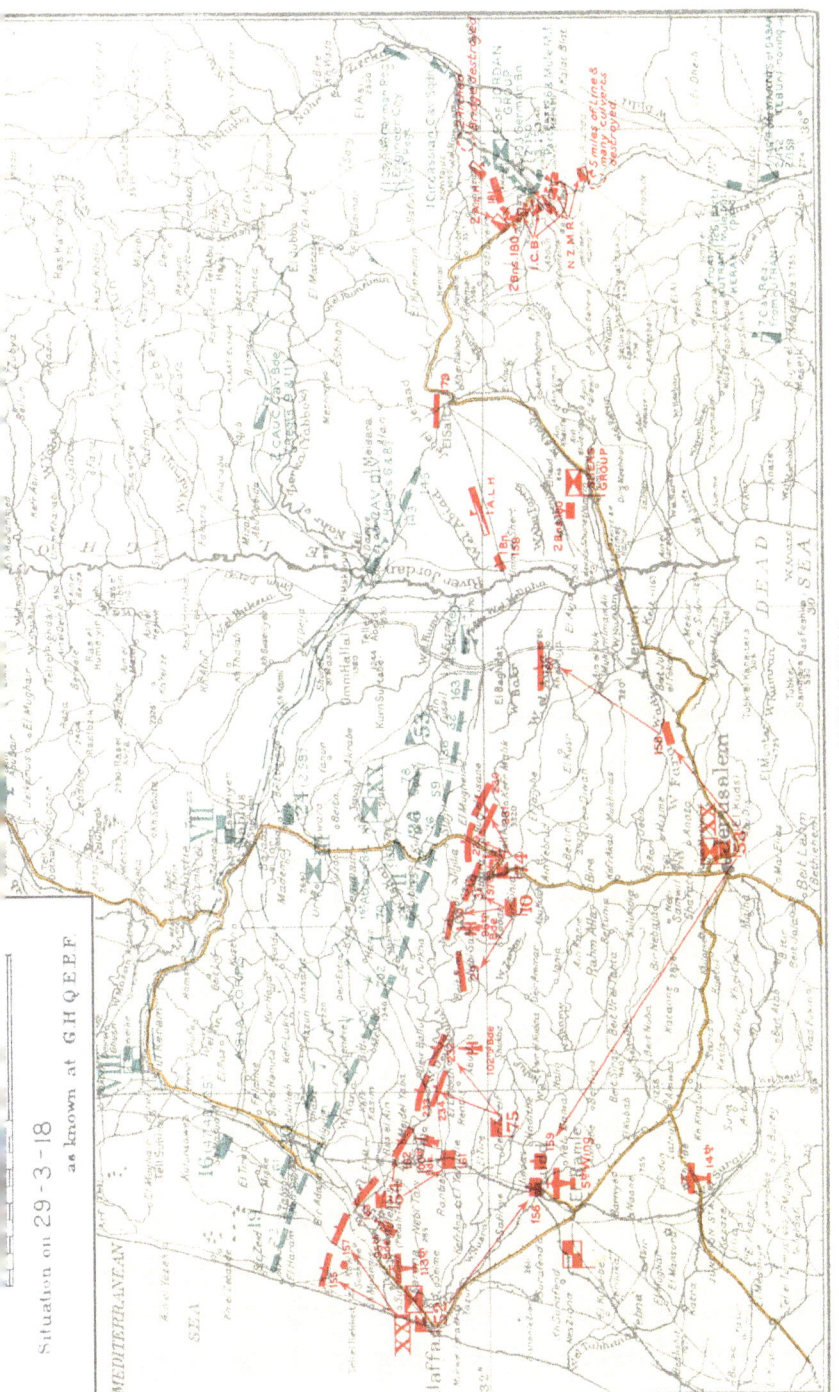

AMMAN RAID.

Situation on 29-3-18 as known at G H Q E.E.F.

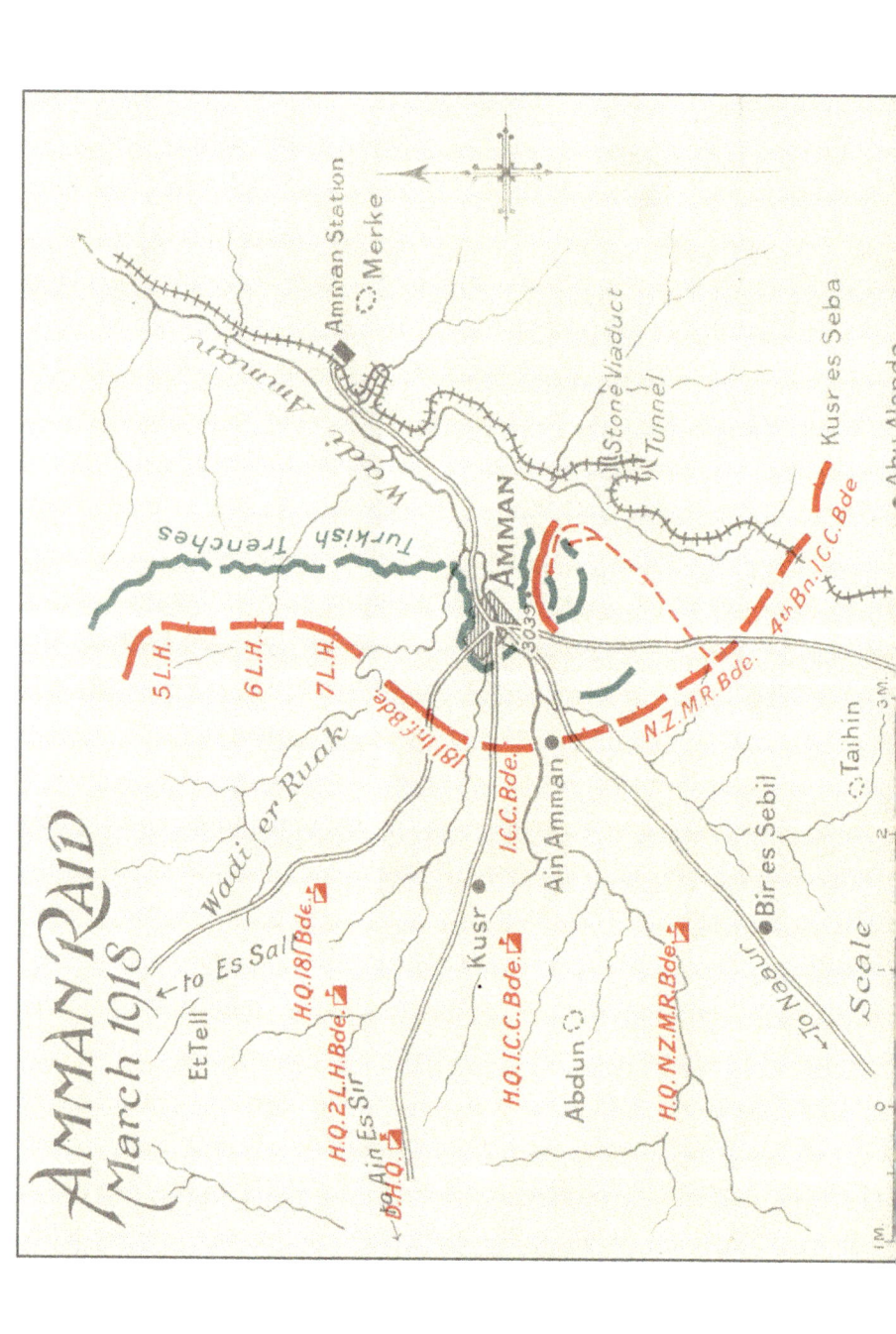

THE FINAL BREAK THROUGH

Situation at 10pm on 18/9/18 as known at GHQ.E.E.F.

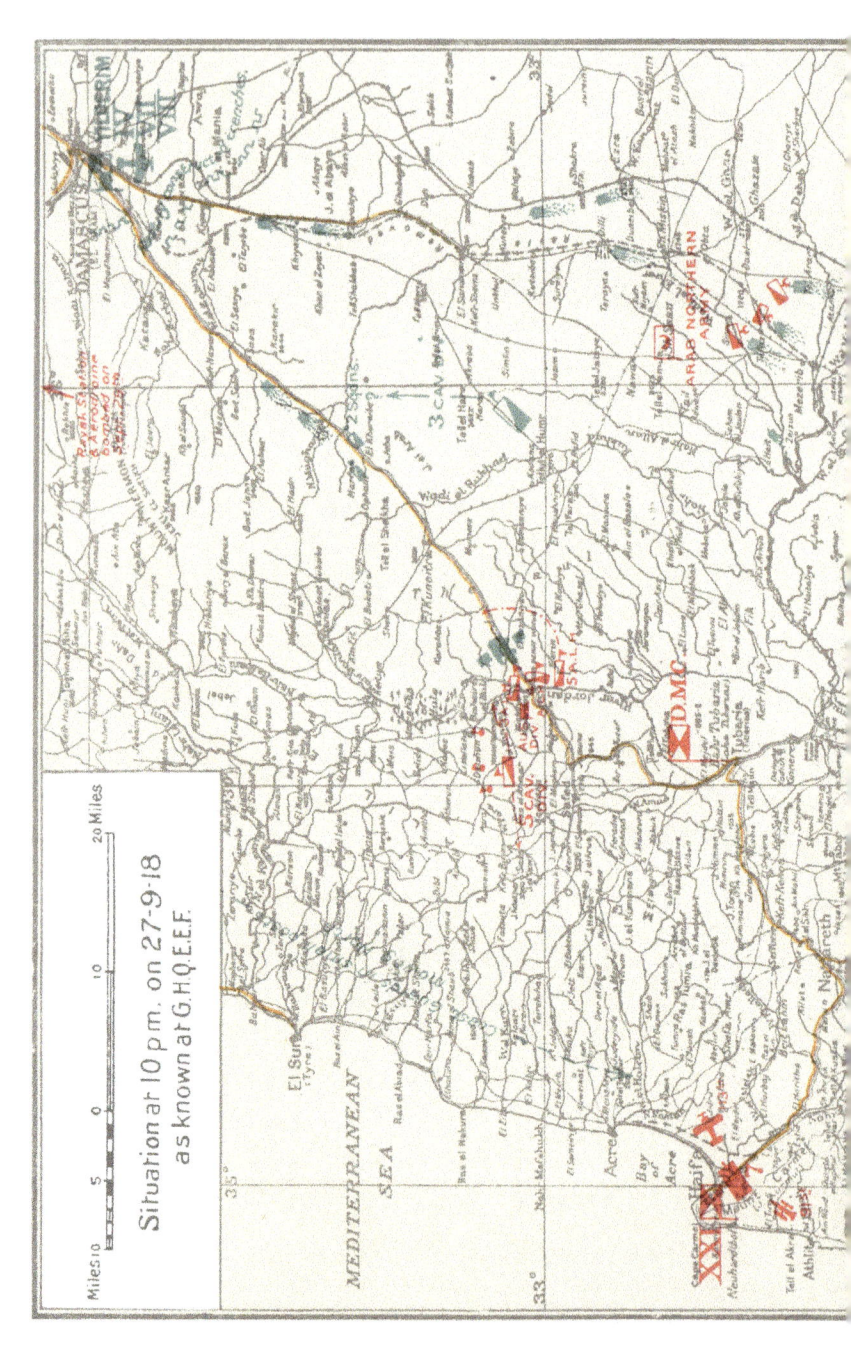

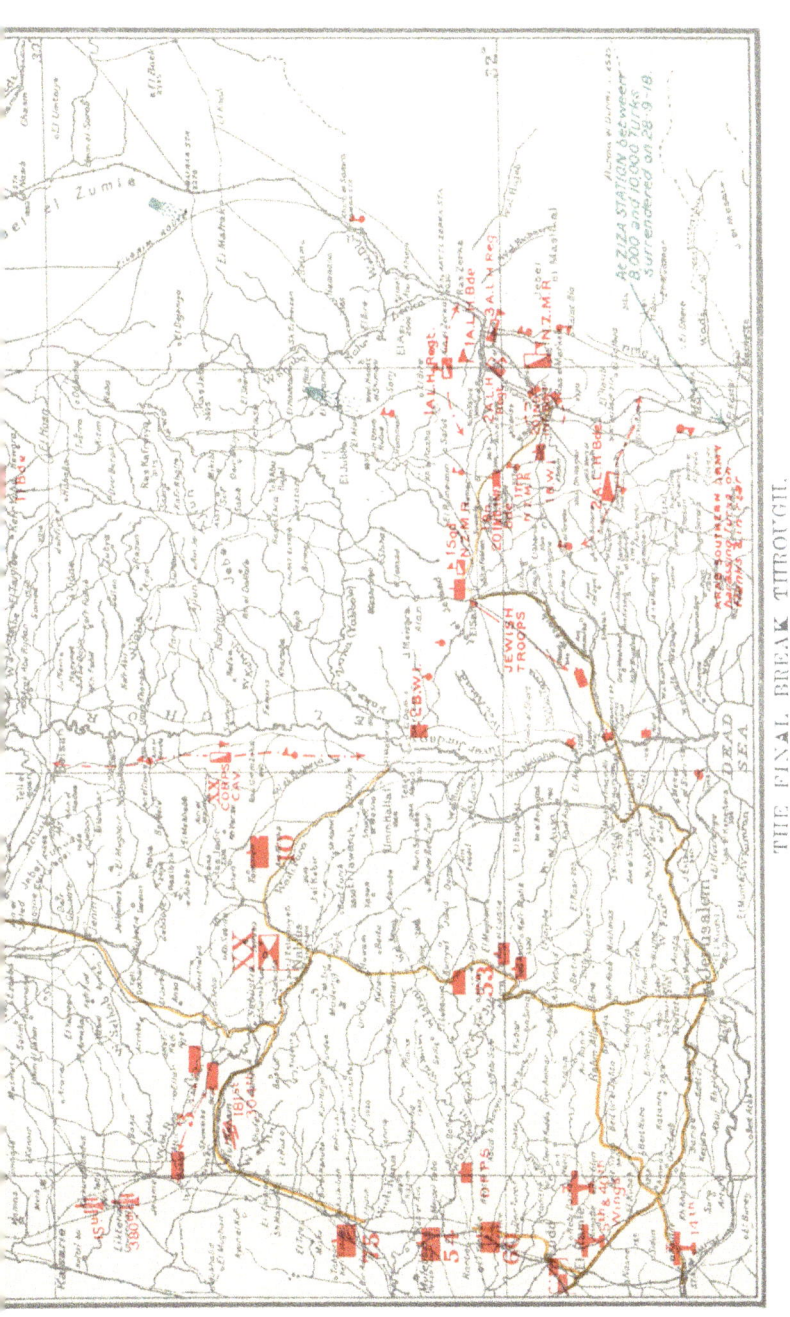

THE FINAL BREAK THROUGH.

Introduction by General Sir John G. Maxwell, G.C.B., K.C.M.G., C.V.O., D.S.O.

The Government of New Zealand having done me the honour of inviting me to write a Foreword to the volume "New Zealanders in Palestine" of the history of New Zealand's share in the Great War, I gladly comply for two reasons: first, an opportunity is given me to record my testimony to, and admiration of, the splendid qualities of the New Zealand Contingent; second, the pleasure with which we will all welcome the history of their achievements.

It may not be out of place to record the events leading up to the arrival of the Australasian Contingents in Egypt.

On August 29th, 1914, I was at the Headquarters of Marshal Joffre, at Vitry le Francois, where I received orders from Field-Marshal Earl Kitchener to proceed at once to Egypt and take over the command there. Somewhat disconcerted, I complied, and arrived September 8th in that country.

When I left France the French and British armies were in full retreat to the line of the Marne. Our little Army, after magnificent and strenuous resistance, had suffered terribly, and the question of reinforcements was paramount. It was, therefore, no surprise when, on my arrival in Egypt, I received orders to send every British soldier at once to England. I was informed that large forces were expected to be passing through the Suez Canal *en route* to Europe, and that a Territorial Division would be sent as soon as possible. The situation I found was by no means a pleasant one. The Turks were sitting on the fence, the Khedive Abbas was in Constantinople intriguing against us. The population of Egypt was some 12 millions, the great majority Moslems, in sympathy with their co-religionists the Turks; of the European population, the majority was Italian, Greek, German and Austrian, with a good proportion of Turks and Turko-Egyptians, Syrians and Armenians. The British and French were in a decided minority.

The extraordinary anomaly was the political situation. With considerable difficulty, and late in August, 1914, General

Sir Julian Byng had got rid of the diplomatic representatives of both Germany and Austria, yet the Nationals of both these countries remained; the Turks were diplomatically represented by a High Commissioner.

The Suez Canal was neutral and full of German ships. Spies abounded.

The situation of our Army in France demanded heroic measures—risks had to be taken; and it was very fortunate for Great Britiain that the late Earl Kitchener was at the helm! No one knew better than he what risks in the Near East could, or could not, be taken! He had already, with that remarkable foresight for which he was famous, begun the formation of the new Armies at Home, and had called on the Empire's great Dependencies and Colonies for far greater efforts than were at one time thought possible. Nobly they responded! But there was a very anxious and delicate period to be bridged over before these forces could be trained and marshalled where wanted.

Simultaneously with the withdrawal to England of all British Colonial troops, the bulk of the trained Indian Army was ordered to France. So long as the Turks did nothing, this stream of troops through the Canal and Egypt astonished the Egyptians and had the effect Lord Kitchener anticipated. They kept quiet. On September 25th, the 42nd East Lancashire Division, with two regiments of Yeomanry arrived.

The Turks during this period had mobilised their armies in Asia Minor and Syria; the Bedouins on the Sinai frontier became more aggressive. Consequently, the political situation in Egypt became more difficult. The only troops guarding the Suez Canal were the IXth Brigade, Lahore Indian Division.

In the meanwhile, the news from Europe was far from reassuring. Large Turkish forces were reported at Deraa on the Hedjaz Railway, at Nazareth, Nablus, Hebron and Beersheba. German officers and agents were said to be assisting.

To avoid their falling into the hands of raiding Bedouins, it was decided to withdraw Anglo-Egyptian authority from Sinai. One British officer, one Egyptian Judge from El Arish, and about twenty policemen from the rest of the Peninsula represented this authority. Steps were also taken to fill up and destroy, as far as possible, all known wells and water supplies. It was no wonder that as the rumours of Turkish activities spread, the uneasiness in Egypt became more and more pronounced. On November 2nd, martial law was proclaimed. On November 16th, a further force from India for the defence of the Canal began to arrive, so on November 22nd the IXth Lahore Brigade proceeded to France to rejoin its Division. On November 20th, Lord Kitchener telegraphed that owing to the Turkish threat, the Australian and New Zealand contingents would disembark and train in Egypt, and that I was to make arrangements for their reception.

This was indeed welcome news—more appreciated by me than by the contingents themselves!

On December 3rd, 1914, the New Zealand troops began to arrive.

On December 18th, Egypt was proclaimed a British Protectorate.

On December 19th, the Khedive Abbas Hilmi was deposed and His Highness Hussein Kamel proclaimed Sultan of Egypt. On December 30th, His Highness the Sultan made his State entry into Cairo, the Australasian contingents assisting at the ceremony.

On December 24th, the Hon. Sir Thomas Mackenzie, G.C.M.G., F.R.G.S., High Commissioner for New Zealand, with the late Rt. Hon. Sir George Reid, G.C.B., High Commissioner for Australia, arrived in Egypt on an official tour of inspection. This visit was peculiarly well-timed and vastly appreciated both by their countrymen and the authorities in Egypt; the former were able to hear from the lips of their representatives to Great Britain exactly how matters stood and, as far as was known, their prospects. The High Commissioners were able to see for themselves the conditions and difficulties prevailing in Egypt. Incalculable benefit was derived from this visit. Both High Commissioners delivered stirring speeches, and put great heart into their contingents. The New Zealanders were addressed by Sir Thomas at their camp at Heliopolis, whilst Sir George did the same to the Australians at Mena, under the shadow of the Great Pyramids.

During this time, the Turkish activities began to take shape, and there was little room for doubt that an attempt to invade Egypt was contemplated.

I have thought it advisable to recount these facts in order to make it clear why the Australasian troops were detained in Egypt and not sent through to France.

It was out of the question to allow the Turk a foothold in Egypt. The troops now settled down to reorganisation and strenuous training until April 25th, 1915, when the Gallipoli campaign opened. It is true that in February, 1915, the Turks carried out their intention of crossing the Sinai Peninsula, and attempting to cross the Canal and invade Egypt. The immense difficulties of such an attempt were speedily manifest, and it required no great effort on our part to throw those who reached the Canal back in confusion.

Some of the Australasian troops assisted in this first serious defeat of Turkish ambitions. The Gallipoli campaign, though the troops performed prodigies of valour and to all intents and purposes destroyed the flower of the Turkish armies, was not the success it was hoped for. The expedition failed, and the evacuation of the Gallipoli Peninsula led up to the Palestine expedition, which happily was gloriously successful.

The Gallipoli campaign showed the world what magnificent soldiers these splendid men from Australia and New Zealand were. The reputation they won there was afterwards fully maintained in many a bloody fight in France and Palestine. It was not my good fortune to accompany them in either of these campaigns. In 1914-15 and the early part of 1916, when these contingents were under my command in Egypt, it was my privilege to see a good deal of them, and I state, without fear of contradiction, that although they subsequently covered themselves with glory, they, during their stay in camp in Egypt, covered themselves with credit by their excellent soldier-like behaviour, notwithstanding the novelty of the conditions prevailing, the cruel temptations and difficulties of language.

It would have been a trial for the most disciplined troops to find themselves in a "halfway house" debarred from proceeding to the battlefield of France, and, as they thought, "out of it." Yet they bore themselves like men. The late Sultan Hussein frequently used to express to me, in no measured terms, his intense admiration for the countries that produced such men—volunteers who gave up everything, prepared to give up their lives, for their King and Mother Country. He could hardly understand it; yet he said, "With such men you *must* win."

The men of Australia and New Zealand were soon destined to find that so far as fighting was concerned, they were very much "in it." Right gloriously they fought, and though we mourn many a brave soldier now resting peacefully in his far-off grave, yet they have not given their lives in vain; for when the history of the Great War is written and incidents are seen in their proper proportion, I am sure it will be conceded that the exploits of our gallant men in Gallipoli, Palestine and Mesopotamia, under the orders of General Sir Ian Hamilton, Field-Marshal Lord Allenby, and Generals Maude and Marshall, were responsible in a great degree for the ultimate defeat of Germany.

New Zealand has every reason to be proud of what her sons have done for the Empire, and in no theatre have they more reason to be so than the glorious and bewilderingly successful campaign in Palestine.

J. G. Maxwell

General.

London, August 12th, 1919.

Introduction by General Sir Archibald Murray, G.C.M.G., K.C.B., C.V.O., D.S.O.

I have been greatly honoured by being asked to write a few words of introduction to the history of the New Zealand Mounted Brigade.

The Brigade served under my command in the Sinai Peninsula during the whole of 1916 and until the end of June, 1917. Fortunate indeed is a commander in the field who has at his disposal New Zealand mounted troops, for he can depend on them at all times to display energy, resource, and endurance. All these three qualities were time after time exemplified by the New Zealanders in the waterless desert country of Sinai.

I have known the Canterbury Mounted Rifles cover forty miles of heavy desert sand in thirty hours.

On May 31st, 1916, the New Zealand Mounted Brigade was in action at Bir Salmana, covering sixty miles in thirty-six hours.

Not only is the Brigade equal to any troops in energy, resource and endurance, but in addition it is second to none in determination and dash. The fine determined action of these troops at Mount Royston, Romani, and their magnificent dash at Magdhaba and Rafa will always be remembered by the Egyptian Field Force to their everlasting credit.

I have had New Zealand troops under my command in other lands than Egypt and have gained a lasting and sincere affection for them, collectively and individually. They are a magnificent lot of men, who play the game at all times.

I feel sure that this History will bring home to all New Zealanders and the Empire generally the grand part played in the Great War by their mounted troops. It will also be cherished as a priceless memento by those who have lost near and dear relatives who gave up their lives for their King and country and now lie buried in a far distant land.

The Empire is proud of the New Zealand Mounted Brigade and I personally owe it a debt of lasting gratitude.

Archibald Murray,
General.

Went House,
West Malling, Kent.

Introduction by Field Marshal Sir Edmund H. H. Allenby, G.C.B., G.C.M.G.

The New Zealand troops who served in Palestine formed part of the Australian and New Zealand Mounted Division, which was composed of Australian and New Zealand Brigades that had fought in Gallipoli.

The Division had its full share of fighting in the conquest of the Sinai Peninsula, and in the first and second battles of Gaza in March and April, 1917.

When I assumed command of the Egyptian Expeditionary Force, in June, 1917, the New Zealanders were already veteran troops proved in many a battle. Two more years of hardship and danger were to pass before they saw the end of their labours. Two years of unceasing toil, crowned with much glory.

The summer of 1917 was spent in preparing for the campaign.

On the evening of October 30th the troops destined for the attack on Beersheba moved from their rendezvous. On the evening of the 31st Beersheba fell.

In this action the New Zealanders took a prominent part; and, thenceforward until the 7th November, they were continually engaged in bitter fighting north of Beersheba. Afterwards, moving to the coastal plain, they joined in the advance through Philistia.

At Richon le Zion, on the 14th November, they defeated a determined and heavy Turkish counter-attack by a brilliant bayonet charge. From November 16th to 25th, in the neighbourhood of Jaffa; and in December, on the river Auja, great deeds of valour were done by the New Zealanders.

In February, 1918, the Jordan Valley became the scene of their activities.

From March 23rd to 31st they fought the Turks and the weather in the daring raid to Amman. Again, they co-operated in the raid to Es Salt, from April 30th to May 4th; and they shared the victory over the Turks and Germans on July 4th.

When the autumn campaign was in progress, the New Zealanders took a leading part in defeating the Turkish IV. Army. In the Jordan Valley, and thence eastward, over their old battlefields of Shunet Nimrin, Es Salt and Amman, to the Hedjaz railway, the men of New Zealand fought and marched to final and complete victory. Nothing daunted these intrepid fighters; to them nothing was impossible.

I am proud to have had the honour of commanding them; and they have my congratulations, my thanks and my good wishes.

Edmund H. H. Allenby
Field Marshal.

The Residency,
Cairo, 30/8/19.

Introduction by Lieut.-General Sir H. Chauvel, K.C.B., K.C.M.G.

It was my good fortune, as well as an honour which I appreciate very highly, to have the New Zealand Mounted Rifles Brigade included in my command during the operations in Sinai and Palestine.

I had previously had considerable experience of the horsemen of New Zealand in the South African War and on the Gallipoli Peninsula (as infantrymen) and knew their sterling qualities and what might be expected of them; but when the Anzac Mounted Division was formed early in 1916, the most confirmed optimist could never have conceived the opportunities which would come in their way; opportunities which, with their Australian brothers, they grasped with both hands.

In the early part of the Great War the day of the mounted man appeared to be gone for ever, and it remained for the Australian Light Horse and New Zealand Mounted Rifles to demonstrate to the world that the horse soldier was as essential in modern warfare as he had ever been in the past. It was the splendid work of these Australians and New Zealanders in the Sinai Peninsula which, in the first place, turned a defensive campaign into an offensive one and, in the second place, led to the enormous increase in the cavalry in the Egyptian theatre of the War. Without large forces of cavalry, the final operations, which destroyed three Turkish armies and forced Germany's allies out of the War, could never have been undertaken.

From the Battle of Romani to the Armistice with Turkey the New Zealand Mounted Rifles Brigade took a prominent part in all the operations, under the brilliant leadership of Major-General Sir Edward Chaytor and Brigadier-General W. Meldrum, and I am personally much indebted to these officers and all ranks of the Brigade for much of the successes achieved, first of all by the Anzac Mounted Division and later by the Desert Mounted Corps.

The achievements of the mounted men of New Zealand form a record of which their country and the Empire have every reason to be proud.

Melbourne.

Harry Chauvel.

Late Commanding the Desert Mounted Corps.

The New Zealanders in Sinai and Palestine

CHAPTER I.

How the Brigade Returned to their Horses after the Campaign in Gallipoli.

*Let oil nor steam, nor wings of dream deprive us of our own
The wide world for a kingdom, the saddle for a throne.*
—*Ogilvie.*

On December 26th, 1915, 62 officers and 1329 other ranks arrived at Alexandria from Gallipoli, under the command of Brigadier-General E. W. C. Chaytor, C.B., and travelled by rail to Cairo, and returned to their old camp at Zeitoun, where the horses had been kept in the best of condition by a devoted band of transport drivers and reinforcements, assisted by native labour.

We New Zealanders are all horse-lovers by our British birthright, and as Colonials we have learned to value the horse as a means of existence, and not merely as a means of recreation. Our Main Body men were horse-lovers by nature, for had they not volunteered and in very many cases brought their own horses? And they were now horse-lovers by conviction, the conviction born of active experience. They had learned that to no man is a horse so essential as to the mounted soldier. His horse is more than a friend, he is a part of the soldier's very life.

We had all read of the Arab's love for his horse, and we learned in these early days in the desert around Cairo the reason of that love. Without a horse in the desert a man is impotent. He perishes miserably. He who has once ridden into action with the bullets whistling past his ears and the shells bursting round him, will never forget his horse; how the good steed became verily a part of his body, a glorified body that carried him whithersoever he willed; escaping this danger by a miracle; leaping over that; and, when all seemed lost, by his very energy and the thunder of his hoofs thrilling his rider to renewed effort.

Organisation as a Mounted Brigade began at once. Main Body men found their own particular horses again, and many happy meetings there were between man and horse.

It was not now a case of training horses. The horses were there in the pink of condition, and the task was to find the men. Horsemanship being an essential accomplishment for success in mounted work, daily riding tests were made, and much care, judgment and patience were exercised in the selection of suitable men from the reinforcements to fill vacancies to complete establishment. Indifferent horsemen were sent to their respective "Detail Squadrons" for further instruction. These "Detail Squadrons" were formed at Zeitoun (one for each regiment) to train reinforcements, and were drawn upon when required by the unit in the field. Selected officers and N.C.Os. were sent to the School of Instruction at Zeitoun, where they and those who from time to time throughout the remainder of the War replaced them, most worthily upheld the honour of New Zealand. Our machine gunners in particular gained much credit, carrying off the highest marks obtained by any unit throughout the whole course of the schools. These schools were instituted early in 1915, and were carried on by selected officers from the British Army and brought to the highest state of efficiency; and well and truly did they take that place in the East which in the West was taken by the training camps at Sling and the cadet battalions at Oxford and Cambridge.

Day by day the work of reconstruction went rapidly on. New arms and equipment were obtained from that generous mother of the Army, the Ordnance Stores. Old arms and equipment were cleaned and repaired, and the machine guns overhauled by our old friends at the Citadel. Here, at Cairo's most ancient fortress, are situated the Egyptian Army's ordnance workshops, and in Mishalany Bey and his assistants the Brigade ever found true friends, for whom no job was too difficult, no repairs too urgent, and no want too small to be instantly and efficiently supplied. And it was very largely owing to the Citadel that the strenuous efforts of every officer and man in each troop bore such good fruit; that the depleted regiments, which had reached Cairo on December 28th, 1915, were enabled in a short twelve days to parade and to form (together with the Signal Troop, Field Troop, Field Ambulance and Ammunition Column) that perfect instrument of war, a Mounted Rifles Brigade—fully armed, magnificently horsed, properly equipped and at full strength.

BRIGADE HEADQUARTERS, ZEITOUN.

The N.Z.M.R. Brigade was composed of three Mounted Rifles Regiments. The Auckland Regiment, the Wellington Regiment, and the Canterbury Regiment. The Otago Mounted Rifles were not with the Brigade during the Sinai and Palestine campaigns. Each regiment was composed of three squadrons; and each of these squadrons was recruited from a regiment of Mounted Rifles in New Zealand; and the squadron bore the name of that regiment in New Zealand. So the Auckland Regiment consisted of the 3rd, 4th and 11th Squadrons coming from their parent regiments, 3rd (Auckland) Mounted Rifles, 4th (Waikato) Mounted Rifles, 11th (North Auckland) Mounted Rifles. The Wellington Regiment was composed of the 2nd, 6th and 9th Squadrons coming from Queen Alexandra's 2nd (Wellington West Coast) Mounted

Rifles, 6th (Manawatu) Mounted Rifles, and the 9th (Wellington East Coast) Mounted Rifles. And the Canterbury Regiment consisted of the 1st, the 8th and the 10th Squadrons, from their parent regiments the 1st Mounted Rifles (Canterbury Yeomanry Cavalry), the 8th (South Canterbury) Mounted Rifles, and the 10th (Nelson) Mounted Rifles. From this it is seen that each of the three military districts, Auckland, Wellington and Canterbury, found one regiment.

In addition to the three regiments the complete Brigade consisted of the Machine Gun Squadron, the Signal Troop, the Field Troop, the Mobile Veterinary Section, and the Mounted Field Ambulance. A battery of R.H.A. also always fought with the Brigade.

The Machine Gun Squadron was formed early in the Sinai campaign from the machine gun sections of each regiment and was therefore recruited from all three regiments. Later as a complete unit the Machine Gun Squadron was reinforced from suitable men from any district in New Zealand.

The Signal Troop were specialists principally from the Post and Telegraph Department and the Railways.

The Field Troop was a unit formed in Sinai. They were the handy men of the Brigade; and among them were civil engineers, mechanical engineers, engine drivers, carpenters, plumbers, draughtsmen, surveyors and mechanics of all kinds. And the Troop was recruited from selected men chosen on account of their special qualification.

The Mobile Veterinary Section was officered chiefly by veterinary officers belonging to the Agricultural Department and recruited from men selected in New Zealand. And, lastly, the Mounted Field Ambulance was kept up to strength by men selected in New Zealand and sent with the other reinforcements.

As to the R.H.A. Battery, for nearly the whole of the campaign the Somerset Territorial Battery, R.H.A., was attached to the New Zealand Brigade, and the men came almost to consider themselves New Zealanders, but the battery was, of course, recruited from England.

Attached to the Brigade, though not actually working with it, were the Rarotongans formed into a company about 250 strong.

In addition to the Brigade and its attached units, two Camel Companies were formed from Mounted Rifles reinforcements. These companies formed a part of the I.C.C. Brigade and fought in the Sinai and Palestine campaigns. On June 10th, 1918, they were disbanded and formed into the 2nd M.G. Squadron, and as such were attached to the 5th Australian L.H. Brigade.

RIGHT TO LEFT: CAPT. BOND, GENERAL CHAYTOR, MAJOR POWLES.

Put shortly the composition of the Brigade was as follows:

	Officers	Other Ranks	Horses
Headquarters	6	43	55
3 Regiments each of 24 Officers, 499 Other Ranks, 616 horses	72	1497	1848
1st Machine Gun Squadron	8	222	321
Signal Troop	1	36	36
Field Troop	2	50	67
No. 2 Mobile Veterinary Section	1	29	28
Mounted Field Ambulance	6	133	127
Auckland M.R. Band	1	36	—
No. 4 Coy. A.S.C.	5	119	156
R.H.A. Battery	5	149	246

In addition there were the following:—
1. 2 Camel Companies each of 6 Officers 117 Other Ranks 12 234
These were formed in 1918 into the No. 2 M.G. Squadron of 8 Officers 221 Other Ranks.

2. N.Z. Rarotongan Coy.	6	240
3. Administrative Headquarters in Cairo	3	30
4. Training Depot, Ismailia	19	79

To keep the Brigade up to strength throughout the war a total of 17,723 all ranks left New Zealand.

The days went by busily spent in drill and "mobilisation parades"—the whole Brigade parading in full mounted order with first line of transport. These parades proved invaluable; and a steady improvement in smartness, in equipment, and in general soldierly bearing was very noticeable.

How the Brigade Marched through the Land of Goshen.

At 9 o'clock on January 23rd, 1916, the complete Brigade moved off from Zeitoun Camp, passing through ancient Heliopolis, which dates from 2433 B.C., and marched by easy stages to the Suez Canal.

Down through the shady lanes of Matarieh we rode, overhead arches of the gorgeous Bougainvillaea, underneath the horses' feet carpets of purple blossoms, past that old garden where is "Mary's Well," and that traditional tree under which Mary and Joseph and the Child took refuge after the "Flight into Egypt," and so to Heliopolis, the On of the Old Testament, now a wide enclosure of earthen mounds partly planted with gardens. And there standing solitary is that wonderful obelisk as tall and straight and as finely cut, even as it stood when first erected nearly 4000 years ago, in front of the Temple of the Sun wherein Moses was educated. It is the oldest known in Egypt, and therefore in the world, the father of all that have arisen since. It saw the coming of Joseph, the education and growth of Moses; it is mentioned by Herodotus; and of all the obelisks that were or still are, it alone has kept its position, and it stands to-day as erected by its makers; and was now looking down upon men from the youngest nation in the world.

Passing on, our way lay along one of those causeways high above the floods. We looked across the green fields to the minarets of Cairo and the mighty Pyramids shimmering there in the sun; even as no doubt Moses beheld them when he, too, turned his face to the East and took his leave of Egypt. So we now, not knowing what lay for us in the future, looked across Cairo to the Pyramids and wondered whether our wanderings would bring us within sight of these mighty monuments ever again.

The weather was delightfully cool, and though rain fell heavily every day and there were no tents, all were in the highest spirits. The strain of the life on Anzac had gone and we were moving off to whatsoever God had in store for us; not this time on our feet, but in our rightful manner upon our beloved horses. And when the nights were wet and cold and the ration train arrived late and there was no firewood, yet the E.S.R. in its wisdom had seen fit at this time to duplicate the railway line from Cairo to Ismailia, and for the purpose had stacked quantities of creosoted sleepers—and creosoted wood *does* make a bright and cheerful fire! And so we journeyed through the land of Goshen, passing the night of January 27th at Abu Sueir, the ancient Pithom—the treasure city which the Israelites of old made for Pharaoh. On the fourth day we had passed through the lines of Tel el Kebir, now filled with sand but distinctly traceable; and on the sixth day, the day after passing Abu Sueir, arrived at Moascar. The next morning we rode through Ismailia and marched past General Sir Archibald Murray, then Commander-in-Chief in Egypt. He was accompanied by General Sir A. Godley—whose headquarters were in Ismailia—and General Sir A. H. Russell, the Brigade's old Commander. And on the evening of the seventh day we arrived at Serapeum and settled down into a comfortable camp in the sand about one mile from the banks of the Canal.

Now began training in earnest—rifle shooting, machine gun shooting, tactical exercises, boxing matches, swimming in the Canal, filled up the days—and happy days they were.

The weather was still cool and the nights bracingly cold. All the old hands were losing the "Gallipoli strain," and to the new hands the life was wonderfully interesting. Then came sorrow, with the breaking of many friendships; for there was being organised at Moascar the New Zealand Infantry Division, for the completion of which the New Zealand Mounted Rifles Brigade was peremptorily ordered to find some 50 officers and 2000 men. They went reluctantly to the artillery and to the infantry, and together with the Maoris, formed the Pioneer Battalion.

This forceful and rigorous policy depleted the Brigade of some of its best officers and "Main Body" N.C.Os. and men. Many of these were in the details camps just out of hospital and recovering from wounds and sickness incurred on the Peninsula, and they were summarily transferred to batteries, transport, or infantry battalions. N.C.Os. of long experience as mounted riflemen were reduced to the ranks where privates or gunners only were required, and were not given a chance to volunteer; nor was the Brigadier given a chance to call for volunteers; for men were seized in the training camps.

In no unit of the Army is there greater *esprit-de-corps* than in a mounted regiment. It goes without saying that a man who willingly and voluntarily chooses a mounted unit, with all its added work of care for his horse in addition to the care of himself, is of necessity a man of steadfast purpose and of wide sympathies. In addition to the Brotherhood of the Regiment he belongs to the Brotherhood of the Horse, and from this twofold love springs a tribal feeling as strong as that which animated the Highland clans of old. And this Brigade had just been through a campaign the like of which for the welding of love and friendship between man and man has scarcely ever been equalled, and which was fought under a leader whose watchword to his men ever was—even as that of King Arthur to his knights of old: "Do everything that comes to you with all your might, and for reward just this--- that to this Table Round ye all belong."

Amongst the officers so transferred was Major G. A. King, D.S.O., who had been the Brigade's Staff Captain since the Brigade was formed in New Zealand in 1914. His departure caused the greatest regret throughout the whole Brigade, for no other officer had so endeared himself to all ranks. His enthusiasm, his unbounded energy, his great knowledge of horses, arms, equipment, and all impedimenta of a mounted soldier's life, and his ever unfailing and smiling good humour proved a tower of strength to the whole Brigade and smoothed away many a difficulty. No one but he who had the good fortune to work intimately with George Augustus King can ever know how much the great reputation made by the Brigade throughout the War was due to him.

A Popular Commander

On February 19th the well-known Commanding Officer of the Canterbury Regiment, Lieut.-Colonel John Findlay, affectionately called by his men "Old John," rejoined. He had been seriously wounded on Gallipoli in the breaking of the Turkish lines on the night of August 6th, and had been in hospital in England for some time. His arrival in his regimental lines was heralded by much cheering. This officer continued to command the Canterbury Regiment throughout the remainder of the War, and justly earned the distinction, conceded by both Australians and New Zealanders, of being the finest Regimental Commander in the Anzac Mounted Division. When it is remembered that this Division was the original cavalry formation in the Sinai Campaign, and the parent of all cavalry formations that eventually took part in the Palestine campaign, among whom it gained for itself the name of being the finest cavalry Division in the Army, it will be seen that the reputation won by Colonel Findlay was of the highest order.

MAJOR G. A. KING WITH MAJOR POWLES AT ZEITOUN.

On February 23rd the 'Otago Mounted Rifles finally left the Brigade. Though never officially a part of the Mounted Brigade, they had fought throughout the Gallipoli campaign under their beloved leader, Colonel Bauchop, as a Brigade unit, and had returned with the Brigade, and with it had gone through the period of re-horsing and reconstruction.

BRIGADE TRANSPORT CROSSING THE PONTOON BRIDGE AT SERAPEUM.
MARCH 6TH, 1916.

At Serapeum began the study of archaeology and ancient history, a study that proved of inestimable value to everyone in the Brigade. In a country of dust, sand, flies and intolerable peoples—and from whom there was no escape, no week-end or other leave—this interest in the old history of the land helped to pass many a weary hour and to brighten many a dreary day.

And it began in this way—on the edge of our camp lay a large mound, much like the sand hills which lay all around but of a more solid formation; and on this mound lay broken slabs of red Assouan granite. A digging party found more granite. And so, gradually a band of enthusiastic excavators began systematic digging; and there came into being the "Serapeum Sand-Shifters' Association," formed by willing volunteers of brawn and muscle from all units in the Brigade. The result after due submission of many pieces of inscribed granite to the Cairo Museum authorities, was interesting and startling. It appears that there was a Pharaoh called Necho who began to cut a canal from the Pelusiac arm of the Nile to the Red Sea, to bring his Mediterranean shipping through to the Indian Ocean. After one hundred thousand of his people had died on the work he was compelled to desist. Soon afterwards Darius the Persian conquered Egypt and he completed the canal and erected at its entrance to the Red Sea a huge monument in red Assouan granite. This was the monument which we had found.

This first excavation was the forerunner of much interesting work done by the Brigade during its career.

BRIGADE HEADQUARTERS OFFICE READY FOR THE ROAD.

Shorn of some of its best officers and men and without the Otago Regiment, the Brigade welcomed with joy a move to rail-head Ferry Post and there on March 6th took over a portion of the front line of the Canal Defences.

Here many days were passed in long patrols into the Desert; in learning how and how not to make defences in the sand; and last and by no means least, in learning how and how not to load the "Ship of the Desert." For the desert on the east of the Canal is so soft that all wheels were left at Serapeum, and the Brigade made its first move on "Camel Transport"—a never-to-be-forgotten day when everything everybody owned had either to be got somehow on to a camel or left behind for ever. And one experienced a mild wonder (a wonder that returned many times in the days to come) how with sand all round and no shops within many miles, one's "Things" multiplied exceedingly immediately a camp was pitched.

Formation of the Anzac Mounted Division

On March 21st the front line was inspected by H.R.H. the Prince of Wales, whose quiet unassuming manner, keen interest in everything he saw, and utter absence of "side" quite captured the hearts of our men.

On March 15th the Australian and New Zealand Mounted Division was formed, consisting of the following Brigades:—
1st Australian Light Horse Brigade.
2nd Australian Light Horse Brigade.
3rd Australian Light Horse Brigade.
New Zealand Mounted Rifles Brigade.
4 Territorial R.H.A. Batteries—2 Scottish and 2 English.—(The Ayrs and Inverness and the Somersets and Leicesters).

These batteries were at this time armed with 18 pounders and were as keen and efficient as any regular batteries and were magnificently horsed.

The Australian and New Zealand Mounted Division which now and hereafter became known as the Anzac Mounted Division, was placed under command of Major-General H. G. Chauvel, who commanded the 1st Light Horse Brigade on Gallipoli, and also the 1st Australian Division, and who afterwards so successfully commanded the "Desert Mounted Corps" —the largest body of mounted troops commanded by one man in the Great War; and which was destined 'to break the Turkish Armies.

Headquarters of the Division was established at Serapeum and the formation of the necessary divisional units—Field Squadron, Signal Squadron, Divisional Train—was taken in hand, the requisite personnel being found from Light Horse and N.Z.M.R. reinforcements.

The Divisional Headquarters was also formed from Light Horsemen and New Zealanders. Major-General H. G. Chauvel (now Sir Harry Chauvel, K.C.B., K.C.M.G.), who commanded for the first year was an Australian, and for the rest of the war the Division was commanded by a New Zealander, Major-General E. W. C. Chaytor (now Sir Edward Chaytor, K.C.M.G., K.C.V.O., C.B., A.D.C.). The A.A. and Q.M.G. and the D.A.D.M.S. were also New Zealanders and so were several of the clerical staff.

The New Zealand Division under the Mounted Brigade's old commander, Major-General Russell, was now leaving for France, and many sad farewells were taken of old and tried friends. A feeling of being "left" took possession of all and any move was welcomed. This came in an order for the Division to concentrate at Salhia, and the Brigade marched there via Moascar on April 6th. Salhia is the place from whence Napoleon set forth upon his attempt to conquer Palestine, and where he organized the Army that reached Acre. It is the extreme eastern town of the Delta and was the "jumping-off" place for all pilgrims journeying to the East in the olden days; and from there in all probability that mighty general, Moses, led forth his people to the Promised Land.

At 4 p.m. on April 23rd, 1916, Easter Day and St. George's Day, the Brigade received an urgent message to move as soon as possible to Kantara, the Pilgrims' stopping place on the Suez Canal. It transpired that a Turkish Force under cover of a fog had attacked and driven in, with heavy casualties, the Yeomanry advanced posts in the Desert at the wells of Katia and Ogratina.

CHAPTER II.

How the Brigade took the Way of the Land of the Philistines.

"You pass over broad plains—you pass over newly-reared hills —you pass through valleys dug out by the last week's storm —and the hills and the valley are sand, sand, sand, still sand, and only sand, and sand, and sand again. The earth is so samely that you turn your eyes towards heaven—towards heaven, I mean in sense of sky. You look to the sun for he is your taskmaster, and by him you know the measure of the work that you have done, and the measure of the work that remains for you to do. He comes when you strike your tents in the early morning, and then, for the first hour of the day, as you move forward on your camel, he stands at your near side, and makes you know that the whole day's toil is before you; then for a while, and a long while, you see him no more, for you are veiled and shrouded, and dare not look upon the greatness of his glory, but you know where he strides overhead by the touch of his flaming sword. No words are spoken, but your Arabs moan, your camels sigh, your skin glows, your shoulders ache, and for sights you see the pattern and web of the silk that veils your eyes, and the glare of the outer light. Time labours on—your skin glows, your shoulders ache, your camels sigh, and you see the same pattern in the silk and the same glare of light beyond; but conquering time marches on, and by-and-by the descending sun has compassed the heaven, and now softly touches your right arm, and throws your lank shadow over the sand right along the way for Persia. Then again you look upon his face for his power is all veiled in his beauty, and the redness of flames has become the redness of roses; the fair, wavy cloud that fled in the morning now comes to his sight once more—comes blushing, yet still comes on—comes burning with blushes, yet comes and clings to his side."—*Kinglake.*

At dawn on April 24th the Brigade crossed the Suez Canal and marched 7 miles east into the Desert to a position called Hill 70, completing a forced march of 37 miles; but word was received that the Turks had made off. The 2nd Light Horse Brigade, which had crossed the Canal just before our men, was in time to exchange a few shots and to pursue the Turkish rear-guard for some miles further.

The Anzac Mounted Division took over the outer line of what was called No. 3 section Canal Defences, and established posts of Light Horsemen at Dueidar and Romani—15 and 20 miles respectively from the Canal; and with the Canterbury Regiment guarding rail-head. The rest of the N.Z.M.R. Brigade remained for some days at Hill 70, spending the time in long patrols into the Desert, in water exploration, and in well-digging.

Kantara (or the "crossing" to give it the Arabic meaning) has been from ancient times the entrance gate to the Desert from Egypt. It stands just on the edge of the great area inundated by the Nile and from it begins "The Oldest Road in the World"—that great highway connecting Africa with Asia, and which runs across the Sinai Desert, and which has been followed from time immemorial by invaders from East and West—by Egyptians and Babylonians, Assyrians and Persians, Greeks and Romans, Crusaders and Saracens, and by Napoleon in his attempted conquest of Palestine. The Child Christ fleeing with His parents from the wrath of King Herod, came down this road to Egypt. And now with their faces

LT.-COL. JOHN FINDLAY, C.B. D.S.O., CANTERBURY MOUNTED RIFLES.

towards the Holy Land came our glorious youth of the Southern Cross, beginning the modern Crusade that was to wrest once more the Holy City from the hands of the Turk.

A glance at the map will show why this great road is just here and not elsewhere. Sinai will be seen to occupy the position of a bridge between Asia and Africa. It is a great waterless tract of glaring desert, all sand along the Mediterranean, and towards the south running up into lofty barren mountains of scorching stone.

Across this fiery bridge two ways only lie. The one, "The way of the Land of the Philistines," runs from the Delta just above the Nile inundations, along the coast, and so into the

HORSE LINES IN THE DESERT.

plain of the Philistines at Gaza; and the other leads through those burnt up mountains. And the reason of it is this—to cross this fiery bridge one must have water. Each winter there is a small rainfall along the coast and there are great thunder showers among the mountains. The sand along the coast soaks up, as a sponge, the rain and yields again to the hand of man in his wells. And in the mountains during the course of the ages, the wisdom of man has caused great cisterns to be excavated to catch the waters of the storm-run torrents. And so by these two routes only can man go. Moses by God's command was directed to go by the mountain route, lest the warlike Philistines should overcome his army of recruits.

These are the two main routes by which invading armies might approach from Palestine—the first the Darb el Sultani, the "Oldest Road in the World," and, the second, the route through the mountains of the Sinai Peninsula which the Turks used for their first attack upon Egypt in February 1915 and along which they were extending their railway from Beersheba.

On this route the only large water supply was at a place called Moya Harab some 30 miles from Serapeum on the Canal.

General Murray decided to occupy the Katia oasis area thus blocking the Darb el Sultani, and to empty the water cisterns at Moya Harab rendering the second route useless to the enemy, and to keep at Suez a small body of troops to ward off any raid in that direction.

The 5th Mounted Brigade (Yeomanry) was sent to the Katia oasis under this plan; and it was the initial attack upon this Brigade that brought the Anzac Mounted Division across the Canal.

Stretching eastward from the Canal almost as far as the eye can reach from the deck of the modern steamer, lies a flat sandy plain. At the end of this some 7 or 8 miles out, are

NEW ZEALAND FIELD AMBULANCE BIR ET MALER, SHOWING THE AEROPLANE SIGN.

great sand hills rising some 200 feet above the plain; and from thence onwards for 100 miles to the "River of Egypt" at El Arish stretches a vast confusion of these great sand hills, with an orderly disorderliness, in that they trend generally to a north-west and south-east direction following the prevailing wind; and in the hollows between lie innumerable "hods"—

little depressions filled with the date palm, and in which brackish water can be found.

Again looking at the map, a great lagoon will be seen following the coast line nearly to El Arish. It is the famous Serbonian Bog of Milton—the Bardawil of the Arabs (called Bardawil or Baldwin after King Baldwin I. of Jerusalem, who died near there is the year 1118 A.D.). It is the remains of the Pelusiac arm of the Nile which in the time of Herodotus was the main outlet of Egypt's trade with the Mediterranean. It is now a great salt marsh some 8 inches lower than the Mediterranean Sea; dry and salt-covered in summer; and filled with water for a short period in winter. Here at its western end on May 5th the Canterbury Regiment cut a canal 550 yards long designed to flood this great swamp and so cover effectually our left. But the force of the waves so persistently silted up the canal that it was eventually abandoned.

On May 12th the Brigade moved out to Bir Etmaler and joined with the 2nd Light Horse Brigade in a line of outposts and in patrolling the Desert to the front. Now ensued a period of great value to the whole Division; and much of the magnificent work done later owed its success to the lessons learnt at this time during which horse and man learnt to live in the Desert—even as do the Bedouins. Long patrols were undertaken to learn the country and to get information of the enemy. Whole Brigades learned to pack up at an hour's notice and to move with the same ease as previously did a squadron.

Herodotus tells the story of the Persian King, who, wishing to invade Egypt, did not know how to get his troops through the waterless desert until he hit upon the idea of utilising the earthern jars that came annually to Egypt from the Grecian Isles filled with wine. He bought up these and paid the Bedouins of that day to fill them with Nile water, and to secrete them in the desert, and so got his men across. But our men learned that water was to be found in many places and they learned how to get it without digging a well.

Well digging in the sand is a very arduous and tedious process, as an immense amount of sand has to be excavated to enable the water to be reached. But our Engineers perfected what was called the "Spear Point Pump." A 2½ inch pipe was pointed, perforated and covered with a sheet of fine perforated brass. This was driven down into the water area by means of a small pulley bar and monkey, or by a sledgehammer; and additional lengths of pipe were added if necessary. The ordinary General Service "Lift and Force Pump" was then attached. This arrangement proved so efficient that "Spear Points" were issued to every Squadron in the Division, and the R.E. Troops carried a number of them. Our men were thus enabled to get water at any of the hods in the desert in a very short space of time.

HORSE TROUGH AND PUMP.

The Khamsin season was now at its height. Day after day blew this dreaded hot wind from the south. The summer sun burned with fiendish ferocity. The air scorched one's face, and sunstroke was frequent. Packets of candles melted until the wicks alone remained. What the temperature was in the blazing sunshine at this time is not recorded. One regimental medico just arrived, in his enthusiasm, put the only thermometer in possession of the regiment out in the sun and was surprised to see the mercury rush up to the top until it could go no farther. Special bathing parades were organised, and whole regiments rode over to the sea at Mahemdiya, an ancient Roman watering place and fortress on the Bay of Tina, showing still standing great walls of stone and the remains of the baths built of brick and lined with plaster, much of which was in a state of perfect preservation.

THE UBIQUITOUS SIGNALLER. CABLE LAYING IN THE DESERT.

That the desert is made of sand we had learnt at school as little children, but we had now to learn that it has yet another ingredient—flies.

They were to be found anywhere and everywhere—near habitations and far away from any sign of man. In or near the hods in the date season they were at their worst, and one continual battle was waged against them from sunrise to sunset. Various poisons were laid out and the "catches" were so great that a tent had to be swept clear of the "casualties" many times a day. But the great thing was to lay in wait for them at night. Then they clustered at the top of the "bivvies" or on the tent pole in drowsy myriads; and the cunning hunter applied swiftly a flaming flare. Eating became one long fight between hungry man and hungry flies. One ate with one hand while the other was continually brushing away the pests. Great was the war waged upon them by our medical officers and the sanitary detachments; and to their lasting credit be it said that the flies always decreased the longer an area was occupied by our forces. Many instances occurred of a regiment moving into a fly infested area and leaving it practically free. The strongest weapon used, was the stamping out of the fly breeding areas; and in finding these our sanitary inspectors became wonderfully expert. One great difficulty there always was, in that, as the Turk was driven back our forces occupied ground lately occupied by him; and he never had with all his German tuition a sanitary system in any way approaching ours. The first few weeks in a Turkish area were very painful.

DAILY RATIONS. A TYPICAL DESERT SCENE.

On the 16th a strong reconnaissance was ordered in the vicinity of Bir El Abd some 20 miles away and to Bir Bayud, and troops from the 2nd Light Horse and New Zealand Brigades were detailed for the work. The duty was successfully carried out, though the men and horses suffered severely, for the worst Khamsin yet experienced was blowing—20 miles out and 20 miles back under such conditions was a test fit to try the stoutest Crusader of old. But the information required was obtained, though many a man had to be carried into the shade of some convenient hod and brought round with bitter water dug from out the sand. At the Mounted Field Ambulance tent in the Et Maler hod under the palm trees, the thermometer rose that day to 123 degrees. Think of 123 degrees in the shade! What it was out in the glaring sunshine must be left to the imagination.

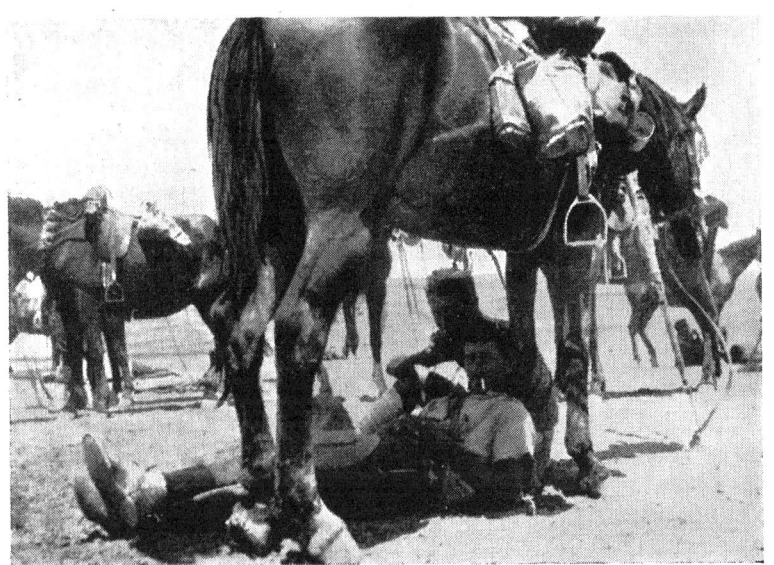

A REST IN THE SHADE!

The following message was received from G.H.Q. "The Commander-in-Chief wishes to convey to General Chauvel and troops of the Anzac Mounted Division his appreciation of the excellent work done in the very arduous reconnaissance yesterday. The Commander-in-Chief does not think that any other troops could have undertaken this operation successfully in the present weather."

On May 20th Turkish troops were discovered in the Maghara mountains; and on May 22nd a long and arduous reconnaissance was undertaken by the New Zealand Brigade to Bir Salmana, a series of brackish wells on the Old Caravan Route and about 20 miles from Romani. A couple of 18 pounders from the Ayrshire Battery mounted on ped-rails accompanied the Brigade. After an all night march Salmana was surrounded just as dawn was breaking and all the Turks in occupation killed or captured. Hod Salmana was held all day and the water thoroughly tested throughout the vicinity, and the Brigade marched back the following night.

On all these patrols nothing but camel transport was used, all wheels having been left at Kantara, where our wagons under Major Smith ("Yorkie") did most excellent work in conveying the supplies of the Division from the main railway station at Kantara to our military railway across the Canal. The wagons with their teams of mules, two in the pole and three in the lead, driven by one man from the box, did such excellent service that the five-mule team was laid down for the Egyptian Expeditionary Force as being the perfect transport for the work; and they ultimately almost superseded the British four or six horse ride-and-drive team.

It is interesting to note that these same five-mule teams some two years later in the Jordan Valley most effectually demonstrated their superiority over the British six horse ride-and-drive team. There they daily drew an average of 1000lbs. more, and in the final operations in the mountains east of the Jordan they simply walked away from the heavy teams.

On June 1st the Division suffered its first casualties from enemy aeroplane bombing. A number of men and horses were killed and wounded in the 1st Light Horse Brigade camp at Romani; and thenceforward for the rest of the campaign, the Turk lost no opportunity of dropping bombs upon the horses. This was particularly so during an action, for then his planes would immediately be over, looking for the led-horses.

On June 24th the New Zealand Brigade handed over its camp and posts to the 2nd Light Horse Brigade and leaving the Wellington Regiment with the Light Horse returned to Hill 70, and took over in place of the Wellington Regiment, the 5th Light Horse Regiment in position at Dueidar. This is the first stopping place on the "Old Road" and is some 15 miles from Kantara.

Advantage was taken of the nearness of the Suez Canal to send to Kantara two squadrons at a time for rest and bathing, their places being taken in the Brigade by two Squadrons of Warwickshire Yeomanry.

At this time, in accordance with the new establishment for Cavalry Brigades, the regimental machine gun sections were formed into a Machine Gun Squadron. This was done throughout the Division; so that each Brigade had now its Machine Gun Squadron as a complete and self-contained unit under its own Commander.

About this time also the Divisional Field Squadron was further enlarged and improved to suit the desert warfare. It consisted of four troops, one to each brigade. These engineers became extraordinarily efficient in the quest and in the getting of water. Attached to each troop was a medical officer, whose duty it was to test all the water found and pronounce and placard it "drinking water"; "horse water" or "not fit for horses" as the case might be. Much of the water passed as fit for drinking was palatable if not boiled. But if boiled some chemical reaction appeared to be set up which let loose certain salts, completely spoiling the water and making a cup of tea undrinkable. The extreme heat and the brackish water caused digestive troubles which however were amenable to early treatment.

The whole area from the Canal bank stretching east for some 50 miles had now been explored and water located and

WATER STORAGE TANKS GOING UP TO THE FRONT.

noted down; and the Division had learned how to live in the desert.

The appreciation of H.Q. was shown in a letter from the Commander-in-Chief (Sir Archibald Murray) to the G.O.C. Division dated 12/7/16 in which he said—"Whatever I ask you people to do is done without the slightest hesitation and with promptness and efficiency. I have the greatest admiration for all your Command."

On the 19th July at a quarter past four in the afternoon an aeroplane reconnaissance, with Brigadier-General Chaytor observing, discovered long lines of Turks advancing westward over the desert in the vicinity of Bir Salmana, Bir Jamiel and Bir Bayud—on approximately a frontage of 8 miles.

LEFT TO RIGHT: MAJOR BATCHELOR, LT.-COLONEL POWLES, GENERAL CHAYTOR, CAPTAIN HULBERT, MAJOR STAFFORD, COLONEL BROWNE, MAJOR SMITH.

This startling information—for no suspicion had been heard of any expected advance of the Turks—was sent in to D.H.Q. by 6 o'clock and by wireless immediately to the 2nd Light Horse Brigade, who had already left Romani on a reconnaissance and were to go as far as Bir El Abd.

The air reconnaissance report, which was proved afterwards to be wonderfully accurate, read as follows:—

"3000 men and 200 camels with from 200 to 300 large "shelters at Bayud also 3 rows of trenches facing west. "At Bir El Abd 3000 to 3500 men 2000 camels 200 to 300 "shelters 20 to 25 bell tents 1 large black hut and 3 "circular trenches."

The 2nd Light Horse Brigade, with which was the Wellington Regiment, was ordered to remain at Katia and to send out patrols to gain touch with the enemy.

The Battle of Romani.

"And the Egyptians lay encamped on the banks of the Nile which runs by Pelusium, awaiting Cambyses. The Persians crossed the desert, and pitching their camp close to the Egyptians, made ready for battle. Stubborn was the fight which followed and it was not until vast numbers had been slain that the Egyptians turned and fled."
—*Herodotus.*

Now the ruins of ancient Pelusium are to this day to be seen some few miles from the wells of Romani; and it was just outside Pelusium in the year 528 B.C. that the invading Persians conquered the Egyptians. Upon this self same ground 2500 years later the invaders of Egypt were to be defeated in the Battle of Romani.

The operations which now ensued and which resulted in the complete defeat of the Turks and of the final overthrow of the German-Turkish dreams of cutting the Suez Canal and of conquering Egypt, may be described as of three phases.

In the first phase our plans were perfected; the railhead at Romani protected with strong works and manned by infantry; and the mounted troops drew the enemy on across the desert until he finally attacked our railhead.

The second phase was the Battle of Romani, which might have been called the second battle of Pelusium, and which consisted of the great Turkish attack and our counter stroke.

In the third phase, the Turk was driven back into the desert and finally defeated in the action of Bir El Abd.

Immediately the news of the enemy's advance was brought in by General Chaytor, there began a busy and an arduous time for the Anzac Mounted Division. At or around the wells of Romani were the 1st and 2nd Light Horse Brigades, and their work was to keep in touch with the enemy and to find out his strength and his movements. It had long been realised that if possible the Turk, when his next advance began, should be induced to come on and to attack us where we could get the support of the infantry; for by practical experience it was definitely known that under the great summer heat and on the burning sand, our infantry could not be expected to march more than six miles per day. Therefore it would be wise to induce the Turk to attack us in position, maintaining at the same time a mobile mounted force with which to strike at his flank, to cut his communications, and so surround him.

A defensive line was therefore constructed by the 52nd Division (Lowland Scots), a magnificent lot of men of fine physique, who played a good game of Rugby and were therefore soon on the best of terms with our men. They were veterans from Helles where they were under the command of Lieut-General the Hon. H. A. Lawrence, afterwards Sir Hubert Lawrence, K.C.B., Chief of Staff to Sir Douglas Haig, and who now commanded all troops in the Romani area. This line rested its left on the sea at Mahemdia (the camp of Chabrias —that famous Athenian Admiral who conquered the Egyptian Fleet about the year 376 B.C. and landed his forces here for the attack upon Egypt) and ran along a series of sand hills protecting railhead at Romani and enclosed with its right a mighty sand hill called Katib Gannit, a total length of some six miles. But though protecting the railhead this fortified line did not include the "Old Road"—the caravan route which runs from Katia through Dueidar and so to Kantara. This was left to the Anzac Mounted Division whose distribution was now as follows:—1st and 2nd L.H. Brigade— vicinity of Romani (with the 2nd L.H. Brigade was the Wellington Regiment); at Hill 70 about five miles behind Dueidar lay the N.Z.M.R. Brigade with the 5th L.H. Regiment at Dueidar itself, and patrols away east along the "Old Road" —the New Zealanders with the addition of two regiments of Yeomanry and two R.H.A. batteries formed the force destined to strike at the enemy's southern flank; further south based upon the Canal was the 3rd Light Horse Brigade.

The 1st and 2nd L.H. Brigades working from Romani took it in turn day by day to harass the enemy, to report his movements, and to draw him on. The work was exceedingly interesting but very arduous, and was carried out day after day in the scorching sun with little or no sleep.

Miniature battles between our own and the enemy's patrols were frequent, and the prisoners thus taken were invaluable sources of information to us.

The Wellington Regiment was still attached to the 2nd L.H. Brigade and remained and fought as a unit therein through the battle of Romani and the operations following, which were preceded by those fatiguing day and night reconnaissances. The regiment bore its full share of the fighting and earned the unstinted praise of the Australians who affectionately termed the Wellingtons the "Well and Trulies." Moreover, at one stage in these operations, the Wellington Regiment temporarily furnished—owing to casualties—the Brigade Commander, the Brigade Major, and the Staff Captain, simultaneously for the 2nd L.H. Brigade.

On the 28th July enemy forces had entered Um Ugba—which formed an advanced salient in their position. Lieut-Colonel Meldrum who commanded the regiment and who loved a fight, asked permission to take the Hod and for two guns to assist in the attack.

The assault was made by two squadrons who advanced under machine gun fire and the well-directed fire of the two 18 pounders, and was made at the point of the bayonet with

LT.-COL. C. E. R. MACKESY, C.M.G., C.B.E., D.S.O., AUCKLAND MOUNTED RIFLES.

a determination and energy that gained great praise from the Light Horsemen who witnessed it. The enemy were driven out of the Hod leaving 16 dead and 8 prisoners in our hands.

A typical day's work at this time was as follows:—

A brigade would leave its bivouac about one in the morning and would get into touch with the Turks about daylight, picking up officer patrols that were left out all night by the preceding brigade. A section of horse artillery from the Ayrshire Battery with guns mounted on ped-rails accompanied the Brigade which soon came to blows with the Turks in finding out his dispositions. After harassing the enemy all day, the Brigade early in the afternoon would begin its return to its bivouac at Romani, leaving out as before a number of officer patrols to watch the Turks. These officer patrols were of the greatest value and the timely information sent in by them on the night of August 3rd gave ample notice of the Turks' great advance.

These tactics were so skilfully carried out that every move of the Turk was known to us; and he daily reported to Constantinople—"British again driven back towards the Canal." By daylight on August 3rd the enemy had advanced to and occupied Katia Oasis—within striking distance of the infantry line at Romani. Immediately in front of Katia lay our open right flank with the Old Caravan Route leading to Dueidar and the Canal. The possibility of the Turkish attack developing in this direction had been considered by General Lawrence in consultation with Divisional Commanders; and the plans for meeting such an attack fully discussed.

Having in view that the morrow, August 4th, was the last day of the Mohammedan Feast of Bairam; and that the Turks would probably attack on that day; General Chauvel decided to leave out for the night the whole of the 1st Light Horse Brigade to hold an out-post line of about 3 miles to cover all the entrances to the sandhill plateau, which formed the Romani position, and which were unprotected by Infantry posts. It was this skilful placing of the 1st L.H. Brigade by the Divisional Commander that upset the Turkish plan—causing the enemy to deploy four hours before he intended to and making one of his columns change direction in the dark, forcing it into the soft and steeply undulating sand dunes lying between Romani and Kantara.

The night was a very quiet one and very dark. At 10 o'clock a light was seen at Katia. It was exposed four times for 10 seconds each time; then ceased; and all was quiet. Just before midnight the 1st Light Horse Brigade called up the Divisional H.Q. by telephone and reported that bodies of the enemy were appearing in front of the out-post line, and that firing had commenced.

This out-post line had been taken up after dark on the evening of the 3rd but nevertheless withstood the enemy's main attack from 12 midnight to 4 a.m. on the 4th, when the 1st Brigade was reinforced by the 2nd Brigade; and then the two Brigades as previously arranged, pivoting on the extreme right of the infantry position, gradually withdrew to a line which had already been decided upon, covering the right flank and rear of the Romani position.

At 3 o'clock in the morning some more information came in from the N.Z. Brigade which had an officer patrol at Bir Abu Raml away out on the Old Caravan road. It appears that the officer in charge had heard the enemy approaching and had sent an N.C.O. with some men to investigate. This N.C.O. soon encountered the enemy, and leaving his patrol in observation hurried back to Bir Abu Raml to warn the party there, but he found himself in between two columns of Turks moving north-west. He then rode quietly to one column, rode along it until he struck a gap in the transport camels, went through and made off with his information apparently unobserved. It soon became apparent that the enemy's attack was made in three columns in numbers about 8000. One, their right column, attacked the 52nd Division in front. This attack was easily held off, but the 52nd Division was subjected to severe shelling during the day. The Turk centre column and his left column were most skilfully led round the open flank on the 52nd Division's right, and on, to seize the camp and the railway. The skill and confidence with which these columns were led was explained some days afterwards when some Turkish orders were captured, signed by Lieut.-Colonel von Stotsein, Commander of the 4th Group. These orders stated, *inter alia,* "Bedouin guides will be required to have a certificate to be able to cross the enemy lines." This meant that only those Bedouins who were in our pay (and supposed to be getting information for us) were to be employed. The enemy were so determined in their attack that they would undoubtedly have reached the railway but for the gallant and skilful resistance put up by the Light Horse Brigades and our Wellington Regiment. There was no moon and the Turkish masses could not be seen. Our men could only fire at the flash of the enemy rifles and beat off his bayonet attack when it came.

As has been said, at daylight the 2nd L.H. Brigade, with the Wellington Regiment reinforced the 1st L.H. Brigade, prolonging the latter's right. The enemy's weight was such that the two Brigades gradually drew back until about 11 a.m. The enemy's main attack, arrested by the well-directed fire of the R.H.A. Batteries of the Anzac Mounted Division, and by our rifle and machine gun fire, which was contributed to considerably by the 52nd Division infantry posts on the right of the Romani position, appeared then to have exhausted itself, but held its ground.

The camps as well as the firing line were heavily shelled by the Turkish guns of various calibres including 5.9″ and 10.5 Cm. guns, and were severely bombed by enemy planes.

The enemy now held a line running from the Bardawil along the front of the 52nd Division entrenched position and thence bending westward through, and including, the great sandhill called Mount Meredith to the great sand dune Mount Royston (named respectively after the G.Os.C. 1st and 2nd L.H. Brigades). This latter position dominated the camp area at Romani and threatened the railway line.

General Royston, under whom the Wellington Regiment was serving and who was a very Knight of the old Crusaders was throughout this momentous day the most conspicuous and ubiquitous figure on the battlefield. Although wounded he rode amongst the men, for whom he always had a cheery word, encouraging them and often exhorting them to take cover, whilst openly exposing himself. It is said that he used up no fewer than 8 horses during the fighting; and a characteristic message came from him to H.Q. late in the day—"General Royston has just been wounded and has gone to get another horse."

It was just at this critical period of the day's fighting that the N.Z.M.R. Brigade with some Yeomanry appeared on the high ground to the west of Mount Royston, and our counter stroke began.

To go back to the movements of this force since early dawn, at 2 o'clock on the morning of the 4th General Chaytor had been advised of the Turkish advance against Romani and moved with his Brigade towards Dueidar along the Old Caravan Route; but events moving so rapidly at Romani and the Turkish attack proving so strong and reaching so close to the railway, that when within a mile of Dueidar he was ordered to move to Canterbury Hill close to Mount Royston, where he arrived at 11 o'clock, finding Yeomanry from the 5th Mounted Brigade already in touch with the enemy on the south west of Mount Royston.

MOUNT ROYSTON, ROMANI.

The attack on Mount Royston at once began; and some infantry from the 42nd Division began to arrive from the Suez Canal at the Pelusium railway station close by. Aided by the accurate and rapid shooting of the Somerset R.H.A. Battery the N.Z. Brigade soon obtained a footing on Mount Royston; and by a very gallant advance in which the Yeomanry took part, the position was captured late in the afternoon; and it was occupied by the infantry, who had arrived too late to take part in the fighting. The mounted men continued to advance until darkness put an end to the fighting, capturing some 1200 unwounded Turks and a mountain battery. The prisoners were sent into the Pelusium railway station and the N.Z. Brigade with the Yeomanry fell back to the railway line to feed and water their horses while the two L.H. Brigades put out an outpost line upon the field of battle. The 3rd L.H. Brigade, which so far had not been engaged, reached Dueidar after dark.

And now began the third phase, the thrusting back of the enemy into the desert.

At 4 o'clock in the morning of August 5th the Division began to move, advancing towards Katia. The 1st and 2nd L.H. Brigades, with them the Wellington Regiment and the Ayrshire and Leicestershire batteries, captured large numbers of prisoners and quantities of material in every mile of their advance. The Wellington Regiment with the 7th L.H. Regiment and supported on the left by infantry posts of the 52nd Division, fixed bayonets and stormed "Wellington Ridge," a position dominating the camps. They encountered heavy rifle and machine gun fire, but rushing up the sandy slope with irresistible dash, they quickly broke through the

SOMERSET BATTERY R.H.A. IN ACTION.

Turkish front line. The enemy became demoralised and our troops pressed forward from ridge to ridge without a pause. At noon the situation was as follows:—Away on the right, south of the Old Caravan Road attacking the enemy in Bir El Hamisah, was the 3rd L.H. Brigade. Next came the N.Z.M.R. close up to the south-west edge of the Katia palms; on their left was 1st, 2nd, and 5th Brigades in that order; and on their left again the 52nd Division was attacking Abu Hamra.

Behind the Mounted Division came the 42nd Infantry Division marching in much distress in the scorching sand.

The Turks were making a very determined stand on the line Bir El Hamisah–Katia–Abu Hamra, using their guns to good effect and with numerous machine guns well placed in the palms fringing on the eastern side of the great flat marsh which stretched right across the front of the enemy's position and gave them a most excellent field of fire.

A general attack was decided upon to commence at 2.30 p.m. at which hour the N.Z. Brigade, and the 1st and 2nd L.H. Brigades advanced at the gallop over the exposed country. The 5th L.H. Regiment fixed bayonets which glittered in the sun, and the great line of galloping horses presented a magnificent spectacle—shell fire was unheeded, bullets buried themselves in the sand dunes as the horses surged over them. The advance continued until the ground became too swampy to carry the horses; and the men dismounted and went in on foot.

This mounted charge considerably shook the morale of the enemy—for in many places he displayed the white flag on the near approach of the horses.

A hot fight ensued and it was here that the popular medical officer of the Wellington Regiment, Captain Wood and his assistant Sgt. Moseley, lost their lives in succouring the wounded.

Meanwhile the 3rd L.H. on the extreme right were held up and failing to work round the enemy's right flank drew off, and this led to the Canterbury Regiment getting the full force of a strong Turkish counter attack.

Darkness put an end to the battle and the Division withdrew to water the horses, leaving Lieut. Johnson with his troop of the Auckland Regiment as a listening post.

THE ACTION OF BIR EL ABD

The 1st and 2nd L.H. Brigades who had borne the heat and burden of the day during the long and arduous days prior to the battle, and who withstood so gallantly the weight of the enemy's attack on the night of August 3rd and early morning of August 4th, were now so tired out that they were sent back to the bivouac lines at Romani and Etmaler. But the 5th Mounted Brigade which had been attached to the Anzac Mounted Division remained under General Chauvel's command. Orders were received to follow up the enemy—while the two infantry divisions, the 42nd and the 52nd, were respectively to advance to Katia and Abu Hamra and to hold these places.

In his cautious advance across the desert the enemy had prepared position after position and these were now invaluable to him in his retreat. He fought a very strong rearguard action well covered by his guns; and after stubborn fighting during the 6th, 7th and 8th, he was pressed back to Bir El Abd some 20 miles from the Romani lines. Assistance to the Division was given on the south by a small flying camel column from the Ballah railhead, who harassed the Turks' left flank working through Bir El Mageibra, Bir El Aweidia and Hod El Bayud.

The 1st and 2nd L.H. Brigades, who had been resting, were now ordered up and being so few in number were formed into a composite brigade under General Royston. At daylight on August 9th the Division began its advance with the New Zealanders in the centre following the telegraph line; the 1st and 2nd Brigades on the left; and the 3rd L.H. Brigade on the right and in touch with the small flying column. The enemy were soon encountered and were driven back on to Bir El Abd on a frontage of about 10 miles.

At 5 o'clock the New Zealand Brigade reached the high ground overlooking El Abd and there withstood a heavy counter attack by the Turks who came on in two columns of 5000 to 6000 each. But well backed up by the Somerset and Leicester batteries the Brigade firmly established itself across the telegraph line and the Old Caravan Road. By mid-day our advance had been completely checked—the Turks bringing up fresh troops and counter-attacking most determinedly. His guns were also well placed and his fire heavy and accurate.

The Ayrshire Battery which was with Royston's column was badly cut up and great difficulty was experienced in moving the guns when he was forced to retire, being obliged to give ground for nearly a mile. The 3rd L.H. Brigade after advancing well up on the right flank was also forced to give ground by the accuracy of the Turkish shell fire, but the New Zealand Brigade held on in the centre and owing to the bending back of both wings were holding a very exposed line on the forward slopes of the hills overlooking the Hod. Though the enemy by the burning of store depots and by movement which could be observed was showing great anxiety to retire, yet finding he could hold his position and that his flanks were not threatened and being reinforced with fresh troops from El Arish, he again delivered a fierce counter-attack on a frontage of about 2½ miles right to our centre. The brunt of this attack was borne by the Canterbury and Auckland Regiments, and by a squadron of Warwickshire Yeomanry, which was under General Chaytor's command. The attack was gallantly withstood and the Turks beaten off just as darkness fell.

A great fight was put up by the machine guns. Lieut. Gordon Harper, the gallant commander of the section of machine guns attached to the Canterbury Regiment, was mortally wounded and brought out with great difficulty by his famous brother, Captain Robin Harper, O.C. Machine Gun Squadron, who had all guns available playing upon the advancing Turks arresting their advance when within 100 yards of the New Zealand position.

This defeat of the last Turkish counter-attack took place just before dusk and continued as the New Zealand Brigade withdrew under cover of these machine guns which were supported by some Yeomanry whose troopers offered many helmets to be used as "flame extinguishers" to hide the machine gun flashes as darkness came on. Each helmet was held over the muzzle and the gun fired through it, and it can be imagined the life of a helmet under such conditions would not be long; but it did its work effectually while it lasted.

Here also fell many gallant officers and men, among them Captain Johnston of the Auckland Regiment and Major Hammond of the Canterbury Regiment, both Squadron leaders.

THE ACTION OF BIR EL ABD

Particularly sad circumstances surrounded the death of this last officer, who was very ill on the morning of the battle, in fact he had been recommended for evacuation to Hospital, but insisted on remaining and leading his squadron; and fought his men with great brilliancy throughout the day. Lieut. A. Martin of the Auckland Regiment also was severely wounded and died in Cairo some weeks later. He had shown exceptional ability as a "water officer," finding and developing wells far ahead of the Main Body. On this day at Bir el Abd after conspicuous good work he fell while leading his troop.

On either side of the "Old Road" they lie, the Aucklanders on the south side and the Canterbury men on the north side—on either side of that road down which those old Crusaders

AFTER BIR EL ABD.

under Baldwin came to oust the infidel from Egypt; and by the same road came that "man of Destiny" eager to conquer a new world for himself; and back again he hurried crushed and shamed; and fled to Europe. And earlier still came Darius and Cambyses the Persians, Alexander the Great with his Greeks, and Anthony with his Romans; and now iron trains thunder by on that selfsame road and They will know—those gallant fellows we left there—They will know that now at last the work is well and truly done.

The three brigades were then withdrawn to water their horses and to rest some few miles back.

At daylight next morning strong patrols went forward and remained in touch with the enemy throughout the day, but the horses were too tired to enable an attack in force to be made.

On the 11th no serious fighting took place, but the enemy was watched and harassed, and plans were made for an attack on the 12th. The advance began at daylight and our patrols soon reported that the enemy was retiring—Bir El Abd was found to be evacuated—and he was followed as far as Salmana, where a small rear-guard was encountered.

Difficulties of transport and feeding the troops precluded the advance being carried any further, and arrangements were made to hold the country as far east as Bir El Abd.

The prisoners captured during the Romani operations amounted to nearly 5000, including 50 officers, some German and Austrians. We also captured a very large number of rifles and a camel-pack machine gun company complete, a mountain battery, quantities of stores and ammunition and two complete field Hospitals most excellently appointed. All the arms and equipment were of German manufacture and the camel-pack machine gun company's equipment had been especially designed for desert warfare. Many of the rifles were of the latest pattern and made of rustless steel. Enemy casualties were estimated at 3000.

The result of these operations was the complete defeat of an enemy force of some 18,000, of which in killed, wounded and prisoners, he lost 9000 men.

The Turk throughout displayed the greatest determination and tenacity. His strength during the rear-guard fighting debarred any serious interference with his flanks. Heavy going and lack of water for our horses assisted the enemy greatly in that they confined our movements. His guns were well served with an unlimited supply of ammunition. The fact that he had transported guns of 5.9 in. calibre across the yielding sand of the desert speaks volumes for his engineering ability. This was accomplished apparently by a large party of workmen who preceded the guns and excavated two parallel wheel tracks through the sand to correspond with the width of the wheels on the gun carriages. These tracks were then filled with brushwood which was firmly packed, and formed an excellent road along which the guns were man-handled; a truly wonderful feat. For those places in the desert where the sand was too soft for this road, strong wooden planks were carried on camels, to be put down as temporary crossings. The same thoroughness and foresight in all branches characterised the enemy's organisation throughout, due no doubt to their German leaders. The heavy guns were manned by Austrians, the machine guns by Germans. The Field Hospitals were complete with all the instruments, fittings and drugs modern science could supply. The bid to break the Suez Canal and to conquer Egypt was a bold one and it was made by picked troops who fought a clean and vigorous fight notwithstanding the tribulation of their wonderful march in midsummer, and this justly earned the admiration of our troops. The attack upon Egypt failed and the attacking force lost at least half its numbers, but the Turkish Government thought so highly of the enterprise that it awarded a special star to the survivors.

The following extract from a captured order by Jemal Pasha is of interest:—

"ARMY ORDER. 30th January, 1915.

1. Grants of money, to be given to the families of officers killed in the attack on the Canal, in addition to legal pensions. (L.T. 250 in one payment apparently).

2. Officers killed, who have shown extraordinary bravery, will be promoted in rank and the pensions of the higher rank will be paid to their families.

3. Privates, corporals and N.C.Os. killed in the attack on the Canal who have shown great bravery will be promoted to a higher rank. The pensions attached to the higher rank will be paid.

4. When the conquest of Egypt has been completed the family of every officer and soldier killed will have a house built for it by the government in its town or village.

5. Claims in this connection must be authenticated by the A. C. Commander.

6. This order applies to all soldiers on the line of battle or behind it.

7. It also includes officers and men disabled by wounds and rendered unable to work.

Commander of the IV. Army, and Minister of Marine.

AHMED JEMAL."

That these operations and the attack upon the Canal in January, 1915, were not merely raids, but were genuine and determined attempts to conquer Egypt, was amply proved afterwards when our forces were able to see the great and thorough preparations in Palestine. A new railway had been built extending the Palestine system to the Wadi El Arish, and alongside it was constructed a fine motor road. Permanent works were constructed for the conservation of water along the route; and at the Wadi El Arish enormous rock cut reservoirs were being made.

THE CACOLET CAMEL.   SITTING-UP CASES FROM THE BATTLE OF ROMANI.

The tenacity and endurance of our own troops of the Mounted Brigades were magnificent. The battle was fought and persevered with through abnormal summer heat, regardless of long periods of thirst suffered by man and beast. The artillery and machine guns covered our advances. In defence they wrought havoc on the enemy's attack. No words can adequately express the untiring devotion of the medical officers, the stretcher bearers and the sand-cart drivers who were ever in the firing line, traversing enormous distances and doing all that lay in their power to alleviate the sufferings of the wounded.

The heavy sand precluded the use of the army ambulance whether motor or horse drawn, and the wounded were collected by the cacolet camel or by the sand-cart, a two-wheeled vehicle with broad tyres on its wheels. The cacolet was a contrivance lashed to a camel's back which carried a man on each side; but the rolling motion which accompanied the camel's gait allows of neither rest nor ease and exacts the full penalty of pain from the unfortunate occupant. Happy indeed was the man whose wound permitted him to be lashed instead to his horse.

Sledges of wood and sheet iron were improvised to cope with the abnormal number of evacuations; but the close contact with the ground surface indelibly impressed upon the occupant of the sledge the rough nature of the country.

CHAPTER III.

Now ensued a period of great activity in railway construction. A line was surveyed and rapidly pushed on to Bir El Abd. Long reconnaissances were made towards El Arish under cover of which the engineers surveyed the line to Mazar, the resting place on the Old Caravan Road halfway between Bir El Abd and El Arish. Led by British Army engineers the Egyptian Labour Corps proved great railway builders. With his "fassee" (or great heavy short handled hoe) and his basket made from palm leaves—there is no finer excavator in the world than the "Gyppy" from the Nile Valley. Always happy and always singing (as long as the weather is not wet and cold) he gets through a great deal of work and shows great muscular endurance. Who has once heard his song will ever forget it! with its chorus

THE HAPPY "GYPPY" LABOURER.

"Allah Il Allah" or "Kham leila, Kham youm"? Many thousands of these men were now at work and the railway advanced by a mile per day—formation, track-laying, sidings, etc., all counted in. Up would steam a "construction train" loaded with sleepers, rails and fish plates, and would stop at the rail end. Out would leap the trained gangs of

"Gyppies" and then just as fast as one could walk, down would go the rails, spiked and coupled and nothing to be done but the ballasting.

By the rail side was brought Nile water in pipes from the Sweet Water Canal which runs from Ismailia to Port

"GYPPY" LABOURERS AT WORK ON THE DESERT RAILWAY.

Said on the western bank of the Suez Canal. The water was brought through two pipe lines which were laid side by side over the desert and eventually took the Nile into Palestine, by a system of pumps and reservoirs in approximately 20 mile stages.

By our occupation of Bir El Abd we had entered an area infected by the dreaded cholera. This was known through our intelligence agents and also from notice boards placed in infected areas by the Turkish medical officers. Precautions had been taken earlier in the campaign to regularly inoculate all ranks, not only against enteric but also cholera; these precautions bore good fruit for though there were mild outbreaks of cholera amongst our men the death rate was practically *nil*.

The whole country to within 20 miles of El Arish was now thoroughly explored and all wells tested and noted down. Many interesting archaeological remains were found. For

THE PIPE-LINE AND RAILWAY ACROSS THE DESERT.

instance, in a beautiful little palm grove south of Bir El Abd was a long Roman trough built for the watering of animals, with the brick work and plaster almost as fresh as the day they were made. Away to the north lay the great Bardawil and many gypsum lakes, whose surfaces, as white and hard as ice, lay glittering in the sun. Huge stretches of the "Serbonian Bog" were as white as if they were covered with snow, the surface being composed of great gypsum crystals whose sharp cutting edges prevented the passage of a horse. Most of this surface was hard and strong enough to bear the weight of a horse, but woe betide the man who strayed from the recognised and tried track, for his horse broke through and floundered hopelessly in that black mud referred to by the poet Milton.

At the extreme point of the curve made by the Bardawil Peninsula lies Katib El Galss—the Mount Cassius of Herodotus. This enormous sand hill, which rises some 200 feet above the sea, now shows a steep cliff-like face to the waves which are encroaching upon it. Along that cliff about 50 feet from the top, stretches a line a few feet in thickness of broken Roman pottery, bricks and stone; clearly showing what was then the top of the hill upon which Cassius built his fortified camp. This is a remarkable instance of the permanency of a sand hill, for Herodotus saw it 300 B.C. Since then it has neither been blow away, nor has it even been moved; it has but added 50 feet to its height.

Farther east, where the Bardawil Peninsula joins the main land, and where is the sea entrance to the Bardawil Lagoon, we found ruins of the ancient towns of Flusiat and

ON THE BARDAWIL.

Khuniat. These once stood at the mouth of that arm of the Nile which ran by Pelusium, and through which all Egypt's trade with the Mediterranean passed; and through which those old navigators used to sail to reach the Red Sea and the land of the Queen of Sheba. What their history was or how old these towns were is not known; but that they were in existence in Christian times is proved by the remains of beautiful marble columns upon which was carved The Cross and many other symbols clearly indicating the remains of Christian Churches. A considerable amount of excavation had recently been done here, it is supposed by the Germans; and near here also, strange to say, was found the famous Stone of Baldwin which had been erected in El Arish by his followers soon after his death in 1118 A.D.

After our occupation of El Arish this stone was taken back and re-erected on that spot where it had been placed so many years ago.

On September 16th-17th a great reconnaissance was made as far as Mazar—half way between Bir el Abd and El Arish— by the 2nd and 3rd L.H. Brigades with a detachment of the Camel Corps, and the New Zealand Machine Gun Squadron. Mazar was surrounded and the strength of the garrison tested and then the Division withdrew. This threat so alarmed the enemy that the garrison fell back upon El Arish and Mazar was abandoned.

Early in November railway construction had advanced so well that the Division moved to Bir El Mazar and preparations were made for the capture of El Arish. All information available showed that this important centre was strongly held by the Turks and aeroplane photographs showed many lines of trenches covering the town both on the sea side and on the west and south. Every effort was made to test all sources of water between Mazar and El Arish.

Now the Wadi El Arish is what the ancients called the "River of Egypt." It is a great dry watercourse coming from the heart of the Sinai Peninsula and there flows down it, two or three times in each year, a great "spate of water." This usually occurs in December or January, at which season there are great thunderstorms among the mountains. For the rest of the year the wadi is dry; though, as we proved afterwards, water can be obtained at certain places by well-digging. Our intelligence reports showed that the Turks were building a railway from Beersheba through Magdhaba, which lies some 30 miles up the wadi from El Arish, and was intended to reach the Suez Canal by way of the route which lay through the mountains.

There was always a danger of an attack by the Turks along this route so that it was necessary that the country to our south should be constantly patrolled. This work was undertaken by the Imperial Camel Corps Brigade, which had been formed from New Zealand, Australian, and Yeomanry reinforcements.

The equipment of this fine body of men included the "Dhurra" bag carrying five days grain for the camel, and a cylindrical five-gallon tank holding the rider's five days

THE CAMEL BRIGADE ON THE MOVE.

water supply. Food for five days, and spare clothing, were carried in a canvas "Pikau" bag slung over the saddle. Strapped over all were blankets, overcoat, rifle, &c., the full weight carried being about 320lb., including the man.

The camels were swift trotting and were supposed to be able to go five days without water. New Zealand contributed two companies, the first of which—the 15th Camel Company—was formed in July under the command of Captain J. G. McCallum, a very keen and efficient young officer, who, backed up by the natural aptitude of the New Zealand soldier to fall in with existing circumstances, very soon had his company fit to take the field. Later a second company was formed, again from volunteers and surplus reinforcements. The two companies took part in all operations undertaken by the I.C.C. Brigade until June, 1918, when they were reorganised, and formed the 2nd N.Z. Machine Gun Squadron in the final operations.

The Commander-in-Chief, General Sir Archibald Murray, came out to Mazar and rode round the outposts, going to the Auckland Regiment who were "farthest east" on the Old Road, and laid his plans for the advance upon El Arish.

More Yeomanry Regiments had by now arrived and with the addition of the Camel Brigade, the mounted force available for future operations had considerably increased. So all available troops were formed into a force called "The Desert Column" under the command of Lieut.-General Sir Philip Chetwode, who had so successfully commanded a cavalry brigade in the retreat from Mons, and a cavalry division later on in France. Plans were laid and orders issued for the advance and attack upon El Arish, when information came that the Turks were evacuating the town.

THE ADVANCE TOWARDS THE HOLY LAND.
Transport on the beach at El Arish.

The Anzac Mounted Division immediately prepared to march out, and on the evening of the 20th of December concentrated at a point on the Old Caravan Road about 15 miles from El Arish, and an all-night march began. The plan was that El Arish was to be completely encircled by dawn—the 1st L.H. Brigade, crossing the wadi to the south of the town, were to close the exits to the north and east; the camels and the N.Z. Brigade to close all escape to the south; while the Yeomanry advanced from the west.

THE N.Z.M.R. BRIGADE "FORD."
The first car to cross the desert and enter El Arish.

The N.Z. Brigade, with whom marched the Divisional Headquarters, was guided by Lieut. Finlayson of the Auckland Regiment who had previously led patrols into this vacinity; and so excellent was his judgment and skill in finding his way that when daylight appeared the column was found to be within 200 yards of the small sand hill to which he had been asked to guide it. As soon as communication could be obtained with the other brigades it was found that all had reached their allotted positions before dawn and so completely isolated the town; and soon afterwards our patrols entered the town and found that the Turks had gone.

The praise for this bloodless victory was in a great measure due to the horses, for the Turk was beginning to feel a wholesome dread of the speed and wide striking range of our mounted arm. He preferred to abandon rather than to defend the well prepared and excellently sited trenches at El Arish. He was so apprehensive about the security of his line of retreat that he made his exit good before the mounted troops could attack. His fears were soon realised however, at Magdhaba, where his retreat was abruptly terminated.

Immediate steps were taken to patrol the country to find out what had become of the garrison, and a line of out-posts was formed well to the east of the town. During the day the Desert Column Commander, General Chetwode, arrived on the beach at El Arish by motor launch from Port Said. Reliable information soon showed that the El Arish garrison had retired to Magdhaba and plans were put in hand for the advance of the Division to this place. The defence of El Arish was handed over to the Yeomanry and to the 52nd Division as they came up, and the Anzac Mounted Division concentrated after dark on the evening of the 21st at a point about five miles south of El Arish on the wadi. Here supplies were issued which had been brought from railhead by camel; and the Division resumed its march about midnight.

The weather was cold but the going admirable, and good progress was made. Each hour was divided into 40 minutes riding, 10 minutes leading to warm the men, and 10 minutes halt.

The fires of the enemy camp at Magdhaba having been observed at 3.50 a.m. the force continued to advance until 10 minutes to five and then halted and dismounted in an open plain some four miles from its objective, while the Divisional Commander went forward to reconnoitre. The number of bivouac fires indicated a considerable force and the brightness of the lights was very misleading as to distance. The position appeared much closer than it really was.

This showing of lights by the enemy clearly indicated how impossible he thought that tired horses and men after an all-night march of 30 miles could possibly set out immediately upon another 30 mile march to the position to which he had retired.

The Battle of Magdhaba

As dawn broke, the bivouac fires disappeared, and a haze of smoke obscured the valley from view for some time. Reconnaissance of the enemy's position was therefore very difficult, and though our aeroplanes were assisting it was not until 8 o'clock that orders could be issued for the attack.

A message which helped to a decision, though entirely unofficial, was that which fell from an aeroplane of the Australian Flying Squadron. The author had flown over an enemy position and had been given such a hot reception there that his feelings prompted him to advise his friends in the Light Horse,—for home consumption only—"the ...... are there all right." This important message however fell near D.H.Q. and the latter immediately took full advantage of its principal information without questioning the pedigree of the Turks concerned.

General Chaytor with his own brigade and the 3rd L.H. Brigade was given orders to move on Magdhaba by the north and north-east and to endeavour to cut off all retreat. The camels advanced straight on Magdhaba following the telegraph line and the 1st L.H. Brigade was for the present in reserve. The Division's batteries soon got to work but targets were extraordinarily hard to find. The enemy's batteries and trenches were exceedingly well concealed, but by 10 o'clock the N.Z. Brigade had closed well in and the news was brought in by an aeroplane that the enemy were beginning to retire and that there was a possibility of their escaping our enveloping movement. So the 1st L.H. Brigade was ordered to move direct on to Magdhaba, but meeting severe shrapnel fire as it trotted over the open plain, was compelled to change direction and take refuge in the wadi bed, up which it advanced against the enemy's left, detaching one regiment to move round to the south of the enemy's position. By 12 o'clock all three brigades and the Camel Brigade were hotly engaged, but on account of mirage and dust-clouds good observations were impossible.

The greatest assistance was, however, given by the aeroplanes whose reports, frequently brought in, and often given verbally by the observer, whose pilot brought him to ground by Headquarters, showed estimated positions, strength, and movements of the enemy at various points.

The information generally indicated that he was preparing to evacuate. The country favoured the enemy who took full advantage of the many folds in the ground to conceal himself. Much drawing of fire was necessary before he could be located.

With the Auckland Regiment in reserve the N.Z. Brigade had advanced with Wellington on the right and Canterbury on the left in "Line of Troop Columns" accompanied by the Vickers and Lewis Guns. On arriving at a point about 2000 yards from the enemy position four enemy mountain guns

THE FIRST CASUALTY, MAGDHABA.

and many snipers opened fire upon the advancing troops, but they pushed forward to a point 1600 yards from the enemy where they dismounted to attack on foot. But the advanced screen under a Wellington officer had pushed up to within 400 yards where they dismounted in a covered position.

At noon the situation was as follows:—

The New Zealanders were engaged with and had partially enveloped the enemy's right; the 3rd L.H. Brigade was still held in reserve by General Chaytor, with the exception of the 10th L.H. regiment, under that well-known New Zealander of the 2nd contingent, Lieut.-Colonel "Barney" Todd, D.S.O., which was engaged in making a wide turning movement to the south to intercept any retirement by the enemy. The I.C.C. was attacking direct on the village and the 1st L.H. Brigade was working on to the enemy's left by way of the wadi bed.

At this time the fire from the enemy mountain guns and from his rifles and machine guns was very heavy, but the guns were very badly served and the small arms fire most inaccurate.

As the attack developed, at 12.30, General Chaytor sent in the 8th and 9th L.H. Regiments between the Wellington and Canterbury regiments, where there was a gap of some 800 yards.

About 1 o'clock word was received that water could not be found at Bir Lahfan, which meant that there was no water for the horses nearer than El Arish, 30 miles away, and it was realised that the enemy was in a very strong position with redoubts well sited and fully manned. Considerable doubt was felt therefore if the position could be taken before dark.

But about 2 p.m. things began to improve; both 1st L.H. and N.Z. Brigades making progress—the 1st L.H. Brigade capturing some trenches and about 100 prisoners.

By 3.30 p.m. the New Zealanders with fixed bayonets were swarming over the trenches to the east of the houses and the Turks were surrendering in all directions.

At four o'clock General Chaytor was enabled to report that his men held the buildings and redoubts on the left and that the 10th L.H. advancing from the south had captured two trenches on that side, so that all retreat to the Turks was cut off.

As darkness came on fighting had practically ceased and prisoners were rounded up and collected, and horses watered at the captured wells.

One of the decisive events of the afternoon was the capture of a battery of four mountain guns. This was effected by Lieut. Johnston, Canterbury regiment. After the surrender of the first batch of prisoners Lieut. Johnston and six men pushed on to where the battery was still firing;

he attacked the position and after firing a few rounds the garrison consisting of two officers and 15 men surrendered.

The Auckland regiment, with the 1st L.H. Regiment (from the 1st L.H. Brigade) and one squadron from the 3rd L.H. Brigade were left to clear the battlefield; and the three brigades began their 30 mile ride back to El Arish, stopping at Bir Lahfan where a convoy of camels had arrived laden with much needed water for the men, who had left El Arish the night before carrying one water bottle per man only.

It must be remembered that they had been marching and fighting for 30 hours without pause and for most of them it meant the third night without sleep. To pass one night without sleep is trying; two nights is absolutely painful; but the third night without sleep after heavy fighting with all the added strain and excitement that it means—is almost an impossibility. Men and horses were dropping off at the oddest times and in the oddest of positions, and many men and horses came down in the dust; and this long night ride may safely be regarded as one of the most trying of the many wearisome marches experienced by the brigade. Apart from the intense cold which penetrated to the bone the lightly clad horsemen, the men were fatigued to such a degree that words fail to adequately describe. They had been called upon to make a superhuman effort immediately following their long march from Mazar; and had succeeded in performing all that had been asked of them.

Dense clouds of dust almost blinded the tired horses, which collided with one another in the dark. Many a man fell asleep, and letting his reins slack, was taken by his horse—who feeling the loss of control had quickened his pace—far in among the troops in front. This caused much amusement and especially so in the case of the Italian Liaison Officer who was among those who fell asleep on their horses. He was riding with the Headquarters of the Division behind one of the brigades and though clad in khaki wore a cap of a different colour and shape from the British cap. Three separate times did his horse take him away in amongst the horses of the leading brigade; and three separate times did tired and dosing troopers wake up with a start to find a stranger riding with them; and three separate times was he brought back to Divisional Headquarters under arrest as a spy! He was a cavalry officer and had lived in England and in New Zealand and was a most popular man amongst all who knew him, but these repeated arrests distressed him considerably and added to the amusement of all concerned and helped to pass away the weary hours.

The powers of endurance of the human brain have their limits and rebel when overtaxed; and on this journey "visions" in various forms appeared to most of the riders. Although the route of the march was practically bare, yet streets and houses well lit up, and curiously shaped animals were seen. The Divisional Commander, usually the most staid of men and who was riding with his staff, was suddenly seen to set spurs to his horse and accompanied by the officer who was riding beside him galloped off to one side in the darkness. The column had gone on its way stumbling and grumbling for a mile or more before the General and his companion quietly slipped back into their places; and it was some time before the explanation of their sudden leaving of the column could be got out of them. It appears that they both, at the same time, thought they saw a fox and thought that they were fox hunting and so went off at a gallop.

That many hundreds of men should see tall buildings lighted up and strange forms—each according to his fancy—is curious, but that two sober sensible well-balanced men should at the same time experience the same hallucination is more than strange. Many discussions have followed these happenings and our wise ones laid it down that the brain had temporarily lost certain of its powers of endurance, which sleep alone could restore. Perhaps this phenomenon accounts for the story told in France of the "Angels of Mons" during the early stages of the war when the British troops were fighting continuously there.

The Brigade eventually arrived at its bivouac ground near Nasmi about three miles from El Arish at about six o'clock on the morning of Christmas Eve; and was almost immediately heavily bombed by enemy planes.

The losses during this action were astonishingly small considering the fighting done and the captures made. The list is an interesting one as showing what is taken from a beaten enemy who is out in the field far from civilization, and it is of course very incomplete, for darkness came on before the last Turk had surrendered, and there was not enough time to collect a quarter of the military material of value. The list is as follows:—

  1282 Prisoners, including 43 officers.
  1 Battery Mountain Guns.
  4 Machine Guns complete.
  1 Broken Machine Gun.
  1052 Rifles.
  180 Bayonets.
  6 Boxes of gun ammunition.
  100,000 Rounds of S.A.A.
  1 Dredger.
  Component parts of an oil engine intact.
  10 Fantasses.
  Telephone wire equipment.
  A number of plans of reservoirs, etc.
  Turkish orders and newspapers.
  40 Horses.
  51 Camels.
  Large quantity of Hospital equipment.

Amongst the officers captured was Khadir Bey commanding the 80th Regiment, Izzet Bey commanding 2/80 Battalion and Rushti Bey commanding 3/80 Battalion. Many hundreds of Turks were killed and wounded yet our casualties in the whole Division were only 12 killed and 134 wounded, of which the N.Z. Brigade contributed two officers, and seven men; and 36 other ranks wounded only. The extremely light casualty list may be attributed to the great adaptability of our men to this class of warfare. The attack was well-planned and well carried out with great skill and boldness, every man showing a skill and intelligent appreciation of the situation and fearless confidence in himself and his comrades. And the fine and sturdy persistence of the Youth from the Southern Cross ultimately placed them in a position to charge with the bayonet; and the line of glistening bayonets at close range with determined men behind them, overcame the enemy who quickly collapsed and surrendered.

It is worthy of note that in an address to the Brigade the following day General Chetwode said "that the mounted men at Magdhaba had done what he had never known cavalry in the history of war to have done before, *i.e.*, they had not only located and surrounded the enemy's position but they had got down to it as infantry and had carried fortified positions at the point of the bayonet."

TURKISH PRISONERS IN EL ARISH.

The season was midwinter in this country; and though the days had been hot the nights had been growing bitterly cold. Throughout the whole of the desert campaign, after the camps at Romani had been left, the troops had had no tents; not even a sun shelter was issued to them. When in the palm groves a certain amount of shelter from the sun could be obtained, but men bivouacing out in the open suffered the full blast from the sun. Many unauthorised "bivvies" were acquired from time to time, pieces of sacking, pieces of canvas, Bedouin cloth, in fact anything that would serve as a sun shelter was pressed into use, to be thrown away again immediately a "stunt" came on. Now however with the bitterly cold nights and the prospect of winter storms coming, every effort was made to get tents from Egypt; but they were not forthcoming until some time after the winter storms had broken upon us.

Another ever present difficulty in the desert is firewood. There is a light scrub growing over many areas and it is good enough to boil the billy under a hot sun, but is never good enough as firewood to make a successful fire. A certain amount of firewood cut in the Mediterranean Islands, principally from Cyprus was available, and it was carried on Greek schooners to Kantara, sawn into two feet lengths and placed upon a military train, brought up to railhead and there distributed to the troops. There was a supposed ration of two lbs. per head per man; but this seldom came; and this thrust forward to El Arish from railhead 20 miles away, brought the firewood question to a climax. There was none: and to-morrow was Christmas Day. By the help of our postal service, the willing co-operation of the railways and camel transport and everybody on the line of communications, fairly large Christmas mails had come in, including amongst other good things—plum puddings and turkeys from the O.C. Training Regiment, Major Samuel. Hence the even more urgent demand for firewood. There were no ruins handy as there were always in France; there was only El Arish, which with our British scrupulous justice to inferior races was protected even more securely than our towns in our own country. But still there were good Christmas fires, and there were good Christmas dinners well cooked! An excited signalling officer rushed into Divisional Headquarters just before sundown and said "your men are cutting down the telegraph poles on the telegraph line which leads from El Arish to Magdhaba." Here was trouble for somebody! It must be remembered that all the way from Kantara to El Arish and on to Rafa and so to Palestine, stretches a telegraph line built of iron and wood. Owing to the action of the wind blowing sand along the surface of the desert, posts are built with iron bases which stand some four feet above the sand level, and to these iron bases the ordinary wooden posts are bolted. Such was the scarcity of timber for poles that the strictest Army Orders had from time to time been issued prohibiting the cutting down or "lifting" of any posts; and to do the Force justice this order was well obeyed. But the urgency of Christmas dinners and cold weather had not before been experienced.

However, just as the wearied Staff began to see what could be done in came the Divisional Commander, who, hearing what was the matter, said with a laugh, that he had just come down this particular telegraph line and that the men removing the poles were the Signallers themselves (which of course they had a right to do for use in other communication lines). "I saw," he said, "two or three wagons being loaded with poles, which several gangs of men had unbolted from off the iron bases, while others took down the wires and rolled them up depositing them in bundles (together with the insulators) against the denuded bases. No other but your own men would be doing this," and the Signalling officer retired discomfited.

Half way through Christmas afternoon he rushed in again more angry and excited than before, saying that he was right after all, they were men from the regiments, and he poured forth many statements in proof. Of course the Staff had now to really act, and it was found that the Camel Brigade had hit upon this clever plan which had deceived even the Divisional Commander himself. There was much said—and written—of course, but the Christmas dinners had been cooked and the men had a little store of wood put away for the cold nights; and H.M. Government Signals was minus five whole miles of telegraph line.

The men had two fine days in which to rest and look about them before the rain came.

El Arish was found to be rather different from the villages of the Delta, though the houses were of the same low flat topped kind; but the town had not outwardly the same dirty appearance. The houses, as in Egypt, were of sun-dried brick, and were washed over with a coating of light yellowish plaster made from the clay found in the El Arish flats. This gave the town a bright and clean appearance. The people, too, were very different. There appeared to be a mixture of many races. Many had blue eyes and fairish skin. One of the native police belonging to the town though unable to speak any language but Arabic, yet with his short close cut beard and blue eyes was a typical Frenchman from the Channel, possibly a descendant of Napoleon's ill-fated army. They were indeed a cosmopolitan, cheerful and vivacious people.

Approaching the town from the west along the Old Caravan Road, one usually follows a track that leads on to the sea beach about four miles from the mouth of the wadi. The beach is here a magnificent one—some 100 to 200 yards wide, and close down to it grow groves of luxuriant young date palms. We soon found the reason of this growth so close to salt water, in the excellent fresh water that was to be found in the sand—the best we had tasted since leaving Egypt, and it was in unlimited quantities.

Looking east there is a bold sand hill jutting right on to the beach; and on the top a domed tomb. This is the tomb of Nebi Yesir, and immediately beyond is a great grove of very tall and feathery palms. Here was the mouth of the wadi—the famous "River of Egypt."

Inland up the wadi some two miles lies in a hollow surrounded on three sides by sandhills, the town of El Arish, on an alluvial flat of yellow soil. The most conspicuous object is the Mosque (with its minaret) on a rise, and beside it is the ruins of a great fort whose stone walls were thrown down by the guns of the British Navy. It was this fort that withstood Napoleon for a whole week.

Looking east across the wadi are great groves of palms and more houses, now the village of El Risa. No doubt when El Arish was Rhinocolura it was a large city on both sides of the "River," and to it in those days were banished thieves from Egypt, whose punishment was not only banishment but disfigurement—by the slitting of their noses.

The Wadi El Arish is for 10 months of the year a dry watercourse, with its shingle beds and low alluvial flats, much resembling a New Zealand river. Debouching from the mountains just above Magdhaba, it bisects a narrow plain which at one time must have been intensely cultivated. Guide books tell us El Arish is famous for its dates, figs and vines. The two first are there but there was no sign of the vines, though there were many acres of excellent vine country.

During December and January the wadi is liable to come down "in spate" on account of thunderstorms in the mountains. Our men were able to see it so on two occasions and both men and horses much enjoyed splashing through the quickly running water on a hard shingle bottom.

THE MOUTH OF THE WADI AT EL ARISH, SHOWING A CAMEL CONVOY CROSSING THE BAR AT THE EDGE OF THE SEA.

On 27th December came a bitter gale from the north-west with much rain and even hail. Horses and men were huddled into all the sheltered nooks that could be found. This gale and rain lasted for twelve days, during which much interest was caused by a trawler dragging her anchor and coming ashore a total wreck. A wharf had been erected in wonderfully quick time by the Australian Bridging Train immediately after our arrival. At this wharf it was intended that store ships should unload; but the gale formed a great sand bar right across its end and it was never used for the purpose.

During the course of the storm great changes were made in the huge sandhills that abut on El Arish on the western side —they were torn about, increased in height, blown flat and great holes excavated among them. In one of these holes, over a mile from the cultivated flat of good soil, which adjoins the town, was laid bare a portion of the plain that had been buried by sand, many many generations ago; and on this bare portion were the clearly marked furrows of a plough. Who had laid those furrows? Perhaps he who paused in his work to watch the hosts of Cambyses the Persian go by; or perhaps one of those noseless inhabitants of Rhinocolura banished from Egypt some thousands of years ago.

The desert with rain and cloud took on a new and absorbing aspect; for the weather was bracing and inducive to effort; and the ground hard with the moisture in it; and many a joyful gallop had man and horse, where before was toil and heat and flies.

About this time our first store ship arrived at El Arish. Native boatmen with their boats from Alexandria were brought over to do the unloading; and it was hoped that our much overworked railway would be greatly eased by these sea-borne rations. But the Egyptian boatmen did not take kindly to the work. This work consisted of rowing their great double ended surf-boats out to the store ship, where she lay at anchor a mile from the shore; loading up their boats with rations and bringing them ashore—the boat being met in the surf by a large party of natives stripped to the waist and carrying a long rope. This rope was attached to the boat as she came through the surf and the team of men then ran away with her up on to the beach. The rate of unloading became so slow that it was seriously considered whether it would be advisable to give up landing stores on the beach, when a happy thought struck someone that the New Zealanders had just received a detachment of Rarotongans, who as Pacific Islanders were no doubt expert boatmen. Enquiries were made and it was found that they were all at home in the water, and they eagerly took on the job of manning two surf boats. These two boats put up wonderful records in unloading stores, shaming the Gyppies into greater effort, and building up a school of competition by which the boat making the greater number of trips in the day, received a flag mounted on a pole which was placed in the bows of the boat and carried throughout the following day.

Our Rarotongans were then withdrawn as there was more important work for them to do. But their example remained for the rest of the campaign, and the victorious flag was carried by the winning boat right up the length of the coast, until Jaffa was reached.

Meanwhile ceaseless patrolling went on—feeling for the enemy—to the southward up the Wadi El Arish as far as the mountains by the Camel Brigade, towards the north and east by the Light Horse. One day soon after Christmas immense excitement and interest followed on the report of a Light Horse Patrol showing how, after following the old road for

THE MONTHLY INOCULATION.   A LEWIS GUN USED AS AN ANTI-AIRCRAFT GUN.

some sixteen miles, they had actually ridden on turf—"turf as green and as smooth and as close as a bowling green," remarked one of the men to a delighted audience. The mere idea of "grass" to men—horse lovers—who had been riding on sand for just over twelve months was delightful. It recalled visions of home paddocks, of gallops over the "run" and instinctively many a man went off and examined his horses feet and got round the blacksmith for a new pair of shoes and wondered what "Old Baldy" would feel like hammering the turf again.

The 1st Light Horse Brigade made a great reconnaissance to the next village, Sheikh Zowaiid, about half-way to Rafa (and therefore to the Turkish border), and brought back stories of great rolling plains; of grass land and of crops just coming through the ground; and of a great lake of water (though they omitted to say it was brackish); and of the village of Sheikh Zowaiid itself with its stone walls and Turkish oil engines and pumps. And the Brigadier exhibited proudly a dozen healthy young hens "all laying" which he had purchased from the Sheikh.

These same hens became well known throughout the Anzac Mounted Division. If one ever wanted to find Brigade Headquarters one looked out for the chicken coops which on the move were carried on a camel; or if one were out riding since early dawn and feeling very hungry directed one's steps to Brigade Headquarters—there was always ready a hearty Australian welcome and a good breakfast with bacon and "eggs." Charlie Cox's chickens became proverbial!

Meanwhile many and anxious were the eyes directed upon the railway line as it crept up to El Arish. The great question of the day—a question which caused as much speculation as the Melbourne Cup—was "would it cross the wadi?" The construction engineers were plagued with questions—but knew nothing. Their instructions were to build to El Arish. Then a rumour went around that a shipload of railway material had just arrived at Kantara, in fact a man coming back from leave said he had seen two of them (and is it not wonderful how one always heard first of what was going to happen at the "Front," from the "Back"?). Then one joyful day, a patrol was ordered as escort to the surveying engineer, our good friend Hay—who went away across the wadi; and we said, looking into each other's eyes, "It seems too good to be true, we *are* for the Promised Land after all!"

A diversion came and put an end to all these debates for a while. News had come in from many sources that there was a strong post of the enemy at Rafa, the last village of Sinai and which is situated on the Old Road where it crosses the Turco-Egyptian Boundary Line.

Intelligence reports showed some 2000 or 3000 men with guns strongly entrenched just out of Rafa, and from good aeroplane photographs capital plans were drawn of the enemy position showing every trench.

The position appeared to be on paper very formidable. There was a central "keep" on a hill called El Magruntein and spreading out fanwise towards the south-east, south and south-west was a system of redoubts connected by trenches.

The position looked one of "all-round defence" with its weaker side to the north-east, or on what would be, to a force

THE TURKISH MAIN POSITION AT RAFA SHOWING THE TURK'S TRENCHES.

advancing from El Arish, the farther side or rear of the position.

The Division received orders to move on the evening of the 8th January, 1917, to attack the enemy at Rafa at dawn next day. This time the Division was to be accompanied by the Camel Brigade (with its Hong Kong and Singapore Mountain Battery) and by the 5th Brigade Yeomanry, with a battery of the Honourable Artillery Company (18-prs.). The whole force was to be under the command of Sir P. Chetwode.

It is necessary to lay some stress upon the difficulties of the undertaking, because the famous cavalry raids of history offer no real standard of comparison.

In the European wars of 1865 and of 1870, cavalry actions did not take place at any great distance from their base and even then there was food and water in plenty in the country. Again in America the great raids of Jeb Stuart and of Morgan were undertaken through country upon which the raiders could live. Our mounted troops (the cavalry of the Great War), on the other hand, have made their raids in the desert, where all supplies even so far as water for the horses had to be carried with the column. Our mounted troops carried out their raids in a country where, if a man fell out of the column and wandered alone, he perished miserably; where, if a water bottle by mischance were overturned or leaked, there was no water for the owner for perhaps another twenty-four hours; and this under a burning sun by day and bitter cold by night, in which he became soaked to the skin with the dew; and man cannot march and fight for more than a very limited time without food and drink.

Then, again, the task set our mounted troops in these raids must be considered. To attack and overcome a stubborn enemy strongly entrenched with both field and machine guns, is at all times a difficult task. How much more so when the attacking force has a few paltry 18-pounders behind them, however well served these be. Yet these difficulties were again and again gloriously overcome by these young soldiers from the Southern Seas. It was a job that required dash and determination, combined with an infinity of painstaking forethought. The last round of ammunition, the last pound of "bully" and biscuits, and the last pint of water had to be worked out. When supplies could not be carried by the men they had to be carried to him and delivered at the very moment when wanted.

Yet all this was done. Men who had hunted and farmed fought as veteran soldiers, full of dash and determination and cunning; and he who had carried on a business or wielded a pen took his place and supplied and fed men and horses as never had been done before, or could have been done, even by the justly famed A.S.C. in the British Army itself.

Late in the afternoon the column assembled on the plain on the east side of the wadi over against El Arish. The wadi was "in spate" and the men and horses much enjoyed fording the River of Egypt—splashing through the water on the shingle was so like New Zealand. With a thirty-mile ride to be considered it was decided that an assembly at dusk (as was the custom) would not give time: so the observation and perhaps bombing of enemy aeroplanes was risked and the column was actually in motion before the sun went down.

The first part of the way lay over very heavy sand-dunes, which tried the double-gun teams and ammunition wagon teams to the utmost; and it was some miles before the Old Road in its defined form appeared, and then the column took to that great shallow trough worked down by the feet of countless generations. The guns and ammunition wagons were given the hardened centre and the horsemen rode on each side.

A HALT IN THE DESERT.

Let us stop and watch them go by in the moonlight. The great wonder of the desert is its all-embracing silence—all sound is swallowed up—and so in silence they go by, each troop riding in line with its troop leader in front. Over the swelling sandhills they come, line upon line—noiseless they go—no song, no laughter, no talking, not a light to be seen; no sound but the snort of a horse as he blows the dust from his nostrils; or the click of two stirrup irons touching as two riders close in together; or the jingle of the links on the pack horses; or perhaps a neck-chain rattling on the pommel. No other sound is heard unless one be very close, then there is a low swish swish as the sand spurts out in front of a horse's foot slithering on from step to step. All are intent upon the work in hand; all with faces turned to the Promised Land.

Here come the Light Horse, with their emu plumes waving —here the quiet grim New Zealanders—here Yeomanry in helmets from many countries—and on the road itself go by the guns with their Scotch and English crews—and away out on the flank stretching out mile after mile into the black darkness of night come the camels, riding in sections four abreast.

There are Australians among them and Yeomen from the British Isles and our own New Zealanders, and following them a band of tall, silent, swarthy Sikhs on huge Indian camels. These are the Hong Kong and Singapore Mountain Battery, who so ably serve the Camel Brigade. And lastly, far behind, softly and slowly and calmly, come long streams of laden camels led by Egyptians bare-footed in the sand.

Very good progress was made to Sheikh Zowaiid which the head of the column, reached about 10 o'clock, and the whole force closed up and rested till 1 a.m. on the 9th, the men dismounting and going to sleep with their bridles on their arms; but to the unbounded surprise of everyone the good steeds instead of standing as usual as quiet and steady as statues and dozing also, immediately got their heads down and began cropping. Delighted investigations showed a halt had been made on cultivated land—with the crop showing about six inches—light sandy soil certainly, but soil it was. Though this caused a loss of much useful sleep, yet the pleasure shown by the horses more than made up for it, and many a man gave up entirely any thought of sleep and helped his horse to a "real green feed."

At 1 a.m. on the 9th the column continued its march, with the Yeomanry following the "Old Road" direct on Rafa, and the Anzac Mounted Division bearing away to the east to get into position to attack from the south, east and north. By the Column Commander's orders all wheels except the guns were to be left at Sheikh Zowaiid. This was done under protest by all Brigadiers as it meant leaving all reserve ammunition behind.

About half a mile after leaving Sheikh Zowaiid an enemy Bedouin Camel Patrol was captured—luckily not a man got away. At half past three the flank guard of the 3rd L.H. Brigade ran into a Turkish post and captured two Turks, but not before they had fired a flare. But this was not answered from anywhere and was possibly not seen.

It was known that there were a great number of Bedouins in this district and aeroplane photos had shown a very large encampment at Karm Ibn Musleh—close on to the Border—so the N.Z. Brigade was sent forward on a special duty to round up these Arabs. This was successfully done at daylight, but not before the warning Arab "lu-lu-ing" had gone wailing over the downs—a most eerie sound in the half light. Immediately daylight came the nearest camp sent up a smoke signal and this was answered from camp to camp.

At six o'clock the Auckland Regiment in the advance reached the Boundary Line between Egypt and Turkey; and having halted his regiment the old Colonel rode forward alone, past the Boundary Pillar, and taking off his hat, there thanked Almighty God that he had at last been permitted to enter the Holy Land (and was the first New Zealander to do so!) and came back smiling—and the sun rose and we were out of Egypt. And for the rest of the day the battle was fought just round about here—in two countries at once—in Palestine and Egypt; one might almost say in two continents—in Asia and Africa; for the Boundary Line between Turkey and Egypt ran its pillared course to the Gulf of Akaba about one mile from the great Redoubt on El Magruntein.

The battle of Rafa took the same course as that of Maghdaba—the long night approach, the contact at dawn, the closing in during the forenoon, the determined attack in the afternoon and the surrender at dusk.

But here the task was greater. At Maghdaba the enemy's strength lay largely in his invisibility—the flat ground and well-sited trenches took hours to find. Here the strength lay not in the flatness of the position, but in its rising ground with its central "keep" on El Magruntein, a conical grassy sloped hill some 200 feet above the surrounding country. Clear for 2000 yards or more all round this position lay a beautiful turf land, slightly rolling, with a background of the great dunes stretching right along the coast in a strip of a half mile to three miles in width—away up to Jaffa. The edges of these sandhills were about a thousand yards from the centre of the Turkish position on its western side.

As the sun came up the enemy lines could be seen with the central keep dominating the whole—providing many tiers of fire to back up the well planned redoubts and lines of trenches. These were laid out by the German Engineer and dug by the Turk—a combination of best field engineer and best "digger" in the world. But forethought and good leading led the attack eventually on to the one place vulnerable.

THE BOUNDARY PILLARS AT RAFA.

At a quarter past six the Division was placed as follows:— Divisional Headquarters, 1st and 3rd L.H. Brigades and the Artillery just south of Karm Ibn Musleh. The N.Z. Brigade was about one and a quarter miles North at Point 350, close to the *i* in Shok El Sufi; and the Camels three-quarters of a mile west of Karm Ibn Musleh. The Divisional Commander and Brigadiers spent a little time in studying the position while the aeroplanes were making their observations. These soon reported that they had been fired upon from all trenches. The airmen, however, performed perhaps their most useful work at a distance from the actual battlefield. They kept the movements of the enemy forces under observation giving timely news of the advance of the relieving columns from Shellal or Khan Yunus.

Shortly after 8 o'clock orders were issued for the attack; the New Zealanders were to attack from the east—taking the group of trenches C4 and C5; and the Brigadier was to make provision for the safety of his own right flank (and rear) which extended to the sea.

The 1st L.H. Brigade was ordered to attack C3, C2 and C1 and when these objectives had been carried both brigades were to rally and attack the central redoubt. The Camels were ordered to attack D Group and the 3rd L.H. Brigade to remain in reserve.

In the meantime a New Zealand patrol had reached to the north of Rafa and cut the telegraph line.

The brigades were soon in motion towards their several objectives and the New Zealanders had some four miles further north to go in order to attack from the east. It was a sight to hearten even a conscientious objector to see those magnificent men and horses moving over the close turfed open downs in "Artillery formation" with the Brigade Headquarters in the lead.

At 10 o'clock the attack began with the Aucklanders leading—supported by two machine guns. The Canterbury Regiment was ordered to prolong the Auckland right and in doing so advanced upon and captured Rafa, intercepting some camels which were seen retiring from the El Magruntein position. Six Germans, 2 Turkish Officers, 16 other ranks and 21 Bedouins together with camels, horses and mules, were taken with a line of half completed works running from Rafa to the south east. In Rafa itself were a few huts, the Police Barracks and the Police Post on the Main Road.

In getting into a position well forward and where the led horses could be left, the Auckland Regiment galloped over some out-lying trenches, and two German Officers and some 20 Turks were captured. Two of the latter attempted to run away, but Major McCarroll cut one down with his sword and severely wounded him. This is probably the first occasion on which a sword was used by a New Zealander in this War.

The Wellington Regiment was ordered to support the Canterbury Regiment and also to protect the brigade from attack from the north and north-east, the direction of Khan Yunus and Shellal, at both of which places the enemy were known to be in numbers. So two troops were sent off for this purpose.

By 11 o'clock the position of the force was as follows:— From the extreme right (or northern flank) Canterbury Regiment, Auckland Regiment, 1st L.H. Brigade, 3rd L.H. Brigade, Camel Brigade and on their left and reaching to the sandhills the 5th Yeomanry Brigade.

At this hour General Chaytor moved his Headquarters to the Boundary Post one mile south-east of Rafa, immediately behind the Auckland Regiment. The Inverness Battery from a position near the Anzac Mounted Division Headquarters covered the advance of the Brigade, later moving to a covered position behind Brigade Headquarters at a range of 2250 yards. During the advance two reserve guns of the N.Z.M.G Squadron were placed in position on a small ridge which afforded cover. Very good shooting was done by these guns, supported by half a troop from one of the regiments, on trenches and parties of the enemy in C group at a range of about 800 yards and the fire greatly assisted the 3rd Brigade in advancing; in fact it eventually forced the enemy to abandon that portion of his position and an enemy machine gun was subsequently found there. The Machine Gun Squadron Commander then took over the four remaining guns and distributed them along the line of attack. The machine gunners advanced with the troops, giving them mutual support, and they were able to bring covering fire to bear on the central redoubt right up to the time of its capture.

By half past 11 the attack was progressing well all along the line. As the "Times" special correspondent who witnessed the operation says:—"The ground in front of the position was so open that the whole action could be seen for miles, and presented a battle picture of a kind seldom witnessed in a modern war. One may mention in passing that the unusual conditions led to some unusual incidents, such as a Padre digging himself in with a spoon, or a man trying to put an ammunition camel down under fire while himself discreetly first adopting kneeling and then the prone position. The enemy had an ideal field of fire as the ground for some 2000 yards in front of the position offered not one inch of cover. Over this perfect glacis our dismounted troops advanced by rushes under very heavy fire, particularly from the enemy machine guns, which were very difficult to locate. That the attack could have made any progress at all in daylight speaks very highly both for the dash and determination of the troops and for the accuracy of the covering fire. The Mounted Division had learned to put great faith in the fine shooting of the Territorial Batteries attached to them, and the gunners

A PART OF THE FIRING LINE AT RAFA.

again gave them admirable support bringing their guns well forward in absolutely open country. They had the rare experience of seeing their targets, but they themselves were even more visible to the enemy who shelled them heavily with his mountain guns. The fire-fight was severe and prolonged but by three o'clock distinct progress had been made in spite of the fact that our men were fighting under every disadvantage against some of the best Turkish Troops. At half-past three the rear face of the enemy position began to be seriously threatened by the pressure of the New Zealanders' attack from the north.''

To bring this pressure to bear at this time the New Zealand Brigade had continued their steady good work. After the capture of Rafa and the clearing of the sandhills to the sea (which was done by the Wellington Regiment) the Brigade settled down about noon to the systematic taking of the great central redoubt.

The Canterburys, on the right of the Brigade's advance, were steadily working their way forward just inside the sand belt and between them and the Aucklanders was the Wellington Regiment less the squadron on the look-out to the north and east. All three regiments continued making steady progress, though owing to the bowling-green nature of the country the pace was necessarily slow, and delay was caused by the "overs" from the H.A.C. battery attached to the Yeomanry. At two p.m. the Canterbury Regiment gained touch with the Yeomanry who were attacking straight along the road from El Arish and whose left was on the sandhills. These two forces junctioning on the sandhills completed the encirclement of the whole Turkish Force.

At 2.45 p.m. most important information was obtained from a Turkish machine gun officer and three Germans who had been captured by a Wellington troop, on the watch towards Khan Yunus. The information disclosed the fact that the 160th Regiment had left Shellal when the attack began with the intention of reinforceing the Rafa Garrison. Shellal is about 10 miles away on the Wadi Ghuzzeh and the going is good. Further information went to show that the Rafa Garrison consisted of two taburs of the 31st Regiment each one thousand strong, with four Krupp mountain guns. At this hour though the 1st L.H. Brigade had been making good progress and had reached the line of the "Big Tree" they were now at a standstill. The 3rd Brigade on their left were also held up and no progress could be made by the Camel Brigade or by the Yeomanry.

At half-past three General Chetwode ordered all guns available to be turned on to the Central Redoubt and that a general assault was to take place; but still no progress was made and the enemy planes at about this time became very active in their bombing. Disquieting reports also came in from the two troops of the Wellington Regiment who were now engaged with the advanced guard of the enemy relieving forces advancing from Khan Yunus and Shellal respectively. These appeared to be about two battalions in number and other troops were seen further back advancing over the hills, but too far off for an estimate of their numbers to be made.

The position at this time was critical. The Turks in the trenches were fighting stubbornly and large bodies of enemy reinforcements were close at hand. Ammunition was running short in the firing line and the Inverness Battery, which had so effectively assisted the New Zealand Brigade throughout the day, ran out completely and was sent back.

A conversation took place on the telephone between the Divisional Commander and the Commander of the Desert Column, as to the advisability of abandoning the attack and withdrawing the troops owing to the advance of the enemy reinforcements. Before, however, any orders could be put into effect the New Zealanders were seen on the crest of the Central Redoubt—having stormed and captured it at the point of the bayonet. After which the remaining enemy positions quickly fell to the other brigades—being dominated and enfiladed by the New Zealanders on the central keep.

The attack which brought about this sudden transformation was carried through in perfect manner and was the culmination of a day of steady methodical and persistent work, exhibiting the characteristic tenacity of the New Zealanders and their fighting Brigadier.

It was New Zealand's day. The Brigade had advanced across grassy slopes, with no cover but an occasional clump of the Iris Lily, planted to show the boundary of a field. The covering fire from the machine guns, Lewis guns, and rifles was perfect, and was the great feature of the attack. At four o'clock, when General Chaytor ordered a general assault, the hail of bullets on the redoubt made it smoke like a furnace. This kept the enemy fire down to such an extent and so disturbed his aim that our men were enabled to cover the last 800 yards of glacis-like slope in two grand rushes, every one having made up his mind to "get home." Another outstanding feature of the Brigade's attack was the determined use of machine guns. These advanced in the firing line, crossing their fire to get better targets, co-operating with one another and with the machine guns of the 1st Light Horse Brigade and advancing to within 400 yards of the Turk's main position. Four guns of the Canterbury Regiment on the right flank gave good covering fire at effective ranges. These guns were placed in a trench, but were afterwards moved forward to a sunken road, from which position they were able to maintain "overhead" covering fire until the assaulting troops were within a few yards of the trenches. The position of these guns was also of such a nature that had the pressure from the enemy reinforcements advancing from Shellal proved too heavy to be held off, and the Brigade forced to retire to the coast, they would have been most useful and effective in covering the retirement.

Another feature of the final charge was the spectacle of many of our men firing as they ran—such was the feeling of "Fire Superiority."

After a short pause to reorganise in the redoubt, an attack was launched upon the "sandy redoubt"—"C" 5— which quickly surrendered. Darkness had now come on and the Brigade assembled close to the great redoubt while prisoners were being collected and sent on to Sheikh Zowaiid.

It was still a race against time, and no one knew what might develop from the Turkish columns from Shellal and Khan Yunus so ably held off all day by the Wellington Regiment. The whole Division was therefore given orders to move back to Sheikh Zowaiid where there was water ready and supplies for horse and man. These were reached about midnight.

The Ambulance Carts and the Stretcher Bearers were still busy and the work of tending and collecting the wounded was carried on far into the night, even though the Ambulances had worked without ceasing throughout the long day. Prisoners, amongst whom were German machine gunners, had to be collected; the captured guns taken away, and a Christian burial given to those gallant fellows who had given their all for their country. A strong rearguard therefore was left and all available empty wagons sent up from Sheikh Zowaiid with which to clear the battlefield.

At Sheikh Zowaiid the Wellington Regiment remained until the morning of the 11th, to enable this to be done.

The Division had marched back to El Arish on the 10th, reaching there tired, but successful, on the evening of the same day.

A lesson, not without its uses, was learned from the failure of the Ammunition Supply during the critical hours of the battle. As has been said, no wheels but the guns were

AMBULANCE WAGONS RETURNING FROM THE BATTLE OF RAFA.

allowed to come past Sheikh Zowaiid during the night march. The intention of Desert Column Headquarters was that the reserve ammunition was to be sent on after daylight, but in many cases it failed to reach the units in the firing line. Major Wilkie, the ubiquitous quartermaster of the Wellington Regiment. remained at Sheikh Zowaiid with the supply convoys; but during the early hours of the battle was so concerned at the small amount of S.A.A. with which his regiment had gone into battle, that he went forward to Rafa and hearing that his regiment was calling for ammunition, seized a cable wagon, emptied out the signalling gear and wire, filled it with boxes of S.A.A. and galloped across to the New Zealand Brigade—thus replenishing the machine guns in time for the great assault on the Redoubt. This foresight and dash on this officer's part very materially helped in the final success.

The 15th Coy I.C.C. Brigade (The New Zealand Company) had some heavy fighting during the day, and their brilliant commander, Captain McCallum, the man who had made the company, was killed.

The work of the Medical Corps and the Stretcher Bearers was again magnificent. The little canvas hooded sand-carts were to be seen on all parts of the field throughout the action, approaching right up to the firing line again and again.

TURKISH PRISONERS ON THE ROAD TO EL ARISH FROM RAFA.

Considering the nature of the battle, the storming of trenches with very little artillery support over a perfectly open plain, the casualties in the New Zealand Brigade were exceptionally light. This can be attributed to the splendid co-operation of the machine guns, and of troops, squadrons and regiments;

The Battle of Rafa

and the natural aptitude of our men for warfare of this nature. It must be remembered that the Brigade was largely seasoned with Anzac veterans and that all ranks had now been fighting the Turk in the desert for 12 months. The Turks were confident almost to the last that they could hold their position; and one captured officer admitted that he thought it was impossible for the attackers to succeed in the time available, and before the arrival of the Turkish Reinforcements. Our captures included:—

- 162 Wounded (and collected by us).
- 1472 Prisoners.
- 4 Krupp Guns.
- 7 Machine Guns.
- 1610 Rifles.
- 45,000 Rounds of S.A.A.
- 71 Belts of S.A.A.
- 134 Pack Saddles.
- 85 Camels.
- 19 Horses.
- 35 Mules; and a large quantity of miscellaneous equipment.

The expenditure of small arms ammunition was large, and adverse comments were afterwards made; but ammunition is cheaper than men, and the free use of machine and Lewis guns undoubtedly enabled the N.Z. Brigade to capture what at one time looked to be an impregnable position.

The capture of Rafa with its Turkish garrison completed the clearing out of the enemy from Sinai, which province he had held since the outbreak of the war. It completed the Sinai Campaign, the Desert Campaign as it was often called, in which the Anzac Mounted Division had borne the chief part and upon which almost the whole of the fighting had fallen. Henceforth the British forces engaged were to be greatly increased and the scope of the fighting greatly extended, but it was in this Desert Campaign in Sinai that the spade work was done, that the experience was gained, and the force forged, that was ultimately so dramatically to overthrow Turkey.

The small force of Australian and New Zealand horsemen and British Territorial horse-gunners which began the campaign at Romani formed the nucleus of the largest body of horse that had ever operated under one commander since the days of Darius the Persian; and with their comrades from Great Britain and India, were to justify without any doubt the retention of cavalry as an indispensable arm of the service.

This small force had grown into the "Desert Column" and was to become "East Force" at the battles of Gaza and ultimately the great "Egyptian Expeditionary Force" that was to overthrow the Turkish Empire.

In this Campaign our men became true horse-masters; and it can be safely said that in no campaign of which history has cognizance has the horse been so well understood in all his needs, and so well fed and tended. A horse not in the pink of condition was a rare sight. The forage was good and on the whole in sufficient quantities and the hot dry climate apparently suited the constitution of the horse. Much care was taken in the early phases of the operations when near the

AFTER RAFA.

Canal to protect the animals from the sun by the erection of sun-shelters made of matting or canvas; but as the campaign progressed and transport became difficult the sun-shelters were left behind and the horses bore the full glare of the sun's rays at all times, and apparently suffered little thereby. This was well shown later on, under the appalling conditions in the Jordan Valley where these same horses maintained their condition and general fitness in a wonderful way. The men learned to live in the desert and to find their way both by day and by night in a manner worthy of the Bedouins themselves; in fact our men were the better guides, the Bedouin

A BURYING PARTY AT RAFA.

as often as not in common with Gyppies, proving to be suffering from night blindness. As has been said there were no tents; palm-leaf shelters, odd pieces of canvas, captured Turkish canvas sheets or Bedouin cloth were all that could be found or carried. Later on, as Palestine was reached, a canvas sheet about five feet by four feet was issued to each man; and two of these laced together made a fairly good "tent d' abri" under which two men could squeeze; but being so short made a poor shelter when the winter rains were met.

The Division settled down into fairly comfortable bivouacs and tents were brought up by train. The New Zealand Brigade was camped on the shore about three miles from El Arish where there was an ample supply of good water. Bathing, football, boxing, were fully indulged in and our men worthily upheld New Zealand's traditions. The absorbing topic of the hour again became the railway, and its progress towards Palestine was eagerly watched.

CHAPTER IV.

How the Brigade entered Palestine and went up against Gaza.

On February 22nd the Division marched to Sheikh Zowaiid and the Brigades camped on the beach, with the New Zealand Brigade farthest east just where the Turko-Egyptian boundary line reaches the coast.

The desert was now far behind and all reconnaissances were into grass country or among cultivated fields, with the green crop showing well above the ground. There were flowers everywhere. A blaze of bright poppies and scarlet ranunculi was characteristic of the country; then there were great stretches of irises both large and small, blue cornflower, pimpernels, anemones in endless variety and many beautiful "bulbs"—gladioli, tulips, acres of narcissi; and many flowers whose names were unknown to our men. And in the strip of sand-hill country that ran along the coast grew the beautiful perfumed desert lily.

The country around Rafa and up to the Wadi Ghuzzeh (Gaza), which was now the limit of our patrolling, was an open and rolling-downs country, with no fences and very few trees. It was either pasture land or under crop and the corn was coming on quickly over many thousands of acres. The Turk had made a great effort at grain growing and had compelled the Bedouin inhabitants to plough every available acre, confiscating their ploughs and animals for the purpose. So that by the time the second battle of Gaza was fought the whole of southern Palestine, from Rafa and Gaza eastwards to the mountains, was one great corn-field. Six miles north of Rafa on the main road to Gaza lies Khan Yunus the southernmost village of Palestine and most likely the "Darum" of the Crusaders of King Richard the Lion Hearted. In those days it was a fort built and held for the protection of the Christian Pilgrims coming from Egypt; and the remains of an old castle still stands there, the first of the many relics of the Crusaders we were to see. Khan Yunus is surrounded by many acres of orchards, each with its great hedge of prickly pear. Here also was the first deep well which afterwards with the help of a modern old engine and pump gave an almost unlimited water supply to the troops. Near Khan Yunus there were several smaller villages, and some six miles further on close down by the sea lay Deir El Belah hidden in its groves of date palms. Here the sand hill strip narrowed to a bare half-mile just where a great lagoon empties into the sea during the height of the rainy season. Each of these villages has its well, and also there were many ancient "harabas," stone cisterns filled by the rain or by some

ARABS BRINGING IN THE HARVEST.

mechanical means. They were usually bottle-shaped with a circular opening of two to three feet in diameter. Sometimes the body of the bottle was excavated into a rectangular chamber. The opening was usually closed by a close fitting stone to prevent evaporation. These cisterns proved of great value to the troops, but the calculating of the capacity of the odd shaped reservoirs was a difficult task for the engineer in whose area they chanced to be.

On February the 23rd, General Chaytor with the New Zealand and 2nd L.H. Brigades, made a reconnaissance of Khan Yunus for the special purpose of capturing the Sheikh Ali El Hirsch and his following. This man was a notorious Turkish Intelligence Agent. At this time the Turks had a line of strong posts, Beersheba–Shellal–Weli Sheikh Nuran–

Khan Yunus, and air photographs showed well dug lines of trenches at these places. The operations failed in capturing the Turkish Agent, but our troops surrounded Khan Yunus and drove into the town detachments of the enemy. The effect of this was such as to make the Turk evacuate Khan Yunus and his splendid system of defences stretching from there to Shellal on the Wadi Ghuzzeh, and retire to the Gaza-Beersheba line wholly on the north and east of the wadi.

By the middle of March the railway had reached Rafa and preparations were made for the capture of Gaza. In the meantime a long looked for event came off, the Rafa Races, held on March 21st, on the old battlefield. The course was excellent going; and with natural grassy slopes for lawn and grandstand, the spectators were happily provided for. The "fields" were good and races keenly contested among the Yeomanry, Australians and New Zealanders. Our D.A.D.M.S. earned undying fame and a win for New Zealand by pulling off the "Promised Land Stakes" with a little horse called "Maori King" (alias "The Rat") from Canterbury.

The First Battle of Gaza.

On the day after the Rafa races the preliminary moves prior to the attack on Gaza began, and all roads and tracks possible for wheels were carefully reconnoitred as far as Belah and allotted to the different formations; for the force to be employed on this undertaking was to consist, for the first time in the campaign, of all arms—infantry, cavalry and guns, and was now called "East Force," consisting of the Anzac Mounted Division, Imperial Mounted Division (one Light Horse Brigade and two Yeomanry Brigades), the Camel Brigade and three Infantry Divisions—the 52nd, 53rd, and 54th, all under the command of General Dobell of West African fame.

The arrangements for feeding this force had to be made in advance and as the country was hard enough to carry wheels, all wagons were brought up from Kantara to supplement the Camel Convoys now much too small for the augmented forces. First Line transport, i.e., baggage wagons, tool carts, etc., were formed into an improvised "Train" and loaded up with supplies. On the night of March 25th, the forward move began and by daylight the whole Division was at Deir El Belah, hidden as far as possible in the palm groves and orchards. The New Zealand Brigade marched up the beach and went out in front to hold a line just south of the Wadi Ghuzzeh—to cover reconnaissances to be made by the Staff in order to determine the best place at which to cross the wadi and to advance upon Gaza.

The crossing place over the wadi was chosen close to Tel El Jemmi and marked so as to be easily found in the dark. With the exception of these reconnaissance parties the whole force of two Cavalry Divisions and two Infantry Divisions (the 52nd remained at Rafa) lay up quietly during the day.

A CAMEL TRANSPORT CAMP.

And so Sinai was left behind not to be returned to until the war was over; and we were fairly launched upon the 10th Crusade.

Gaza is one of the very oldest cities in the world. It is mentioned in the 10th Chapter of Genesis and again many times in connection with Samson, the strong man of Israel, who fought the Philistines. It was at Gaza, that being warned that his enemies were upon him, he rushed away with the city gates carrying them up to the top of the hill now called Ali el Muntar, to the east of the town. Here also he gave the most wonderful exhibition of his strength and performed the last great act of his life by pulling down the Temple of Dagon destroying some three thousand Philistines.

Gaza was always the fortress city of southern Palestine. Alexander took it on his way to conquer Egypt and it put up a great defence against him, seriously delaying his march; and when at various times in the course of the history of these rich plains the yoke of Egypt was thrown off, Gaza then became the frontier city and bulwark against the Pharaoh's armies.

LT.-GENERAL SIR HARRY CHAUVEL, K.C.B., K.C.M.G.

It was one of the five capital cities of the Philistines and was an important and populous city under the Romans.

Nowadays the town lies in the midst of orchards and is an important depot for barley, wheat and dhurra, and has a population of 40,000 souls.

The capture of Gaza presented a similar problem to that of Rafa, but upon a larger scale.

Rafa, the railhead, to Gaza is twenty miles. Gaza was held by its own garrison and there were enemy troops who could be sent up to support from Beersheba away to the east, on the flank of an attacking force, and from Huj eight miles north-east; and both these places were on the Turkish system of railways. In addition there was a line of Turkish posts from Gaza to Beersheba which would have to be forced.

The plan was as follows:—The Anzac Mounted Division by a night march was to place itself astride the main road on the far side of the town, so closing all avenues of escape to the north and ready to co-operate in the attack upon the town by the infantry who were to operate from the south. The Imperial Mounted Division was set the task of holding off the enemy forces from the direction of Huj; and the 54th Division those who might advance from Beersheba or the railway leading to that town.

In order to protect the lines of communications back to Rafa the 52nd Division took up a position watching the crossing of the wadi towards the east and covering Khan Yunus.

The 53rd (Welsh) Division was selected to make the attack upon the town from the south.

And all these things were done in due order, the Anzac Mounted Division encircled Gaza and cut off all retreat of the

LANDING STORES NEAR GAZA.

garrison, the enemy's reinforcing troops from Huj and from the Beersheba railway line were successfully held off; and the infantry, aided by the New Zealanders, captured Ali Muntar and all the principal defences of Gaza; yet the town, twenty-four hours afterwards, was still in the hands of the Turks, and the East Force was back again on the south side of the Wadi Ghuzzeh. What happened was as follows:

At 2.30 in the morning of the 26th March, the New Zealand Brigade left its bivouac at Belah with the Anzac Mounted Division to cross the Wadi Ghuzzeh. As there was a constant stream of Infantry transport coming up from Rafa crossing and re-crossing the Belah flat no starting point was fixed, but units were ordered to march straight from their

LT.-COL. J. H. WHYTE, D.S.O. (AND BAR), D.C.M., WELLINGTON MOUNTED RIFLES.

lines and to take up their positions in the column as it advanced. To make matters more difficult a heavy fog came down and there was no moon. The leading brigade, which had left its bivouac riding in "sections" upon reaching the open flat to the north of Belah, shortened up into "column of troops." This caused a break in the column, and if it had not been for the good leading of the next brigade serious delay would have been caused. But our men had developed an almost uncanny sense of finding their way in the dark, and in spite of all these difficulties the wadi was reached and the crossing made twenty minutes only beyond the estimated time; and moving by compass the Division skilfully avoided the broken ground on the east bank and reached Sheikh Abbas at seven o'clock. Simultaneously the Advanced Guard ran into a Turkish post on the Gaza–Beersheba road and the first shots were fired.

Shortly after eight o'clock enemy planes appeared and flying low attacked the column with their machine guns.

At half-past nine the Division reached Beit Durdis to the north-east of Gaza where Headquarters were established and the 2nd Light Horse Brigade sent on towards the sea, which they reached by 11 o'clock. Communication by cable and helio was established with Desert Column Headquarters, which were at Point 310 on the south side of the wadi close to In Seirat. A wireless station was also set up, but a powerful enemy plant in Gaza nullified its work throughout the day.

On its way to the sea the 2nd Light Horse Brigade captured on the main road a Turkish officer and staff, who was proceeding from Huj to Gaza to take over the command there.

This officer, a divisional commander, took his capture most philosophically, as the fortune of war; but he sadly deplored the absence of his servant who was riding behind with a pack horse upon which was his master's kit. The latter earnestly begged the Light Horse into whose hands he had fallen to capture this servant also. However, much to the Turkish Commandant's disappointment the servant and the pack horse got away. Curiously enough some three weeks later when our forces were holding the south bank of the Wadi Ghuzzeh an unarmed Turk gave himself up to the outposts. He was the missing servant come in quest of his master, but without the pack horse!

Patrols were sent out towards Huj and northwards along the main road by the Auckland Regiment. Gaza was now completely invested and the infantry attack was progressing from the south. This attack met with stubborn opposition. The 53rd Division lost very heavily and was reinforced by one brigade of the 54th Division, which had taken up a covering position at Sheikh Abbas, effectually blocking any relief from the direction of Beersheba.

The Imperial Mounted Division which had followed behind the Anzac Mounted Division throughout the night, was now in position due east of Gaza watching Huj.

All mounted troops were more or less under shell fire from Gaza, but very little fighting had yet taken place so far as they were concerned; and the infantry attack was not making much progress.

News was now beginning to come in from the watching patrols of both mounted divisions, of activity in the direction of Huj and the Beersheba railway. Columns of dust in the

A DESERT SHELTER.

direction of Tel el Sharia showed where enemy movement in large numbers was in progress.

At 2 o'clock orders were received from Desert Column Headquarters for the Anzac Mounted Division to attack Gaza in support of the infantry attack, and for the Imperial Mounted Division to take over all observation duties; and to assist the latter in this duty the Camel Brigade was sent up.

As soon as these posts had been taken over the attack began as follows—the 2nd L.H. Brigade advanced on a front extending from the sea to the Gaza–Jebalieh road (inclusive); the N.Z.M.R. from the Gaza–Jebalieh road to the top of the ridge running north and south just east of the town; and the 22nd Mounted Brigade (which for the day was taking the place in the Division of the 1st L.H. Brigade) on the left of the New Zealanders.

An enemy deserter who had been caught confirmed the intelligence reports of the enemy's strength in Gaza. He estimated the infantry at two battalions, with 500 Austrians and 200 cavalry, with four large guns in addition to small field guns. He said that support had been asked for from Huj, 8 miles away, at 10 o'clock this morning; also that there were in Gaza 24 hours' supplies only, and all the wells except three had been blown in.

Gaza lies in a hollow in the midst of orchards, each of which is surrounded by a tall impenetrable prickly pear hedge. These orchards reach out to the north, west, and south, some three or four miles.

On the eastern side the town is shut out from the cultivated plain by a low ridge running north and south, called afterwards "Anzac Ridge," which culminates at its south end in Ali el Muntar, the hill up which Samson carried the gates of the city.

This ridge was strongly entrenched and strongly held by the Turks and it was in attacking Ali el Muntar from the south that the Welsh Division suffered terrible casualties.

The attack of the Anzacs soon developed and in spite of prickly pear hedges progress was rapid. Horses had to be left behind and the hedges penetrated on foot and the Turks driven out by hand-to-hand fighting.

THE CACTUS HEDGES OF GAZA THROUGH WHICH OUR MEN HAD TO FIGHT THEIR WAY.

The New Zealand Brigade Headquarters took up a position on the ridge, on a knob afterwards called Chaytor's Hill, and the Wellington and Canterbury Regiments pressed on towards Gaza. Four machine guns were attached to each of these regiments and the remaining four held in reserve. Of the Auckland Regiment there were available three troops only, the rest of the regiment not yet having come in from its observation duties away to the north and east.

By five o'clock the Canterburys had worked along "The Ridge" attacking the Ali el Muntar defences practically in the rear; and in conjunction with the Infantry entered this strong position about dusk.

The Wellington Regiment pushing from cactus hedge to cactus hedge and cutting gaps with their bayonets, had captured several trenches and many prisoners, and, finally, by some very fine work they took two Turkish guns with limbers and ammunition all complete. Further progress was here

THE TWO KRUPP GUNS CAPTURED IN GAZA BY THE WELLINGTON MOUNTED RIFLES.

held up by several houses filled with Turks from which it was impossible to dislodge them. One large building in particular drew special attention by the incessant fire which came from its occupants, and this prompted the Wellington men to make use of the captured guns to blow the snipers out of the house; and the formation of an extemporised gun crew of mounted riflemen was complete in a moment. The gun was a Krupp, but its intricacies were quickly solved, probably not in conformity with gunnery regulations, but with splendid results.

The gun was directed at the house and Corporal Rouse who was "O/C Gun Detachment" looked through the barrel until the "target" was well in view, inserted a shell, closed the breach and fired the gun. Result, large hole in the house and twenty terrified Turks covered with debris ran out and surrendered. Three shots were fired from the captured gun in the manner described, each of which took effect on its objective. One of the latter in fact caused such destruction to the buildings along the line it traversed that Corporal Rouse was heard to remark that "the New Zealanders had made, at any rate, a new street in Gaza."

Another gallant little enterprise was carried out by Lieuts. Allison and Foley with their troops. On the left of the Wellington Regiment's front was a trench from which came a galling fire and which was protected by a narrow lagoon. These two officers with their men charged across the lagoon into the trench and bayoneted its thirty-two occupants.

While this attack by New Zealand was going on the 2nd L.H. Brigade had been meeting with considerable opposition among the sandhills to the north-west of the town, but continued to slowly advance through the orchards.

At six o'clock the situation so far as the attacking forces upon the Gaza position were concerned was most satisfactory, the Wellington Regiment and the 2nd L.H. Brigade were well into the northern outskirts of the town; and the Canterbury Regiment, with men of the 53rd Infantry Division were in Ali el Muntar; and the trenches south of the town were held by the 53rd Division; but at this hour a message was received by the Division: "owing to the lateness of the hour and the strength and position of the enemy forces pressing in from the north and east and the difficulty of continuing the attack in the dark in the town of Gaza, the G.O.C. Desert Column has decided to withdraw the Mounted Troops," and orders were received to break off the action after dark and to withdraw to Deir el Belah.

The artillery were soon on their way back and the wounded collected and brought to the ambulances and the prisoners sent back under escort. These included a Divisional Commander (the Commandant of Gaza) and 462 other ranks, two Austrian Krupp 77 mm. Field guns complete, one Artillery Observation Station complete with instruments, one convoy of six wagons loaded with stores, six camels, 16 horses and 12 mules.

The guns were taken back by ammunition wagon teams under the supervision of the Brigade Veterinary Officer, Major Stafford.

The greatest difficulty lay in extricating the 2nd L.H. Brigade from the labyrinth of cactus hedges and crooked lanes in which it had been fighting.

This brigade's horses were some four miles to the north and the night was a very dark one. However, it was done; and the troops of the Auckland Regiment that had been all

A VICKERS GUN IN THE TRENCHES.

day helping to hold off the Turkish reinforcements, were collected; and the Division began its march back at midnight, reaching Belah at half-past eight on the morning of the 27th.

Until the Division was clear the enemy was held off by the Imperial Mounted Division and the Camel Brigade, assisted by a Motor Car Patrol, and then these followed across the wadi.

The infantry had preceded the mounted troops in the retirement, with the exception of the 54th Division, which remained until the following day at Sheikh Abbas engaged with the enemy forces from Beersheba. By the 28th the whole force was back behind the Wadi Ghuzzeh.

At Gaza, fell Trooper A. R. FitzHerbert a well known settler of Rangitikei, age 64 years, but with the heart of a boy. He was loved by all who knew him and was an inspiration to the whole brigade. He found it difficult to enlist where he was known, on account of his age, but being of a very erect figure and filled with youthful vigour he at last managed to pass for a hale and hearty man of 40; and so, got away, with reinforcements for the Canterbury Regiment, reaching Egypt towards the end of 1915. Immediately upon the return of the brigade from the Peninsula he applied to be transferred to the Wellington Regiment and became "No. 3" in his own son's section in a troop commanded by a man whom as a boy he had taught to ride and to shoot. His great knowledge of horses soon won for him a place in the regiment, and his unfailing cheerfulness under troubles and trials of every kind endeared him to all.

Who could resist that gay laugh or that happy song as he worked away on the horse lines, whether the temperature was 120° in the shade and there blew a khamsin, or the night was shiveringly cold? The story is told of him that once when down with a touch of dysentery he was sent to hospital and there fell among a room full of "leadswingers," ages well in the early twenties. The consternation he caused was most amusing when after a mere three days in bed he announced his intention of going back to the front; and go he did, though a conspiracy of the matron and nurses managed to keep him in hospital for a week.

Early in the advance on the town through the orchards he was wounded in the neck, but after being bound up he insisted upon going on. Later, however, he was compelled to seek medical aid, and on his way to the dressing station he stopped to attend to a wounded comrade, on whom he was tying a bandage when a burst of shrapnel mortally wounded him.

As the regiment was still advancing, and there was no ambulance cart in sight he was bound up carefully and left for the stretcher bearers; but even then he insisted upon having his rifle beside him.

Many times during the campaign in the desert he was asked to take up clerical work for the regiment, such work being thought more suitable to his age, but he invariably refused, saying with a laugh that he had enlisted as a fighting soldier and as such he would remain.

He died as he would have wished in the midst of battle with his rifle in his hand.

The opinion was freely expressed subsequent to the operations that, had the infantry taken advantage of a fog (which formed a natural screen in the morning), Gaza would have fallen. The attack was commenced too late in the day by both infantry and mounted troops.

LT.-COL. J. N. MCCARROLL, C.M.G., D.S.O. (AND BAR), AUCKLAND MOUNTED RIFLES

Many hours, fraught with tremendous possibilities and worth thousands of reinforcements were frittered away. The mounted troops were idle till about 4 o'clock in the afternoon, but immediately they commenced to advance the pressure they brought to bear was such that they were enabled to penetrate a part of the town before dark. The subsequent orders to withdraw were mystifying, as the enemy appeared to be overcome.   A Turkish prisoner captured later by the 2nd L.H. Brigade confirmed this, as he stated that the Turks were ready to hoist the white flag.   The outside pressure by the Turkish reinforcements from Beersheba and Huj however, apparently decided the course of action taken by the East Force Commander.

A few days were now spent down on the beach at Belah where good water was to be found in any quantity in the

MEN AND HORSES IN THE SURF ON THE PALESTINE COAST.

lagoon.   Active patrolling was kept up towards Sharia and Beersheba.

The Second Battle of Gaza.

On April 16th orders were received for the second attack upon Gaza.

The Turks had by now practically a continuous defensive line from the sea to Tel el Sharia on the Beersheba–Ramleh railway which they were occupying with some 25 thousand men, reported by our Intelligence Department to be distributed as follows:—

    8,500 at Gaza.

    4,500 immediately east of Gaza.

    2,000 in the great Atawineh redoubt, about 10 miles along the Gaza–Beersheba road.

    6,000 Abu Hareira, and Tel el Sharia about half way to Beersheba.

    A garrison strength unknown in Beersheba.

East Force for this attack was about the same strength as at the first battle of Gaza with the addition of some tanks, but this time full use was made of all formations.

The attack upon the Gaza position was to be made by the Infantry upon a line extending from the sea to and including the Sheikh Abbas position. This latter consisted of a great mass of broken ground thrust out as it were into the plain; and up which were excellent covered lines of approach from the Wadi Ghuzzeh; and together with the Mansura ridge formed the most important tactical feature south of the Ali Muntar position at Gaza itself.

The Sheikh Abbas and Mansura ridges were to form the principal objectives and when captured would be used as a point d'appui for the final thrust upon Gaza.

The role of the Imperial Mounted Division was to protect the right flank of this attack from a position of concentration at Tel el Jimmi and to hold a general line Kh. Erk–El Munkheileh–Atawineh, cutting the Gaza–Beersheba road.

The I.C.C. Brigade was to be in support of this operation.

WATERING HORSES IN THE WADI GHUZZEH.

The Anzac Mounted Division was ordered to demonstrate towards the enemy positions about Tel el Sharia and Abu Hareira, to prevent the enemy there and at Beersheba from detaching troops towards Gaza. For this purpose the Division was to cross the wadi at Shellal.

THE SECOND BATTLE OF GAZA

At half-past six in the evening of 16th April, therefore, the Anzac Mounted Division marched from its bivouac at Deir el Belah with the N.Z.M.R. leading; and after an all night march the Canterburys crossed the wadi at the Shellal ford at half-past four in the morning of April 17th, and were shortly followed by the remainder of the Division.

There was a small Turkish post here with a machine gun on a conical hill commanding the ford. This hill was afterwards to become famous as the site of the "Shellal Mosaic," which was actually discovered about two hours after the New Zealanders had crossed over by two Officers of the Divisional Staff, an Australian and a New Zealander. This mosaic is worthy of more than a passing word and will be described later on.

Enemy aircraft were very active and bombed the column as it was crossing the wadi. The engineers had about a ton of gun-cotton on a wagon, ready for use in demolitions, and the driver halted with his Squadron beside the ford, unyoked his horses and took them off to water. All around, men and horses in hundreds were crossing the wadi, moving out towards Beersheba or watering their horses. At this particular moment the bombs were dropped by the enemy aircraft; but by the Hand of Providence they missed the gun-cotton, though the 2nd L.H. Brigade Headquarters were badly hit. Had the gun-cotton wagon been struck, few of the many hundreds in that crowded space would have survived.

By mid-day the New Zealand Brigade was holding a line about Hill 550, near Im Siri, on the Shellal–Beersheba road. Much movement was seen in the enemy lines about Tel el Sharia; and the great railway viaduct at Abu Irgeig was plainly visible on the Beersheba–Ramleh railway.

At dusk the Division retired to Shellal to water and to get supplies, leaving a brigade of yeomanry holding an outpost line.

The attack by the infantry on the Sheikh Abbas position was successful, but made no progress elsewhere.

The next day the New Zealand Brigade with the Aucklanders in the advance moved out at dawn and occupied much the same line, keeping up a harassing fire on the enemy outposts. Much attention was again paid to the mounted troops by enemy aircraft, but little damage was done. At dusk the Division again withdrew to Shellal, leaving the 22nd Brigade (Yeomanry) on outpost duty.

This day, the 2nd day of battle, had proved a hard and costly one for the infantry. They had been reinforced on their right by every available man of the Imperial Mounted Division and of the Camel Brigade. Both horsemen and camelmen had been dismounted and had gone in on foot. Very little progress had been made beyond the line captured at dawn on the first day. The Sheikh Abbas and Mansura Ridges were in our hands and from there we held a line to

C.M.R. AWAITING ORDERS TO ATTACK AT THE 2ND BATTLE OF GAZA.
Col. Findlay watching bombs dropping among the horses.

the sea, about two miles in advance of the Wadi Ghuzzeh. Orders were received for the Anzac Mounted Division to leave the 22nd Mounted Brigade in position covering the Shellal ford, and to march during the night to the support of the Imperial Mounted Division in its attack on the Atawineh redoubt.

The march took up the greater part of the night and reached a point near Kh. Erk by daylight, close to the junction of the El Sharia and Imleih wadis. Whilst waiting here the Canterbury Regiment was rather badly bombed, many men and horses being hit.

By nine o'clock on this the third day of battle, all guns of the Division were in action. The Inverness and Ayrshire

LIEUT.-COL. J. FINDLAY, COMMANDING CANTERBURY MOUNTED RIFLES.

Batteries with the third squadron of the Auckland Regiment as escort were supporting the Imperial Mounted Division in its attack upon Atawineh.

At half-past nine the Wellington Regiment was sent up to support the 5th Mounted Brigade (Yeomanry) who formed the right of the Imperial Mounted Division. The regiment attacked "Sausage" ridge, a spur strongly held by the enemy and forming the southern flank of the Atawineh position. Here the regiment with four machine guns and supported by the fire of the Ayrshire Battery made a good advance, taking most of the pressure away from the 5th Mounted Brigade. At one time Colonel Meldrum had two and a half Horse

Artillery Batteries supporting his attack and he made great use of them at excellent targets.

About noon the remainder of the New Zealand Brigade was ordered forward and went in at the trot. The Canterburys went into the line on the left of the Wellington Regiment to fill up a gap between that regiment and the left of the Imperial Mounted Division.

Colonel Findlay brought his Regiment up under heavy shell-fire and was also bombed by enemy planes. One section of machine guns had severe casualties from shell-fire whilst advancing behind the first line of troops; but owing to the courage and resource of 2nd Lieut. L. A. Craven the guns were placed in position and obtained good targets at from 1000 to 1600 yards on a redoubt, and also on enemy parties advancing through crops at a bare 400 yards. Just before the close of the day's operations this fine young officer was severely wounded, so severely that he never rejoined his unit.

THE VICKERS GUN SECTION UNDER LIEUT. CRAVEN UNDER SHELL-FIRE.

But his splendid work did not go unrecognised; for he received accelerated promotion and the Military Cross for the exceptionally good work he did this day.

A feature of the battle at this time, so far as it concerned the New Zealand Brigade, was the fine shooting of the Horse Artillery under Major Meikle, who on this day was in command

MAJOR E. J. HULBERT, D.S.O.

MAJOR H. C. HURST, D.S.O., CANTERBURY MOUNTED RIFLES.

of the R.H.A. Brigade that had put up such a fine record with the division. Six of these guns were in a position facing "Sausage Ridge" and their close proximity to the enemy positions, enabled observations to be made from the batteries themselves.

Shell-fire and bombing throughout the afternoon was very severe; and the groups of led horses out in the open plain had the most wonderful escapes. At times shells and bombs fell all around them and among them, so that they were

15TH COY. I.C.C. GOING INTO ACTION.

obscured from view for long intervals of time. Yet owing largely to the skilful way in which they were disposed the casualties were fairly light, amounting to 40 horses killed and 60 wounded.

The Camel Brigade had a very difficult task, of attacking the Atawineh position over perfectly open slopes and with very little effective artillery support. The 15th New Zealand Company bore its full share of the three days' fighting, and lost its commander, Captain Priest, who had so ably taken the place of Captain McCallum, killed at Rafa.

Towards dark the enemy from Beersheba made a bold counter attack on the extreme right of the line held by the Division, pushing in the outposts of the 22nd Yeomanry Brigade and shelling the Divisional watering places in the wadi at Heseia, causing some casualties and much consternation to the popular Field Squadron who were resting after a 20 hour bout of "developing water." After this if anyone ever wished to annoy an engineer all that was required was to mention the "evacuation of Heseia" and he got all the fun in the next 10 minutes that he wanted.

Darkness at length put an end to the third days' bitter fighting. During the night the Division crossed the wadi at Tel el Jemmi leaving an outpost line connecting with the Imperial Mounted Division on the left about El Magan and thence south across the wadi at Heseia and so to the old Turkish position at Weli Sheikh Nuran covering the Shellal crossing.

The troops dug in on this line in anticipation of an enemy attack. To the left the infantry remained on the Sheikh Abbas–El Mansura line and thence to the sea.

Thus ended the second battle of Gaza.

Of all the formations engaged the Anzac Mounted Division suffered the least, owing to its function on the first two days of the battle, being to protect the British right flank. The

THE WELLS AT BELAH. FILLED FANTASSES AWAITING THE CAMELS.

New Zealand Brigade lost seven killed and 81 wounded only for the three days, while the total casualties to the British Forces during the second Gaza operations amounted to approximately 14,000 men.

The battle was fought against superior enemy forces who were well entrenched upon higher ground with many and well-served guns skilfully placed. The advance to the enemy position was not only uphill but over perfectly open grassy slopes, without an atom of cover. The country was too exposed and the distances too great for the successful use of tanks. And the water problem at all times gave the greatest anxiety. All drinking water had to be carried on camels from the wells at Belah to the firing line; and the courage and resource shown by the Camel Transport Corps was magnificent. This corps, which had borne the burden and heat of the day in the Sinai Campaign, was recruited chiefly from Egypt. The camel drivers were all "Gyppies," recruited mainly from the Delta, and the officers nearly all Egyptian Government Officials who had volunteered for the work. Many of the N.C.Os. were volunteers from the Australian Light Horse Regiments and these afterwards in many cases were given commissions and proved invaluable officers.

The occupation of the line of the Wadi Ghuzzeh.

The Wadi Ghuzzeh now formed the general line of the British position. It is much like one of our river beds, but carries water only two or three times in the year. But the flow of water, such as it is, has cut deep down into the great Gaza-Beersheba plain, leaving perpendicular banks some 50 to 60 feet high. When our forces occupied this position there were four crossings of the wadi, leaving out the sea beach. The first was on the main road to Gaza; the next at Tel el Jemmi, which was used by the Division at the first battle of Gaza; the third was at Shellal on the Khan Yunus-Beersheba road; and the fourth at Tel el Fara on the Rafa-Beersheba road. But many more were made by the troops until it became possible to cross almost anywhere. The Wadi Ghuzzeh in common with the Wadi El Arish comes down "in spate" at intervals during the rainy season, and it was in this condition when our patrols were examining it, prior to the first Gaza battle; for they found three or four feet of water running in it. By the time the wadi was occupied as our line of defence, however, there remained a few pools of water only and these were carefully conserved and used for horses and men. At Shellal there was a remarkable spring of clear water gushing forth from out the eastern bank. And there were remains there of large Roman masonry cisterns, showing that in the old days this spring was used. But it was highly impregnated with salts, tasting not unlike the "table waters" of commerce. The troops stationed at Shellal drank regularly of this spring, but continuance of the practice brought on stomach troubles.

Palestine abounds in "tels." The glossary attached to our maps gives the meaning of the Arabic word as "mounds of earth"; and so far as our experience goes they were always made by the hand of man. Usually they appear to be the

CROSSING THE WADI GHUZZEH AT SHELLAL.

remains of old cities, such as Tel el Farama (Pelusium) Tel el Saba (ancient Beersheba). But there were two great "tels" on the Wadi Ghuzzeh about which nothing could be found. These were Tel el Jemmi, where the division crossed to make the first attack on Gaza, and Tel el Fara, seven miles further south on the wadi where the Rafa–Beersheba road crosses. These two "tels" stand up above the plain and can be seen for many miles on all sides. They are each flat on top with what were apparently once perpendicular sides. Both drop sheer down into the wadi bed, and Fara has been built up in ages gone by at the water line with huge masonry buttresses and courses of cut stone.

Just north of Tel el Jemmi is Um Jerrar, the ancient Gerar mentioned in Genesis. Abraham lived here and also Isaac and it was here that the trouble arose between Isaac and the men of Gerar over the wells of water which the former had dug. And it was rather remarkable that the only use made by us of this ancient site (for no buildings remain of any sort) was to clean out some seven or eight cisterns found there choked up with earth (and certainly many centuries old) and to fill them with water carried on camel-back from Belah. This water was used by the troops holding the line. So again were the wells of Gerar made to be of use.

The Division now took over the right flank, an open flank, which joining with the infantry line about Tel el Jemmi extended southward along the Wadi Ghuzzeh to Tel el Fara. Trenches were dug and strong points constructed, but the chief work consisted in active patrolling of the great plain which stretches east and south. Wells and cisterns were located, the enemy was continually harassed and he was induced to prolong his line to Beersheba.

This arduous work was carried out for the next few months in conformity with General Murray's plans for the systematic attack upon the now strongly entrenched Turks. The construction of the railway was continued to Belah and a branch line to Shellal; and a large body of men and horses was collected to form the "Egyptian Expeditionary Force," a great army of three corps—two infantry and one cavalry; and in addition there was one extra infantry division and an extra yeomanry brigade and the I.C.C. Brigade.

The Cavalry Corps was called the Desert Mounted Corps, to preserve the identity of the force which fought the Sinai Campaign; and consisted of the Anzac Mounted Division, the Imperial Mounted Division and the Yeomanry Mounted Division with the I.C.C. Brigade and an additional yeomanry brigade attached. The formation of the corps was made possible by the arrival of several yeomanry brigades and by the formation of the 4th L.H. Brigade, which consisted of the 4th, 11th and 12th L.H. Regiments. This Brigade took the place of a yeomanry brigade in the Imperial Mounted Division and so the latter now consisted of two L.H. Brigades and one Yeomanry Brigade and was in future called the Australian Mounted Division.

Major General Sir H. G. Chauvel, who had commanded the Anzac Mounted Division since its formation, took command of the Desert Mounted Corps, and Brigadier-General E. W. C.

Chaytor, our N.Z.M.R. Brigade Commander, took over the command of the Anzac Mounted Division, leaving the New Zealand Brigade to the command of Lieut-Col. W. Meldrum of the Wellington Regiment.

Included in the line held by the Division was a portion of the old Turkish line stretching through the great mound of Weli Sheikh Nuran to Khan Yunus designed by von Kressenstein to defend Palestine.

For reasons unknown this strong position was evacuated after General Chaytor's reconnaissance of Khan Yunus on February 23rd, and the Turks then took up the Gaza–Beersheba line.

At Weli Sheikh Nuran and Tel el Fara a great deal of work had been done. Intricate trench lines elaborately defended from an approach by the dreaded Anzacs upon their horses had been constructed. These "horse-proof" defences consisted in double lines of circular holes some five feet deep

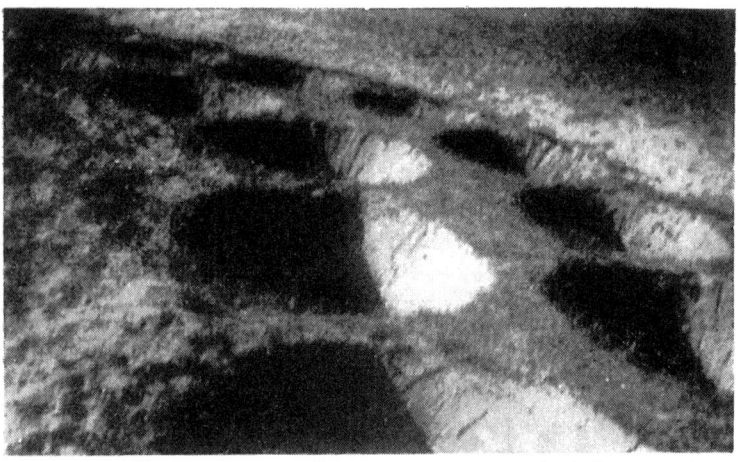

HOLES DUG BY THE TURKS TO KEEP OFF THE ANZACS.

and four feet in diameter and egg shaped, that is they were tapered to a point at the bottom in which it was evident a sharpened stake was to be placed.

It was found to be quite impossible to ride over these double lines of holes and there is no doubt but that we should have found them formidable obstacles.

On May 23rd a highly successful enterprise was undertaken by the Division in conjunction with the Imperial Mounted Division and the I.C.C. Brigade.

For their conquest of Egypt the Turks had constructed a railway from Ramleh (a town on the Jaffa–Jerusalem railway) to Beersheba, using material taken from the Jaffa–Ramleh railway which they had pulled up. This line was then extended south and it had almost reached the Wadi el Arish when we captured Magdhaba. It was exceedingly well built

OFFICERS OF THE 15TH COY. I.C.C. CAPT. McCALLUM IN THE CENTRE.

under the direction of German engineers with all bridges and culverts of masonry, of fine Ashlar work.

Now that our advance had reached to within five miles of Gaza this railway line proved a constant menace to our communications and it was decided that it should be destroyed.

So the Field Squadrons from the two Mounted Divisions and the Australian Field Troop attached to the Camels, took in hand a few days intensive training in railway demolitions, and were reinforced for this special work by about 100 men from the regiments, forming in each division and in the Camel Brigade a "Demolition Squadron."

THE RAID UPON THE ASLUJ RAILWAY

At seven o'clock in the evening of May 22nd the Division moved out and marched all night. A particularly unpleasant "Khamsin" was blowing from the south covering the whole face of the earth in an impenetrable pall of dust. The column marched against this and the usual difficulties of a night ride were increased a thousand-fold. It was impossible to see and difficult to breathe.

The air was full of electricity. A horse's mane on being stroked gave forth a shower of sparks.

The Divisional Commander's and a Brigade Commander's lance bearers chanced to be riding side by side and an eerie sight was the will-o'-the-wisp dancing between their spear points as the lances swung together.

The Divisional Commander put up a record in the manner of leading a raid. He had been very unwell for some days but insisted upon going with the Division and the united endeavours of the Staff backed up by the A.D.M.S. and D.A.D.M.S. were powerless to persuade him to stay. It being impossible to get a motor car through the country to be encountered, he was with difficulty dissuaded from riding; but his great tenacity of purpose overcoming the weakness of the body, he eventually led the Division in a sand-cart.

THE GREAT 18 ARCH BRIDGE AT ASLUJ.

At daylight on the 23rd the New Zealand Brigade was in position to the north (on the Beersheba end) of the scene of the "demolition" and in touch with the Imperial Mounted Division, whose mission for the day was a demonstration against the Beersheba line so as to prevent any enemy troops from there interfering with the railway destruction.

The work went "according to plan" in every detail. Some 15 miles of railway were destroyed including many masonry bridges, in particular a great eighteen arch bridge at Asluj.

LAYING THE GUN-COTTON CHARGES AT THE BASE OF A PIER IN THE BIG BRIDGE.

Such was the perfection of the training of the "demolition squadrons," that the destruction went on just as fast as a man could walk. In front went the led horses of the demolition party, straight along the railway as fast as they could walk. Then came two teams of men on foot in single file on each rail. The leading man put down a slab of gun cotton in the middle of a rail and then doubled on to the next but one, doing the same there, his vis-a-vis on the other side meanwhile putting down a slab of gun-cotton in the middle of the rail on his own side that paired with the rail missed on the other side Then the next man following (on either side) wired the slab to the rail and doubled on, the third man put in the detonator and fuse which he carried ready, and the fourth man lighted the charge. And so they went on, each squadron doing it five miles. The gun-cotton blew a piece of rail clean away of some twelve to fifteen inches in length. The bridges were destroyed by blowing down each alternate arch with gun cotton charges fired electrically.

THE RAID UPON THE ASLUJ RAILWAY

ONE OF THE ARCHES OF THE BIG BRIDGE BEING BLOWN UP.

The 15 miles of railway and all bridges were finished by one o'clock and the troops reached their bivouacs soon after dusk, tired and overwhelmed with dust, but successful.

The constant movement of troops over the alluvial plain converted all roads and tracks into dust beds some 12 inches or more in depth. The dust was very fine and lifted to every breath of wind and enveloped every moving man horse or vehicle in a white cloud. This white cloud gave away movement and so it had long become the established custom to make no offensive during the hours of daylight. At about 10 o'clock in the morning the sea breeze began blowing from the west or north-west and continued until dark making life in a "bivvy" a torment, one breathed dust and ate dust and at night wrapped oneself up in dust.

THE ASLUJ BRIDGE AFTER THE EXPLOSIONS.

The chief roads and tracks were swept bare of dust by gangs of natives which helped matters somewhat; and many miles of motor track were laid down in wire netting. This wire netting, well pegged down on top of the sand in Sinai,

LAYING THE GUN-COTTON CHARGES.

had proved of inestimable benefit to the infantry when advancing upon El Arish.

In order to minimise as far as possible the dust nuisance in and near camp all traffic was restricted to certain roads—usually indicated by heaps of sand or dust which served as a "curb" and were popularly called "lighthouses."

Great pride was taken by certain units in the way in which their camps were laid out and in the cleanliness of their lines. At the corners of intersecting roads and tracks well painted direction boards were placed so that a stranger coming near had no difficulty in finding his way about.

The Shellal Mosaic.

After the return of the Division to the vicinity of Shellal following upon the second battle of Gaza the top of the small conical hill upon which had been found some fragments of mosaic, was thoroughly explored under the supervision of Chaplain Maitland-Woods, an Australian padre. He was an enthusiastic archaeologist with a sound knowledge of handling ancient works of art.

The mosaic was carefully uncovered and proved to be the remains of a Christian Chapel floor done in beautiful colours.

with a Greek inscription at each end. From the inscriptions it was found that this chapel had been built in the 622nd year after the Roman foundation of the city of Gaza. The Roman era of Gaza began 61 B.C., which would give the date of the chapel as 561 A.D.

In the 6th century, A.D., the coast district of Palestine was an important radiating centre of Christianity. The two churches built by Constantine, the "Holy Sepulchre" and the "Nativity," founded in 326 A.D., were the objects of the greatest veneration of all Christianity. This chapel must have stood on the road from Jerusalem to Egypt. Down this road came the Ethiopian Eunuch when he met Philip and it was just here that he was baptised.

The mosaic is executed in marbles of many colours which must have been gathered from many lands and the colours

A PORTION OF THE PARTLY UNCOVERED MOSAIC AT SHELLAL.

to-day are as fresh as if the stones had been newly cut. "I am the True Vine; ye are the branches," is the theme on which the mosaic is composed.

The "True Vine" issues from a Greek Amphora of brilliant colouring in which is placed a cross in red marble, with a bright green glory shining from it. Above is a cage enclosing a bird symbolising the Holy Spirit. On either side above this, is a representation of a hare escaping from a hound —the soul escaping from temptation. And all around the central idea are representations of animals, lions, tigers, flamingoes and peacocks in glorious colours, all doing homage to the central chalice. It may be possible that each animal and bird represents some Eastern Race which had embraced Christianity. The Shellal mosaic awaits interpretation at the hands of competent experts who will be able to give to the world the full meaning of a message delivered over a thousand years ago.

After the mosaic had been fully uncovered it was carefully drawn and painted by a New Zealand sergeant with a faithful representation of its original colours, from which the Egyptian Survey Department turned out a beautiful lithograph. The padre took in hand its removal and cleverly lifted it in sections, which were, with the assistance of the engineers, securely packed in boxes and sent to Cairo.

The padre had always been of the opinion that the chapel had been built to the memory of some Saint and for a long time he was inclined to believe that our Saint George was buried there. And he became greatly excited when during the removal of the mosaic it became apparent that there was a chamber under the floor; and his enthusiasm rose to bursting point when in a small cavity there were found the bones of a skeleton. His brother officers in the Division had always viewed sceptically the idea of anyone having been buried under the floor, and so the padre, hot with his discovery, rushed off to the nearest telegraph station and sent the following wire to D.H.Q.: "Have found bones of saint"! By a strange coincidence the telegram went to Cairo, where it was sent to the Records Office, Cairo, without any alteration or explanation. In due course the padre received the following: "Send full name, No. and Regiment of Trooper Saint"! The laugh was against the padre, but he eventually scored, for the London papers took up the subject of the mosaic and devoted much space to it, and a discussion as to whose bones they might be.

At the end of May the Brigade was withdrawn from the front line and went into bivouac near Abasan el Kebir. Here for a week steady training was the order of the day; musketry, bombing, instruction in the Hotchkiss gun (of which each troop now had one), and the building up of the horses took up the whole of the men's time.

A great pleasure to the men was given by the arrival of the New Zealand Band. This popular unit had left the Brigade when the advance into Palestine had begun and had remained with the Training Regiment at Moascar. Its arrival with new music and plenty of "wind," just at a time when training and dust were spoiling the sweetest of tempers, was welcomed with joy; and there was no more popular man among all the camps than Auckland's "Wally."

A Light Horse Pierrot Troupe also made its appearance about this time and cheered many a dull evening. But the greatest treat was given by the "Palestine Pops," a troupe belonging to the 74th Division, the dismounted yeomanry division who had fought as infantry on Gallipoli and were still doing so, and whose divisional badge was a broken spur. The "Palestine Pops" were talented vocalists and comedians and the "lady" was inimitable. "She" was fair, slim and graceful and "with a way with her" that took by storm the hearts of the boys.

Their first performance was given a few days after one by another troupe, in which there were several "ladies" whose antics provoked uproarious mirth; and many sallies of wit (?) passed between them and the audience. So when the 74th Division's "maiden" came upon the stage she was greeted with applause which her "get-up" and deportment justly earned. But when a few "broad" remarks were indulged in by someone in the audience she turned him down as skilfully and withal as sweetly as any Queen of the May could have done secure in her elected position and surrounded by her court. Before she had been on the stage many minutes, by the mere power of her "womanhood," she had that rough audience in the hollow of her hand, a remarkable tribute not only to her fine acting, but to the innate chivalry of that great crowd of men bowing down to "woman" merely acted.

Hot discussions followed when the performance was over as to whether "she" was really a man or a girl and one reckless man, to settle a heavy wager, stayed behind and boldly invaded the "Green Room," but was met with a good round sentence full of the expletives that none but a Tommy can use, and so returned a disappointed man.

This clever "girl" who nightly delighted the hearts of hundreds of home-sick men with her winning ways was killed in the attack of the 74th Division which broke the Turkish lines on November 6th, near Sharia.

On June 1st new rifles were issued and the rifles brought from New Zealand returned to Ordnance.

The new rifle fired Mark VII. ammunition and had a flatter trajectory and a greater muzzle velocity than the old rifle, but our men were sorry to lose Mark VI. New Zealand ammunition for the machine and Hotchkiss guns. This ammunition was tested by the makers and gave a very small percentage of stoppages, a smaller percentage than any other make of S.A.A. used whether made in England, America or India.

A HOTCHKISS GUN AND CREW. WELLINGTON MOUNTED RIFLES.

On June 3rd the whole Brigade marched over to Khan Yunus where on the railway there was a steam disinfecting plant; and all ranks stripped off all clothing for putting through the steam chamber, a very necessary operation in this dirty country as anyone who cared to stroll down the lines any evening would have soon satisfied himself. He would probably have heard something of this sort—"Bill I've had a regular Melbourne Cup Day. I've turned my bally breeches inside out and outside in 45 blithering times and I have broken the blighters little hearts." Or he might have overheard a verse of an improvised song sung to the Brigade's popular march "John Peel," which once "brought down the house" at a camp fire concert in the desert.

> "I went down the lines the other day
> When I heard a fellow in the Waikatos say
> I've caught 22 which is 30 less than you
> But I hope to get some sleep before the morning."

On June 8th, much to everyones joy, the Brigade marched to the sea at Marakeb, immediately west of Khan Yunus, and stayed there resting and bathing for ten days. The camp was on the sea beach and there was plenty of good water for man and horse.

Advantage was taken to overhaul and improve the Hotchkiss gun saddlery. Captain Herrick, who had been a Lewis Gun enthusiast and who was in charge of the training of the Hotchkiss gunners of the Wellington Regiment, made some great improvements. He devised a carrier by which the gun was carried on the centre of the saddle and so did away with the constant galling of the horses back, an ever present source of trouble with the pack saddle as issued. The improvements designed by this officer were carried out in the field by the Brigade's farriers. These men were invaluable. No work came amiss to them and no hours were too long.

A TYPICAL TROOP HORSE SADDLED UP FOR A MARCH.

The New Zealand Brigade had long before this justly earned the reputation among the mounted troops of being the finest horse-masters in the Egyptian Expeditionary Force, a reputation which they maintained until the end of the war. To the farriers and to Major J. Stafford, D.S.O. the Brigade Veterinary Officer, the Brigade owes more than can ever be told.

On June 17th a report was sent in to Divisional Headquarters showing the numbers of "original" horses still with the regiments. These original horses were horses from Australia or New Zealand and which crossed the Canal in April, 1916, with the brigades. The return is as follows:— 1st L. H. Brigade, 671; 2nd L.H. Brigade, 742; N.Z.M.R. Brigade, 1056. All brigades had suffered much the same casualties.

"BESS." A TYPICAL NEW ZEALAND MARE.
Her record is as follows:—Left N.Z. with Main Body, October, 1914; Egypt, 1915; Sinai, 1916; Palestine, 1917-1918; France, 1918; Germany, 1919; England, 1920; Returned to N.Z. July, 1920. Photographed in the Jordan Valley, June, 1918.

The brigadiers concurred in that the ideal horse should be from 15 to 15.3 and as near 15 hands as possible and should be stout and cobby and if possible with plenty of blood.

Steady training continued, interspersed with football and boxing tournaments; and the health of all ranks rapidly improved. A glorious surf rides in on to the Palestine coast and men and horses spent a great deal of their time in the water.

A little leave to Egypt was now given and the New Zealand Brigade's quota of three officers and thirty-seven other ranks went off for ten days.

Here one puts one's finger upon one of the greatest disabilities suffered by the troops campaigning in the East. There was absolutely no respite from the glare of the sun or the torment of the flies or from the association with alien peoples. There were no quiet restful back areas. To go from Sinai to Egypt or from Palestine to Egypt was simply out of the frying pan into the fire, the same sun, the same flies, the same smelly East and unsociable people. There was of course a very warm-hearted English Colony in Cairo and there were exceptions even among the natives; but the Arab Mahommedan is without humour, sympathy, or the elements of cleanliness; and his only smile is a smile of deceit. Later on a Rest Camp for the Division was established at Port Said chiefly by the help of the Australian Red Cross. Here our men could get good food and sea bathing and rest; but the help of intercourse with friends, to cure war weariness, was entirely lacking. The Aotea Home was a haven of refuge to our New Zealanders, but to get there a man had to be a "convalescent" from a hospital and it was ever a point of honour not to go near a hospital until absolutely forced.

Aotea was a home indeed and the only home our men ever knew throughout the campaign in the East. But as has been said, to get there one had to be first evacuated to hospital. It was this absence of home life as the years went on that told on all alike and the great spaces and great silences of the desert intensified the home hunger. The few Bedouin children met with were made much of by our men, for in spite of their dirt and the natural unattractiveness of the Arab they were children and as children brought memories of home. Two war worn hard-bitten veterans were riding in from the desert in the dusk and passing a Bedouin Camp heard the wail of a baby. "Gee, is'nt that like home, let's take the little beggar into camp Bill"! said one, "Let's" said Bill, and for the sum of two piastres the bargain was clinched. Crowds surrounded their bivvy for hours and much and varied was the advice poured upon them. It was a good little baby, fat and round, and it caused the greatest of interest to the regiment, but biscuits and bully and tea, how ever tenderly administered, is a food for a hard-doing man. The wailing grew in intensity as the days went by and their mates finally firmly and emphatically demanded some rest at night. So the foster fathers sadly went back and returned the infant to its mother.

The last days of June were spent in the bivouacs near Abasan and training went on steadily. All ranks were instructed in anti-gas methods and all officers and N.C.Os. in the handling of carrier pigeons.

On June 28th General Sir Edmund Allenby took over the command of the Egyptian Expeditionary Force bringing a spirit of great optimism; and war material of all kinds poured into the area. Heavy guns arrived, a multitude of motor transport reached railhead and last, but not least, new and fast aeroplanes appeared. These gave our men intense pleasure. The mounted troops had always suffered greatly from bombing from the air, and our own planes had been powerless to prevent it. Equipped with obsolete machines the air men had done extraordinarily good work under the most unfavourable conditions for they were always a prey to the German Fokker or Albatross Scout. Now at last we were to see the tables turned and a general shout of joy went up from the whole Division when a German in an Albatross Scout was brought down in our lines by one of our airmen.

The mastery of the air after this gradually passed from the Turks, who had held it since Sinai days, to our British and Australian airmen.

July found the Brigade back in the front line at Tel el Fara, patrolling, reconnoitring and stirring up the Turk. This, as has been explained, was on the open flank of the Turkish line of defence. Towards Gaza, where the opposing lines drew together, a steady trench warfare with all its accessories was carried on by the infantry divisions. But on the right flank, owing to the distance apart of the lines and the great open flank to the east which nothing but the want of water precluded from use, all work was done on horseback. A small patrol under an officer would go out at night to test or examine some portion of the Turk's line. The party would ride on a compass bearing close up to the objective. Then a selected few would dismount and spend a few hours on foot in among the Turkish patrols, examining, listening and noting down tracks, movement, trenches and above all water.

Then many reconnaissances were made to verify air intelligence. This work brought out all the hunter's instinct in man and much good work was done and the training to officers and men was invaluable. Confidence in the dark is one of the most valuable of military qualities and our men increased this native quality an hundredfold.

On the 19th the enemy were reported advancing upon Shellal; and the Division turned out with the two L.H. Brigades in front and the New Zealand Brigade in reserve. The enemy was encountered about five miles out and after a good deal of shelling by both sides he withdrew.

On July 23rd the Brigade went out with some guns to reconnoitre the enemy line before Beersheba, as intelligence had been received that the enemy had evacuated this part of his line. But he was found to be fully occupying all his works.

On August the 5th and 6th a water reconnaissance was made away to Esani in the south by the New Zealand Field Troop. Their report showed that there was ample water to sustain indefinitely two Divisions at least. About this time the Railway Construction Engineers made a flying survey of a line towards Beersheba under the protection of the New Zealand troops.

Towards the end of August the Brigade went out to the beach and there again steady training became the order of the day.

On the beach at Maraker.

General Allenby presenting decorations to officers and men of the Anzac Mounted Division. September 28th, 1917.

Great progress was made in musketry and on September 13th a Brigade Rifle Meeting was held, bringing out some excellent shooting.

On September 18th the Brigade moved back to its old bivouac at Abasan and came into reserve for the front line.

On September 28th the Commander-in-Chief inspected the men and horses, and on October 16th he presented medals to officers and men of the Division; and the New Zealanders to be so decorated were: Captain R. P. Harper, Machine Gun Squadron; Lieut. L. J. Armstrong and Trooper D. O'Connor, for distinguished service in the field.

During this month steady training had been continued, relieved by tactical exercises and work in conjunction with aeroplanes.

On October 24th the first move of the Great Attack on the Turkish line began.

It was now nearly six months since our men had been looking at the Promised Land from behind the Gaza-Beersheba lines, and many were the speculations as to what it was like. Day after day we had gazed at the mountains of Judea showing up like a great blue wall away to the east, and we wondered just where Jerusalem stood. We were to find

Palestine a rich country sharply divided into plain and mountain. Straight before us lay the plain of the Philistines stretching away north to Jaffa and thence continuing in an ever narrowing strip as the plain of Sharon to Mount Carmel. And marching with the plains on our right was the Judean plateau which rising from the desert at Beersheba reaches its average height of 2500 feet between that city and Hebron and continues north until the great bisecting plain of Armaggedon is reached to the east of Mount Carmel. Here the blue mountains meet the sea and the plains are ended.

The great blue wall of this plateau of Judea is the most characteristic sight from the plain and from it the Israelites of old looked down upon the country that was filled with corn and wine and olives. The highlands are healthly pasture land, but to grow crops of corn much and unceasing industry is required and the luxuriantly fertile plains of the Philistines must at all times have been a great temptation to the Israelites.

TYPICAL PLOUGH TEAMS OF THE PALESTINE PLAINS.

For these plains grow all that man requires. Barley and wheat cover the land as far as the eye can reach. It is the country of the fig, the olive, the orange and the vine. Its flocks and herds are many and numerous and its climate though hot in summer is not unduly so under ordinary conditions. It has its wells, its springs and its running rivers and a copious never failing rainfall in winter. On the coast still struggling gamely with the encroaching sand lie Gaza,

CAPTAIN ROBIN HARPER, D.S.O., M.C., D.C.M.
Commanding the Machine Gun Squadron.

LT. GORDON HARPER, M.C., D.C.M., MACHINE GUN SQUADRON.

Ascalon and Ashdod, which with Gath and Ekron were the five capital cities of the Philistines. Gaza is still a flourishing town, but upon Ascalon has fallen to the full the prophecy, "O .man, savage, ferocious, brutal, what desolations thou hast wrought on the earth! They have stretched out upon Ascalon the line of confusion and the stones of emptyness. Thorns have come up in her places and brambles in the fortresses thereof; and it is a habitation of dragons and a court for owls."—Isaiah.

Ascalon, Ashdod, Jaffa, all were full of people and hives of industry, even down to the time of the Crusade. Now there is a great silence everywhere along that coast, silence and the desolation of sand blowing where so e'er it wills. Ashdod the proud city that withstood the seige of Psammetichus for 29 years is now a Bedouin hovel, and the old Crusader castle that stood so proudly on guard at the harbour is making its last battle with the waves.

On the great ride that was to follow the fall of Beersheba we were to pass through ancient history in every mile. The old Hebrew cities are still there with their Roman and Crusader ruins. We were to pass from Um Gerar and Beersheba in the land of Abraham and Isaac by Gaza (so identified with the life of Samson) and between that city and Um Lakis (the Lachish of the Old Testament) away north past Ascalon where Herod the Great was born, Tel el Safi the ancient Gath of the Scriptures and the Blanche Garde or White Custody of the Crusaders of Richard I. Thence by Ashdod, the Azotus of the New Testament, and Yebna, celebrated of the Maccabees, and Akir (Ekron), and so to Ayun Kara where was Samson's exploit with the lion; next to Ramleh and Ludd, the Romula of the Crusaders and the Lod or Lydda of the Bible and so to Jaffa "the beautiful."

CHAPTER V.

How the Turkish Line was Broken at Beersheba.

It was now that the benefit of the constant patrolling and reconnoitring was felt. The Turk had become so accustomed to our mounted troops riding about the plains that our preliminary movements to the south to obtain a concentration point from which to descend upon Beersheba passed unnoticed. Every care was taken to conceal these movements, however, and no marches were made in daylight. A further protection came from our air service, now far ahead of the enemy's in speed, numbers and personnel; for our airmen kept the enemy planes away or forced them to fly so high that they apparently saw nothing.

The long line before which we had remained for the past six months extended from the sea at Gaza to Beersheba—a distance of close upon thirty miles—and was an almost continuous trench line and followed the Gaza-Beersheba road. That portion from the sea at Gaza to the great Atawineh redoubt we knew well—to our cost. From there on towards Beersheba our reconnaissances—both air and mounted—and our Intelligence Department, told us that there was a great system of trenches at Abu Hareira, where the Wadi Sharia crosses the road; that there was also another great system at Kh. Kauwukah—covering the bend in the railway and the Sharia viaduct on the railway. From there through Bir Abu Irgeig ran a continuous line of strong works to the south of Beersheba. Practically the whole of this thirty-mile line lay upon higher ground than that held by us—giving the Turk good observation and an excellent field of fire.

Beersheba itself was entirely hidden behind a range of hills running up to a height of 960 feet, and along these hills lay the enemy trenches.

General Allenby's plan was to strike at Beersheba—the enemy's extreme left—and having taken the town with its invaluable water supply, to roll up the whole Turk line back upon Gaza. To do this the XX Corps was to attack Beersheba from the west and south-west, while the Desert Mounted Corps came in from the south, east and north.

PREPARATIONS FOR THE ADVANCE UPON BEERSHEBA 129

To cover these operations the XXI Corps, aided by the Navy, was to begin a heavy bombardment of Gaza and its defences 24 hours before the move against Beersheba began.

To enable the attack upon Beersheba to be so made, preparatory measures had to be undertaken some days before, to provide water for those troops taking part in the encircling movement and also to advance the front line towards the west of Beersheba—sufficiently near to enable the attack to be launched by the infantry. The preparatory measures included placing one mounted division at Asluj, one mounted division at Khalasa, and one mounted brigade at Bir el Esani.

LIEUT.-COL. J. N. MCCARROLL, AUCKLAND MOUNTED RIFLES.

The mounted corps was required also to protect the advance of the XX Corps to its preliminary position on the line Abu Ghalyun–Rashid Bek–El Buggar. The water required was to be sufficient for one mounted division at Asluj, for one mounted division at Khalasa and also for two mounted divisions passing through Esani, where they would each stay one night; and finally at Abu Ghalyun (between Esani and Khalasa) water was required for one infantry brigade group. A supply depot had to be formed at Esani (and protection found for it) for the feeding of the mounted corps.

The preliminary moves therefore consisted of: (a) an advance of the front line eastward as far as the line Rashid Bek–Point 720 ($2\frac{1}{2}$ miles north of the Tel el Fara–Beersheba road)–Point 630–Point 510–Point 300; (b) a gradual extension of our line southward as far as Asluj.

General Allenby says:—"It is not uninteresting to review the enemy situation at this period.

The German Staff in Palestine had, so far back as August, decided that the British would make another effort to break through on that front, and with such forces that, unless the Turks were heavily reinforced, the result could only be in favour of the British. That the weaknesses of their position were its extent and the exposed left flank at Beersheba, was fully realised by the command in the field, and during August and September repeated requests were made to the Higher Command for a shortening of the line by withdrawing from Beersheba, or generous reinforcements so that Beersheba could be held à l'outrance.

"The soundness of these demands was fully realised by the German advisers of the Turks, but there existed a policy which was a veritable millstone to those who wished to conduct the operations in accordance with clear strategic principles. This policy was directed towards the recovery of Baghdad. A composite German force had been formed, and one of the first of German soldiers—Marshal Erich von Falkenhayn—was lent for the carrying through of this undertaking. If Baghdad was to be taken, every man and gun must be sent to Irak, and every man sent to Sinai decreased the chance of success. But to this was the unanswerable argument of those who asked that reinforcements should be sent to Sinai: "If the Sinai front is broken, Palestine and Syria will fall into the enemy's hands, and not only will Baghdad not be retaken, but the armies in Irak will be caught like a rat in a trap, with the British across their lines of communication at Aleppo." It was not until mid-October that this argument prevailed, and then it was too late. Troops being diverted from Mesopotamia were still on the lines of communication and the aircraft were still being unpacked and put together when the British troops attacked and captured Beersheba on October 31st, 1917.

"The German command had, however, estimated the date of the British attack with fair accuracy, which they considered would take place, owing to weather conditions, early in November. But they were totally incorrect in their estimate of its direction.

"Various circumstances made them believe that it would consist of a third and final assault on Gaza, combined with a landing to the north, which would turn their right flank and enable the British to occupy the fertile coastal plain. To meet this all defensive work was concentrated for many weeks on the Gaza sector, and their main reserves—the 7th and 19th Infantry Divisions, were concentrated behind Gaza. Von Falkenhayn proposed, by a concentration of forces, to deliver an attack on the British right flank, and so drive General Allenby out of Palestine into the waterless and difficult country east of the Wadi el Arish. In addition to its strategical effect this would have had the political result of clearing that portion of the Turkish Empire from the invader.

"This attack was originally timed for the latter half of October, to precede and forestall the British attack. Owing, however, to indecision, general procrastination, poor transport facilities, and, above all, to the jealousy and opposition of Ahmed Jemal Pasha, G.O.C. IV Army and Governor of Syria, it had to be postponed and was eventually timed for early December.

"By October the 28th the organisation of the Turkish forces under the Yildirim Army Group into the VII and VIII Armies was nearing completion. The Headquarters of General Kress von Kressenstein (G.O.C. VIII Army) had moved back from Huj to Huleikat, so that the former now connected to the main railway by a light line, might be used as a reserve area, and Fevzi Pasha (G.O.C. VII Army) was about to move forward his Headquarters from Hebron to near Beersheba, finally to take over the troops allotted to his command. Marshal von Falkenhayn was at Aleppo, en route for Jerusalem.

"The front had been strengthened by three fresh divisions (giving a total of one cavalry and nine infantry divisions), and an additional division was moving towards the front on the lines of communication south of Aleppo.

"The Gaza sector was a network of trenches, wire entanglements, and strongly fortified posts, conveniently sited for mutual support and cross fire, which extended to the southeast until the defences of Beersheba were reached. The German Staff appeared to have been very well satisfied as to the security of the line against frontal attack, and any second line system of defence had been almost totally neglected. A wide turning movement on the east was considered impossible owing to the broken nature of the country and lack of water."

The advance to the Rashid Bek line took place on October 24th by the Australian Mounted Division, under General Hodson, and was entrenched.

Early on October 27th, Points 720 and 630 were attacked by an enemy force, estimated at six battalions, two squadrons and two batteries. The line was then held by the 8th Mounted Brigade, detached from the Yeomanry Division. The enemy succeeded in occupying the tops of both hills in spite of heavy casualties caused to him during his advance. The position was very gallantly defended by the County of London Yeomanry and the 21st M.G. Squadron. The garrison of the post on Point 720 were all killed or wounded with the exception of three men; that on Point 630 held on in a support trench close behind the crest in spite of heavy casualties and though almost surrounded. It was eventually relieved by the 53rd Division.

This gallant little affair helped materially to keep the enemy's attention away from what was going on further south, and caused him to think that this was the southern limit of the expected attack.

The extension southwards was begun on October 22nd, when the 2nd L.H. Brigade moved to Bir el Esani and the I.C.C. Brigade to Abu Ghalyun.

Thenceforward work on water development was carried on at high pressure night and day. Tracks were improved and marked. The supply difficulties were successfully contended with, though much trouble was entailed in the transport, for the whole of the country to be traversed was sandy and cut up badly with the heavy traffic.

The bulk of the work of finding and developing the water supply fell on the two brigades just mentioned, who, together with the field squadrons of the Anzac Mounted Division and Australian Mounted Division, performed wonders and earned the unstinted praise of the Commander-in-Chief (General Allenby), who, following his custom of visiting the scene of any new move and becoming personally acquainted with those about to make it, had come down to Asluj on the day before the final advance on Beersheba.

The work at Khalasa and Asluj consisted in clearing out the deep wells that the Turks had blown in and installing oil engine-driven pumps and long rows of canvas horse troughs.

MAJOR S. C. P. NICHOLLS, D.S.O.

So completely had the Turks wrecked these ancient wells that the task of clearing them down to the level of the water (over 100 feet) was no light one.

On the 24th October the N.Z.M.R. (strength 95 officers and 1878 other ranks) moved to Esani, and on the 29th to Asluj.

By the evening of October 30th, the day upon which the XXI Corps with the Navy, began the great bombardment of

Gaza, the concentration of the Desert Mounted Corps was complete. The Corps now consisted of three complete divisional groups (Anzacs, Australian Division and Yeomanry Division), the 7th Mounted Brigade, and the I.C.C. Brigade, in all 11 brigades, each with its horse artillery battery—approximately 28,000 mounted men.

The units were disposed as follows—the Anzac Mounted Division at Asluj ready to encircle Beersheba; the Australian Mounted Division at Khalasa, with orders to follow the Anzacs to the vicinity of Beersheba, where it was to come into action on the left of the Anzac Mounted Division. At Bir el Esani was the 7th Mounted Brigade, and at Shellal the Yeomanry Division, with the I.C.C. Brigade at Hiseia, a few miles away.

At 6 in the evening of October 30th the Anzac Mounted Division moved off by a track leading up the Wadi el Imshash over the mountain range just east of Thaffha. The watershed was reached at midnight, and the advanced guard halted for 2½ hours to enable the column to close up and the track to G. el Shegeib to be reconnoitred and an enemy post there to be dealt with.

Here the 2nd L.H. Brigade took the road down to the Beersheba plains through Bir Arara and the remainder of the Division pushed down the track over G. el Shegeib, followed by the Australian Division, who had orders to halt at Iswaiwin until the situation developed.

The only wheels taken with the brigades were the guns and first-line transport (ammunition limbers and limbered wagons containing watering gear and tools). "B" eschelon (*i.e.*, all other wagons), loaded with rations, was left at Asluj with the ammunition column, with orders to await directions. But the ammunition column was to follow on after the division at daylight on the 31st.

Camel water convoys with a small reserve of drinking water for the men were left also at Asluj in readiness to be sent up.

No. 1 Light Car Patrol (Ford cars) and No. 11 Light Armoured Motor Battery (No. 11 L.A.M.B.) were attached to the Division with orders to follow on, leaving Asluj at 5 o'clock on the morning of the 31st.

Supplies were organised as follows:—Each man carried two days' rations for himself and one day's forage for his horse. In addition he carried in a sandbag strapped across the pommel of the saddle a small emergency ration of grain for his horse. "B" eschelon (an improvised train of all baggage wagons) carried two days' emergency rations for the man and one day's forage for the horse.

The medical arrangements made provision for the mobile sections of the field ambulances to march from Asluj with their respective brigades; and for all cacolet camels to march together in rear of the Australian Mounted Division.

A divisional collecting station was ordered to be formed of tent subdivisions of Field Ambulances, at points to be decided upon by the A.D.M.S., and evacuations were to be made by sand-carts and camels to the farthest point to which light motor ambulances could be brought; thence to the Australian Mounted Division receiving station at Asluj; thence to the Anzac Mounted Division receiving station at Rashid Bek by light motor ambulance; and thence to railhead near Shellal by heavy motor ambulance.

The 7th Mounted Brigade left Bir el Esani at 9.30 p.m. and came across country to the vicinity of G. Itwail el Semin on the Asluj–Beersheba road to act as a connecting link between the Desert Mounted Corps and the XX Corps, whose right was on the Khalasa–Beersheba road.

The Anzac Division met with some opposition on the road leading over G. el Shegeib, but this was brushed aside by the Wellingtons—the leading regiment—and by 8 o'clock in the morning of October 31st the Division had reached the line Bir el Hamman (2nd L.H. Brigade); Bir Salim Abu Irgeig (N.Z.M.R.) with the 1st L.H. Brigade in reserve behind the New Zealanders.

The Division's next objective was the line Tel el Sakaty–Tel el Saba and the cutting of the Beersheba–Hebron motor road; and its final objective the line Point 1020 (two miles north-west of Tel el Saba)–Point 970 (immediately north of the town)–Mosque. The importance of finding and developing water during the operations was impressed upon all units.

About 9 o'clock the advance began, and the leading brigades were soon under a hot artillery fire from the hills on the north side of the Hebron road and the advance slowed down. The plains were found also to be much cut up by narrow and deep wadi beds, and this made rapid movement on horseback impossible.

At the same time the infantry attack from the west was proceeding satisfactorily, and their shells could be seen bursting on the hills covering Beersheba to the west.

The mission of the 2nd L.H. Brigade, besides the capture of Tel el Sakaty and the wells there and the cutting of the enemy main line of communication along the Hebron road, included

GEN. MELDRUM JUST BEFORE THE ATTACK UPON BEERSHEBA.

protection from counter-attack from the east and north-east; and in pushing across the open plain the Brigade encountered considerable opposition. By 11 a.m., however, they gained command of the road and by half-past twelve had captured Tel el Sakaty and the wells.

Divisional Headquarters was established on the hills at Khashm Zanna, distant from Beersheba five miles and from Tel el Saba three miles; and from this position a birdseye view of the great Beersheba plain was obtained and the movements of the troops could be watched, even as one does upon a "Field Day"; and with the added interest that it was occasionally shelled by enemy batteries from the hills behind Tel el Saba.

The New Zealand Brigade began the attack on this key position, which appeared to be strongly held, at 10 minutes past nine with the Auckland Regiment in the place of honour. The Canterburys moved forward on its right with the intention of enveloping the tel from the north; and the Somerset Battery went forward with the Brigade coming into action at 3000 yards.

The plain is much broken up by the winding of wadi beds with steep banks almost uncrossable. But these in the end proved of great value giving covered approaches; and the Auckland Regiment soon worked its way up to about 800 yards of the enemy main position, where excellent cover for the horses was found. Good covering fire from here was given by the machine guns; and the regiment slowly, but steadily, worked forward.

At 11 o'clock the Inverness Battery, attached to the 1st L.H. Brigade came into action and covered the advance of the 3rd L.H. Regiment across the open plain to the south of Tel el Saba.

At this hour the Somerset Battery moved up and ranged on the tel at 1300 yards. Enemy machine guns were giving much trouble and were not located until the afternoon, when Lieut. Hatrick the Signalling Officer of the Auckland Regiment, from a concealed position in the front line, observed for the Somerset Battery and directed the fire by flag signal. A section of this Battery was moved round to the east of the tel to deal with machine guns in position on the high ground to the north of the hill. These machine guns were holding up the Canterbury Regiment.

About this time the 2nd L.H. Regiment (from the 1st L.H. Brigade in reserve) went forward under heavy fire and attacked some mud huts lying on the wadi edge and which formed the southern flank of the Tel el Saba position. By half-past one the Auckland Regiment had worked its way close up to the hill. Machine guns under Lieut. Picot and supported by a troop under Lieut. Johns had secured a position from which enfilade fire was brought to bear on the enemy front trenches and eventually these guns got up to within 300 yards. During this fine advance Lieut. Johns was killed.

The Canterbury Regiment was now across the Wadi Khalil and bringing fire to bear on the rear of the position, but could not get any further owing to enemy fire from the slopes of the hills overlooking the Hebron road.

At 10 minutes past two the Aucklanders began the assault and advanced by short rushes under cover of all available guns and machine guns and at 2.40 gained the enemy trenches on a hill on the east flank of the tel, capturing 60 prisoners and three machine guns. Two of these machine guns were used with great effect on the Turks' main position, which was rushed at three o'clock.

Tel el Saba (or the hill of Sheba) formed the "keep" of the Beersheba position in the rear of the town and its fall precipitated a general retirement northwards. But the Turk still had plenty of "fight" left and heavily shelled Tel el Saba and the adjacent wadis from the hills above the town.

JUST AFTER THE CAPTURE OF TEL EL GABA.
Horses closing up under the tel to obtain cover from heavy enemy shelling.

The advance was pressed forward on to the line 1020–970–Mosque by the 1st L.H. Brigade; and the 2nd L.H. Brigade pushed well up into the hills west of Tel el Sakaty. The 3rd L.H. Brigade from the Australian Division was sent across to reinforce the New Zealanders.

This Division had during the day come up, and at four p.m. the 4th L.H. Brigade moved forward over the plain on the left of the Anzac Mounted Division and directly upon the town, galloping over successive lines of trenches in a most gallant charge, in the face of severe machine gun and rifle fire. The plain was covered with fine dust and the spectacle of "lines of troop columns" advancing at the gallop, each with its cloud of "smoke," as it were, enveloping it and trailing away up into the air as the troop went forward, was a magnificent sight.

This charge completed the discomforture of the Turk who had been giving way for some hours before the infantry attack from the west; and the town was soon in our hands. In the town were captured 58 officers, 1090 other ranks, 10 field guns, and four machine guns, besides a huge quantity of military stores, an aerodrome, and much railway rolling stock. The total captures for the Mounted Corps for the day were 70 officers and 1458 other ranks.

The general situation on the morning of November 1st was as follows:—The Australian Mounted Division lay to the south-east of Beersheba with the Anzac Mounted Division immediately east and north-east of the town and the 53rd Infantry Division in the hills to the north, the three divisions occupying a line whose perimeter lay some five miles from Beersheba. To the west of the town and connecting with the 53rd Division were the 60th, 74th and 10th Divisions in that order, the last named occupying the railway line to Abu Irgeig where the railway leaves the Beersheba-Gaza motor road. From this point the line stretched away west to the old front line on the Wadi Ghuzzeh.

Along the whole of this new portion of the line the enemy was putting up a stout resistance.

The XXI Corps opposite Gaza was still pounding away at the enemy defences, aided by the Navy whose fire was directed at the town of Gaza.

So it will be seen that, though we had captured the great bastion at the end of the wall, we were faced with a new line, a bending back of the end of the wall as it were. But Beersheba gave us water and an excellent position from which to again hammer at the wall.

The next few days the role of the mounted corps was to protect the right of the XX Corps and some very hard fighting ensued as the enemy brought up his general reserve against the line Ras el Nagb–Tel Khuweilfeh.

On November 1st the Australian Division was withdrawn into reserve at Beersheba and the Anzac Mounted Division ordered to occupy the line Bir el Makruneh–Towal Abu Jerwal, to the north-east of Beersheba. This was done by nine o'clock and the New Zealand Brigade captured some prisoners and a machine gun and was relieved after dark by the 1st L.H. Brigade. For the next few days the Division carried on a mountain warfare against the Turks' left which, with fresh reinforcements brought into the strong position at Tel Khuweilfeh and into the town of Dhaheriyeh on the Hebron road, put up a very stubborn fight. Water was the great difficulty and our troops could not have carried out these

AN ANXIOUS MOMENT. IS THERE WATER IN THE WELL?

operations if it had not been for several providential thunderstorms which occurred on the two or three days previous to the advance from Asluj.

Patrols from the 2nd L.H. Brigade at one time worked their way to the east of Dhaheriyeh, within sight of the Hebron road to the north of the town, and watched there the busy motor traffic with reinforcements coming down from the north.

On November 4th the Australian Mounted Division was sent back to Karm near the Wadi Ghuzzeh for water and on the same day the New Zealanders relieved the 5th Mounted Brigade on the left of the 2nd L.H. Brigade in the hills in front of Tel Khuweilfeh. Here at Ras el Nagb the Brigade spent the next two days and experienced some heavy fighting. A fine performance was put up by L.-Cpl. L. G. Greenslade, 8th Squadron, C.M.R., who was assisting another man to get in one of the wounded. The bringing in of the wounded

BRIGADE 1ST LINE TRANSPORT AND LED-HORSES IN SHRAPNEL GULLY DURING THE FIGHTING AT TEL KHUWEILFEH.

from the firing line was a very difficult matter. There were no regular trenches and the communication from front to rear lay through a shrapnel beaten zone. Both men were hit but Greenslade succeeded in placing the man who had been helping him out of danger and then in attempting to bring in the man they were both going for, Greenslade was killed.

There was no water for the horses so they were all sent back to Beersheba, though not before 37 horses had been killed and 84 wounded. The Brigade was to have been relieved on the 5th by the I.C.C. Brigade, but the latter missed the way in the darkness; and the New Zealand Brigade was forced to remain in the line until the afternoon of the 6th, when they marched out on foot and came into local reserve a few miles behind the front line, with their horses still at Beersheba. Here owing to the strength of the enemy facing the 53rd

Division they remained in reserve. The water problem was still to be faced and the horses went in daily to Beersheba, a distance there and back of 20 miles. The Brigade furnished one squadron as a connecting link between the I.C.C. Brigade and the 53rd Division and also furnished one regiment (the A.M.R.) to the 53rd Division.

On the 10th the Brigade withdrew to Beersheba under orders to rejoin the Anzac Mounted Division.

How the Brigade Rode through to Jaffa

To go back to the situation on November 1st, it must be remembered that the Turkish line had been thrown back on its left, but not broken. General Allenby's plan now was to break through at the foot of the hills immediately to the north of Beersheba. This plan would cut the Turkish force in two, separating the troops in the lines on the plains, whose communications were the roads and railways running north to Ramleh, from the troops on the Judean Hills, who were supplied by the motor road from Jerusalem through Hebron.

A containing force for the Turks in the hills was formed of the 53rd Infantry Division opposite Tel Khuweilfeh, with the I.C.C. Brigade, Yeomanry Mounted Division, N.Z.M.R. Brigade and two squadrons of the M.G. squadron of the 2nd L.H. Brigade.

On the night of 6th November, the XX Corps, in a most gallant attack, broke the enemy's trench system at Kauwukah and at daylight on the 7th the Anzac Mounted Division went through and headed north along the great Philistian plain with the Australian Division behind it, and by nine o'clock was crossing the Wadi Sharia immediately east of Tel el Sharia where the 60th Division was fighting heavily. By 10 o'clock the Anzacs had reached Kh. Ameidat a station on the Ramleh-Beersheba line where a huge ammunition dump was captured with many prisoners.

One of the cavalryman's dreams was now realised. For one looked back, having passed the enemy front line by some 10 miles, and watched the great battle from the rear of the enemy position. His heavy guns at Hareira and Atawineh were firing away at the XX and XXI Corps and huge columns of smoke and dust shrouded the whole country now behind. It was the moment of a lifetime; but there was no pause for reflection, as the Division was being shelled from the Judean hills on the right, from the enemy thrown back from the Sharia lines on the front, and from the Atawineh redoubts on the left.

The Division, shorn of one brigade and with no support from the Australian Mounted Division, who were held up two miles north of Sharia, could get no further this day and bivouaced for the night near Ameidat.

During the night news came through of the evacuation of Gaza by the Turk, and orders were received to use every endeavour to cut these forces off, more especially as the enemy still clung to the Hareira–Atawineh lines. The orders included the certain capture of the wells at the Wadi Jemmameh where was known to be a plentiful supply of water. This was of the greatest importance to the Division for there was no water at Ameidat. To strengthen the Division the 7th Mounted Brigade (Yeomanry) was sent up.

From now on, to the occupation of Jaffa, the two factors which had most influence upon the advance of the mounted troops were (*a*) the frequent counter-attacks which the enemy made against our flanks (most of these being directed against our right where the enemy was able to take advantage of the positions afforded him by the foothills of the Judean Mountains); (*b*) and scarcity of water.

At daylight on the 8th the advance was continued and the 2nd L.H. Brigade by a brilliant piece of work captured two guns that had been holding them up the evening before; but opposition stiffened, the enemy making a very determined stand on the Wadi Hesi, which was forced late in the afternoon. Also he made a fierce counter-attack against the Division's right which was most gallantly held off by the 7th Mounted Brigade, a very efficient Yeomanry brigade of two regiments with the Essex Battery R.H.A. (Territorial) attached.

The result of the day's fighting was an advance of eight miles to a position due east of Huj, the Turkish Headquarters and terminus of their military railway from the coast line. Here our guns got into a position just before dusk from which a fire was kept up during the night on to the main road leading north from Huj, with disastrous effects to the retreating Turks, as next morning was shown by the litter of guns, limbers, ammunition wagons and transport of all descriptions, jumbled up into heaps with their teams shot down.

The Jemmameh wells were captured and found in good order and a great proportion of the 1st L.H. Brigade horses were watered. But the work was too important to water any but those not actually in contact with the Turk.

Late in the afternoon the Australian Mounted Division had reached Huj where the Yeomanry by a fine charge captured 30 prisoners, 11 field guns and four machine guns.

By the evening of the 8th all Turkish positions in the Gaza-Beersheba line had fallen and the enemy was in full retreat.

During the night news came through that the Australian Division could go no further for want of water and that the Yeomanry Division, which had now rejoined the corps, was held up for the same reason and that therefore the Anzac Mounted Division would have to go on without support.

At daylight the three brigades were on the move and Bureir and Simsim were soon occupied and then Huleikat, Von Kressenstein's Headquarters (the G.O.C. VIII Army), where huge supplies of war material were captured and a very fine German Field Hospital was found abandoned. By mid-day the great Arab town of Mejdel was occupied and the ancient Ascalon passed by. In the afternoon an enormous convoy was overtaken consisting of the greatest variety of transport imaginable. There were camels, pack mules, pack donkeys, carts and wagons drawn by donkeys, mules, ponies and bullocks. The wagons were of every make and description evidently commandeered from the Bedouin population. All the unfortunate animals had been driven to a standstill, so hot was the pursuit.

By night-fall the main road and rail running north from Gaza was cut at Julis and a position taken up running from thence to the sea.

On the 10th stubborn fighting took place and the Division was unable to move its right further forward, but on the left the 1st L.H. Brigade occupied Esdud (the ancient Ashdod) and obtained a footing across the Wadi Sukerier.

The Advance Resumed

The water question had now become so acute that the Division had to call a halt while the Australian Division came up on its right and the 52nd Division, our old friends of the Sinai Campaign, came up and took over the line.

The Division then went across to Hamemeh where ample water was found on the beach.

Here the New Zealand Brigade rejoined the Division after a forced march of 52 miles, and of 62 miles for the Auckland Regiment which was in the line with the 53rd Division when the orders came for the Brigade to rejoin.

On the 11th and 12th the Division rested and the "B" echelon (Improvised Train) at last caught up the brigades with welcome supplies for man and horse.

On the morning of the 13th November the Division resumed its advance crossing the Nahr Sukereir, a flowing river, the first real river we had yet seen, by a fine stone bridge at Esdud, the ancient Ashdod of the Old Testament and the Azotus of the New Testament, and the town that played a great part in the time of the Crusaders—our own Richard I. captured it and fortified it in the year 1192.

On the beach there is still the ruins of an enormously strong castle built by him to defend the landing place.

The Division was reduced again to two brigades, as the 7th Mounted Brigade had been withdrawn to reserve and the 2nd L.H. Brigade sent away east to reinforce the Australian Mounted Division in its attack upon the Turkish positions covering Junction Station where the railway to Jerusalem leaves the Ramleh-Beersheba railway and takes its way up the great Wadi es Surar, called in the Book of Judges "the Valley of Sorek."

It leads right up to Jerusalem and it was up this natural entry into the hill that the Philistines sent the Ark of God when they returned it to the Israelites.

The Division bivouaced this night close to Yebna, the biblical Jamnia, which is situated just inside the sand dune belt on the banks of the Wadi es Surar, known where it enters the sea as the Nahr Rubin.

On the 14th the New Zealanders crossed the river close to the sand dunes with the 1st L.H. Brigade on its right. By nine o'clock in the morning the village of El Kubeibeh was occupied, and pushing on, the Brigade encountered the enemy in the orange groves of Wadi Hanein and on the hills between this village and the sand dunes.

On the right the 1st L.H. Brigade encountered and drove back the enemy into the Jewish Colony of Deiran (called by the Jews Rechoboth) which they occupied during the day.

The Brigade passing over the old Crusader Bridge at Yebna.

By noon the situation had sufficiently developed to enable General Meldrum to attack. The Canterbury Regiment was held up on the right against the enemy in the orange groves. In the centre the Wellington Regiment was in contact with the main Turkish position where the enemy held trenches on a high ridge with a steep face to the orange groves and sloping gradually towards the sand dunes, and presenting the top of the long arm of an inverted "L" towards our advance. The foot of the "L" bent westward until it touched the sand dunes.

The Aucklanders advanced on the Wellington Regiment's left, towards this foot, and were much troubled by machine gun fire from the long ridge against the end of which the Wellingtons were pressing.

The Somerset Battery supported the attack of the Brigade. The enemy appeared to be in fair strength and as it turned out numbered about 1500 men with 18 machine guns and one field battery. They were fresh troops brought up by our old friend of Sinai days, Kress von Kressenstein, for the express purpose of turning the left flank of the British advance and of relieving the pressure of the British attack on Junction

Station. They fought throughout the day with the greatest determination.

By half-past one the Wellington Regiment obtained a footing on the ridge and the 9th Squadron under Major Wilder, and supported by the 2nd Squadron, rushed the enemy's first position with the bayonet, and one machine gun and one Lewis gun were captured. These guns were used with great effect upon the enemy's second position, which was captured by another bayonet charge, and two more machine guns taken. The methodical attack on the enemy's third position was then proceeded with. By this time the Wellington Regiment was getting well along the ridge forming the long leg to the "L" and the Aucklanders on their left were coming under fire from the enemy holding the short leg that stretched across their front to the sand dunes.

Each regiment had a section of machine guns attached and these were used throughout, well up in the firing line, in such positions that each regiment gave covering fire to the other.

Close to the junction of the short leg of the "L" position with the long leg (the ridge along which the Wellingtons were making good progress), was a red knoll practically in front of the dividing line between our two attacking regiments. From this knoll the enemy maintained a most troublesome fire on the two regiments. Another position from which a galling fire was being received was captured by the 4th Auckland Squadron by a magnificent dash, two troops galloping right into the enemy. The boldness of this attack minimised the enemy fire to such an extent that few casualties were suffered.

The capture of this position and some high ground in the vicinity protected the left flank of the Wellington Regiment sufficiently to enable it to proceed with its attack upon the enemy's third position on the long ridge.

The Auckland Regiment by pushing small parties up along the sand dunes, discovered, shortly after two o'clock, that numbers of the enemy were gathering in some orchards in front of the regiment in a basin formed by the head of a shallow wadi that had at one time flowed westward towards the sea, but which the encroaching sand had cut off. This basin was just over and behind the short leg of the "L" and so completely out of sight of either attacking regiments.

Every available man was hurried as far forward as possible to deal with this threatened attack, and Colonel McCarroll put into the firing line signallers, gallopers and batmen from his own Regimental Headquarters to hold on until the 3rd Squadron could be brought up. The latter advanced in magnificent style under the command of Major Twistleton. This gallant officer brought his men mounted to within a few yards of the heavily attacked line, where they dismounted and engaged the enemy. Major Twistleton here fell badly wounded, and subsequently died of his wounds.

This gallant officer was the Commander of the Legion of Frontiersmen in New Zealand. He had served with the Otago Mounted Regiment on Gallipoli with distinction. He had gone to France with the Pioneer Battalion, and after serving on the Western Front for some 12 months had come back to the Mounted Brigade—joining the Wellington Regiment just before the advance against Beersheba.

For his good work during these operations he had been given a squadron, and it was in leading his men at a critical period of this day's fighting that he fell. He was a man of great soldierly qualities and of fearless courage, and he was a splendid horseman. He was born in Yorkshire and came to New Zealand as a young man, where he had proved to be of that stuff of which the pioneers of the British Empire are made. Simple and direct in speech, his shrewd judgment and strong practical common sense proved at all times a tower of strength to his companions.

About this time the Wellingtons captured the enemy's third position, gaining practically the whole of the long ridge, but they were greatly troubled by fire from the red knoll already mentioned.

The Divisional Headquarters, situated on a high point called Neby Kunda, close to the village of Kubeibeh, sent word that large enemy reinforcements could be seen moving into the basin in front of the Auckland and Wellington Regiments, but there were no reinforcements available owing to the 2nd L.H. Brigade having been taken away by the Corps to reinforce the Australian Division in its attack upon Junction Station. But every available spare man at Divisional Headquarters, including signallers not on duty, grooms and messengers from the brigades, were formed into a troop in case they were needed.

At half-past 2 the first enemy counter-attack began, and it fell against Wellington's left. But being met with a heavy cross-fire from the Auckland and Wellington machine guns, it withered away. A quarter of an hour later two companies of Turks attacked the Aucklanders. This attack was a very determined one and was well supported by a battery, and at some places reached to within 15 yards of our line, where the enemy made great use of bombs. He occupied also a small hill on which all our men had been either killed or wounded, and from this position brought an oblique fire to bear upon the Auckland main position.

The enemy's machine guns also were most active, and from the excellent positions held they continued to enfilade our troops, one gun in particular on the red knoll between the Auckland and Wellington Regiments, inflicting many casualties.

The situation was serious, and prompt action was necessary to drive the enemy from the knoll. The approach to it was devoid of cover and presented a splendid field of fire to the enemy, but it also favoured the rapid transit of mounted troops. This advantage was quickly seized, for Captain Herrick and two troops of the 2nd Wellington Squadron galloped up a long shallow approach under terrific fire to relieve the pressure. On reaching the foot of the knoll the men dismounted and rushed their objective, engaging the enemy in hand-to-hand fighting.

The fearlessness and determination of Captain Herrick so inspired his little force that the position, with its machine gun, was taken. The two remaining troops of Herrick's squadron immediately came up to reinforce ,and a fine body of fire was brought to bear upon the Turks in front of the Aucklanders, whose commander quickly seized the opportunity caused by the success of the 2nd Squadron and advanced his right to a position where enfilade fire could be brought to bear into the basin. This movement was greatly helped by the Wellington Regiment, who advanced machine guns and brought up more men to reinforce their left.

It was now about 4 o'clock in the afternoon, and this hot fight had been going on since half-past 1.

The determined attack and stubborn defence of our men began to tell upon the enemy, and his fighting strength gave way. He was pursued with rifle and machine-gun fire, but neither regiment was in a fit state to follow him, and there were no fresh troops that could be used for this purpose. So darkness came with our men resting on the ground they had so hardly won.

Thus ended a brilliant battle, in which the Brigade had attacked and captured a strong natural position held by an enemy in superior numbers, and this enemy force was backed up by a well-concealed battery and held trenches with the aid of numerous machine guns. The enemy force was estimated at 1500 men, with 18 machine guns and a battery of artillery. The Auckland and Wellington Regiments combined would not have numbered more than 1000, and of these some 200 were in charge of the led horses; but the rapidity of the movements of the two regiments, combined with a splendid co-operation—a co-operation which continued all day and existed between each troop in each squadron, and between each squadron in either regiment, and between the two regiments.

The day's action brought into play the full attacking powers of the mounted arm against an enemy in position. There was the mounted advance to the first fire position by one regiment, and then its systematic capture of enemy trenches on foot as infantry with rifle and bayonet and Hotchkiss and machine guns, and its rapid reinforcing on horseback of the successive positions when captured.

With the other regiment there was the advance mounted under cover of artillery fire to successive fire positions; the rapid seizing of small tactical features at the gallop; the outflanking of the enemy position by aid of the mounted man's mobility; and finally there was the magnificent mounted charge by which the red knoll was captured.

During the day the Canterbury Regiment drove large bodies of the enemy through the orchards of the Wadi Hanein, and by its action successfully covered the right of the two regiments fighting on the hills.

The casualties suffered by the Brigade in this action were 5 officers and 39 other ranks killed, and 12 officers and 129 other ranks wounded, 41 horses killed and 22 wounded.

The effect of this smashing of the enemy's determined counter-attack was far reaching. The next day, November 15th, the Australian Mounted Division captured Junction Station; the 1st L.H. Brigade occupied the towns of Ramleh and Ludd, capturing large numbers of prisoners and much

OUR BRIDGE OVER THE SUKEREIR RIVER, BUILT OF PLANKS LAID UPON EMPTY WINE CASKS.

abandoned war material; and on the 16th the Wellington Regiment entered Jaffa, thus completing the great drive made by the Anzac Mounted Division from Beersheba to Jaffa, a distance of 65 miles in eight days.

The captures made by the Mounted Corps were 5720 prisoners and upwards of 60 guns and 50 machine guns with an enormous quantity of ammunition and war material of all kinds and railway rolling stock.

Among those killed was Captain A. Herrick, M.C., of the Wellington Regiment.

He had gained his commission on Gallipoli. Early in the Sinai Campaign he had devoted himself to the study and handling of the Lewis gun in which he became an acknowledged authority. And when the Lewis guns were replaced by the Hotchkiss he took these up with equal enthusiasm and effected many improvements in the manner of carrying this gun. He was absolutely fearless and showed a wonderful judgment in the attack. These qualities were well shown on this day. At one of the most critical moments of the Ayun Kara action he galloped his squadron right into the firing line, capturing the "red knoll" position that threatened the whole of our line. This brilliant piece of work turned the tide of battle, but at the cost of his life.

It will be gathered from the foregoing narrative that the Anzac Mounted Division was the only division able to carry on without falling back for water. This is explained by the splendid horsemastership of all ranks. It must be remembered that this division had spent 12 months in the deserts of Sinai and the lessons learnt there were never forgotten. The horses were ever the first care; and they started upon the Beersheba operations in the very pink of condition.

So remarkable was the performance put up in the advance from Beersheba to Jaffa, that an enquiry was set up upon the receipt of certain questions from G.H.Q.

For the information of horse lovers the letter and the answer sent through Desert Mounted Corps are here set out:—

G.O.C., DESERT MOUNTED CORPS.

I shall be glad if you will be so good as to let me have the following details as regards the animals of any of the units under your command during the period 1/11/17 to 31/12/17:—

1. The longest period they were continuously without water.
2. The work performed during this period.
3. Whether they fed well when they were thirsty.
4. The average number of times they were watered daily during the period specified or during any intermediate period.
5. The smallest amount of grain and fodder they received at any time and for what period.
6. The average amount of grain and fodder they received during the whole or any intermediate period.
7. The maximum amount of grain and fodder they received at any time and for what period.
8. To what extent were units able to supplement their forage locally, by grazing or otherwise.
9. When was there any noticeable change in their condition and vigour as a result of work and privation.

(Signed) G. R. BUTLER, Brig.-General.
G.H.Q.,   Director of Veterinary Services,
   1st Echelon,   E.E.F.
      31/1/1918.

Headquarters,
DESERT MOUNTED CORPS.
With reference to your . . . . herewith report in detail as asked for:—
1. (a) One cable wagon team from D.H.Q. was without water for a period of 84 hours.
  (b) Several regiments in the two Australian Brigades were without water for a period of 60 hours.
  (c) The N.Z.M.R. Brigade was without water for 72 hours.
2. By (a) above, almost continuous work, cable laying, which entailed heavy work partly over rough country.
  By (b) above, fast travelling and reconnaissance, averaging about 20 miles each day.
  By (c) above, first two days reconnaissance, averaging about 20 miles per day, remainder of period practically no movement.
3. Yes, up to 36 hours; after that, in most cases, they refused to eat.
4. During the period of advance, once per day, i.e., to 15/11/17, after that twice daily.
5. 4 lbs. grain and no bulk fodder for 24 hours.
6. An average of 9 lbs. grain with average 4 lbs. Tibbin requisitioned from inhabitants up to 17/12/17. From 17/12/17 to 31/12/17, 12 lbs. grain and average 4 lbs. haystuffs.
7. As shown in last period in para. 6.
8. An average of 4 lbs. haystuff per horse was obtained from the inhabitants throughout the whole period of operations. Grazing nil.
9. Decided falling off in condition and vigour after 36 hours without water. With good food and water horses picked up remarkably, though it is to be observed that all units report that issue of grain on five consecutive days caused serious trouble, the horses suffering from diarrhoea and laminitis and losing vigour. With reference to the cable wagon team which was without water for 84 hours, though much distressed at the end of that period, these horses quickly recovered. It is to be remembered that the horses of the Division commenced operations about 26/10/17, in excellent condition, which is largely responsible for the fact that evacuations on account of debility have been extremely small, both during operations and afterwards.

(Signed) E. W. C. CHAYTOR, Major-General.
12/2/18 Commanding,
AUSTRALIAN AND NEW ZEALAND MOUNTED DIVISION.

NOTE.—The horses of one Brigade had an indifferent watering only on morning of 6th, and watering next during the action on the 8th, no more water until during the night of 10/11th. They were greatly distressed on the 10th, but by the 13th were, with the good water and rest, fit for work again, though they lost considerably in condition.

The 14th November, the day of the action of Ayun Kara, was a day of surprises, for on this day our men encountered the first white civilised people since leaving Egypt, and also made their first acquaintance with the famous Jaffa orange groves and the vineyards of Palestine.

About mid-day the 1st L.H. Brigade drove the Turks from a ridge facing Yebna, where the Division had bivouaced the night before, and breasting the rise were astonished to see in front of them, nestling in the hollow, a modern village with red tiled houses so different to the flat-topped oriental architecture our men had become accustomed to. It was a sight to make one rub one's eyes and fear that it were a dream; more especially so, as no such town was shown on our maps, which bore the words "Khurbet Deiran" (or the cistern of Deiran). We found this new garden city to be the Jewish Colony of Rechoboth, founded in the year 1890 by Russians and now famous for its almond groves.

The Light Horsemen were met by an enthusiastic crowd of Zionists—men, women and children.

That evening the mayor of the town, hearing that the commander of the Division was a New Zealander, sent across to his bivouac at Neby Kunda a huge flagon of rich wine with a message "From the Oldest Colony in the World to the Youngest," no doubt alluding to the Israelites in their colonization of the land of Caanan.

There were many strange happenings during this day in the luxuriant orchards belonging to this village and to the neighbouring colony of Wadi Hanein. Fierce fighting with the Turk who suffered heavily had filled the villages with his wounded. There were happy meetings with English speaking Jewish Colonists, for quite a number had been in Australia at a time of distress in the history of these colonies. The story is told of a party riding in the dusk through the lanes among the orange groves, and coming to a cross roads, were in doubt as to the way. They were startled to hear a voice say with an unmistakable Yankee twang "Waal, I guess you are looking for the road." This was the first time for two years that any of that party had heard English spoken by an inhabitant of the land. The friendly American turned out to be an American Jew who had settled down to orange growing just before the war.

Yet more strange was a little episode that occurred as the Divisional Headquarters rode through the village of Wadi Hanein, a very prosperous Jewish Colony set in the midst of luxuriant orange groves and called by the Jews Nachalat Reuben (or the heritage of Reuben).

The road lay through a deep lane bounded on either side with huge mimosa hedges in full bloom and the sweet smell reminded one of Kipling's lines about the smell of the wattle "Riding down to Lichtenburg" and one felt not a little homesick. The lane led out into an open space where crowds of white men, women and children welcomed us with loud cries of "Shallome, Shallome" and much talking in Yiddish. Suddenly came a clear cut question in excellent English from a woman, "Do you know a soldier of the name of ―――?" An audible smile went down the little column and the Staff Officer leading suggested that there doubtless were many soldiers of that name in the Division, but that if she knew his regiment enquiries could be made. Quickly the answer came, "Yes, he is a New Zealander and is in a N.Z. Mounted Regiment, but I do not know which. I would much like to find him for he is my son." And before any further answer could be given a burly policeman, who had been riding behind the Provost Marshal and who had been chosen by that officer quite haphazard that morning from the Divisional Mounted Police as his horse holder for the day, rode forward and said he had a letter for a Mrs. ―――― which had been given to the Divisional Police by Trooper ―――― of the Auckland Regiment about a year ago with the request that all enquiries possible be made for his mother in the villages in Palestine. And here we found her after riding 200 miles through an alien land; and she was the first white woman we had spoken to in all that ride.

Needless to say that Trooper ――――'s C.O. was at once communicated with, and the son was given leave to go to his mother.

Jaffa was taken over by the New Zealand Brigade on November 16th, when the town was surrendered to Lieut.-Colonel J. H. Whyte, O.C. Wellington Regiment.

Three days later the Navy put in an appearance and a naval officer was appointed to manage the port, such as it was, and to improve facilities for the landing of stores. But the town was administered by the New Zealanders for the next fortnight, until a representative of the director of "Occupied Enemy Territory" was appointed. It was an interesting work and fortunately the population upon our arrival was small, all but Turkish sympathisers having been expelled by Jemal Pasha eight months before. Out of a population of 50,000 inhabitants only some 10,000 remained; so the town for an Oriental one was fairly clean.

It is a picturesque city, the old portion built upon and completely covering, with a veritable nest of masonry, a

WELLINGTON MOUNTED RIFLES IN OCCUPATION OF JAFFA, NOVEMBER 16TH, 1917.

conical hill which overlooks the harbour. The modern city spreads round this and away northwards along the shore where it forms the modern Jewish suburb of Tel Aviv (the hill of Spring), consisting of large and well-built stone houses with beautiful gardens.

The word Jaffa means "beautiful" and indeed it is a beautiful city. The great sweep of the green orange groves comes in from the plains melting into the gardens of the town. At the foot of the old city is the solid stone quay, as sound as the day the Crusaders of old tied up their ships; and protecting this old quay from the waves of the Mediterranean lies the reef of Andromeda, and the great rock to which she was tied is still shown. Facing it is Simon the Tanner's house, of which Dean Stanley in his classic book says, "One of the few localities which can claim to represent an historical scene of the New Testament, is the site of the house of Simon the Tanner at Jaffa."

JAFFA (FROM THE NORTH), SHOWING ANDROMEDA'S ROCK.

JAFFA FROM THE SOUTH, SHOWING THE LANDING PLACE.

It was here at Jaffa that Napoleon massacred his prisoners and when he retreated it was here that he poisoned his sick.

Almost immediately after the occupation of Jaffa by the New Zealanders the inhabitants who had been expelled by Jemal Pasha began to flock back to their homes. They arrived from many villages in the plains where they had been in hiding. Many also came even from the country still occupied by the Turk. They came on camel back and on donkeys and on foot, with all the worldly goods they still possessed packed upon camels, mules and donkeys. It was a motley crowd that arrived day after day and it showed many signs of the privations of war. Food had been exceedingly scarce and many had actually starved to death. One of the most pitiable effects of war upon a civilian population was shown by an orphan's home, which had been established in the English Mission buildings during the war. Here some 300 waifs and strays had been collected and cared for by the native

SIX NATIONS AT JAFFA.
Left to right:—Major Davis, U.S.A.; Major St. Quentin, France; Lt.-Col. Bruxner, Australia; Lt.-Col. Powles, New Zealand; Capt. Patterson, Scotland; Major Caccia, Italy.

staff of the Mission. But food had become so scarce during the few months before we arrived that the children had been fed on almost nothing but flour made from dhurra, a coarse native grain. Two-thirds had died and the remainder became the care of our medical people, who secured all food and blankets possible to save the poor little mites that remained.

After a few days supplies became easier and the children were put upon a good ration and warmly clad and given plenty of blankets for protection against the cold nights.

The staff had shown great devotion to these children. They were native women trained by Miss McConachy, who before the war was in charge of the Mission School here, and who since the war had so ably carried on the Soldiers' Club in the Ezebekieh Gardens, Cairo, and by her untiring work at the Australian Red Cross Rooms had endeared herself to every Australian and New Zealander in the Force. Much interest was taken by those who came first into Jaffa in searching for and in finding her house and in placing over it a guard.

The New Zealand Brigade took up a protective line covering Jaffa, just south of the river Auja, and connecting with the Light Horsemen who prolonged the line across the plain to the hills north of Ludd.

Reconnaissances of the river were made and it was found to be deep and unfordable, except at known places. These were a ford on the sea beach where the water reached about half way up the saddle flaps; at the Jeriseh Mill, where men on foot could cross on the mill dam; and at the bridge on the main Jaffa–Nablus road there was a stone bridge, and close by it a mill dam upon which men on foot could cross. These crossings were all held by the enemy.

CHAPTER VI.

The Capture of Jerusalem.

"The Turks in general left the plains and withdrew to the mountains. In consequence of this our men were commanded by voice of herald to move towards the foot of the mountains and when all arrangements were completed they marched towards a castle called Beit Noble. Then the rain and the hail began to beat upon our men and killed many of their beasts of burden. The storm was so violent, that it tore up the pegs of the tents, drowned the horses and spoiled all their biscuits and bacon. The armour and coats of mail, also, were so rusted that the greatest labour was required to restore them to their former brightness. Their clothes were dissolved by the wet and the men themselves suffered from the unwonted severity of the climate. Under all these sufferings their only consolation arose from their zeal in the service of God and a desire to finish their pilgrimage!—Chronicles of the Crusaders."—D. E. Vinsauf.

Following upon the occupation of Jaffa by the New Zealanders the advance against Jerusalem by the remainder of the Army had steadily proceeded, though much hampered by the weather and the winter storms. Upon the crest of the great wave which had rolled up the plains from Beersheba to

THE SURRENDER OF THE TOWN OF JAFFA.
The ceremony at the Town Hall.

Jaffa the Yeomanry were borne far into the hills and reached to within 10 miles of Jerusalem. Here fighting, at a great disadvantage they held on for some days until reinforced by the infantry. But the Turkish resistance daily stiffened as the weather became colder and wetter and no progress was made for some weeks. Both horse and man had become inured to the great heat of the plains, and the men were clothed in the lightest dress possible. All blankets had been left behind and the men were in possession of a water-proof sheet and greatcoat only, and felt keenly this great extreme of cold and bitter rain.

In order to relieve the pressure here the Division was ordered to cross the river Auja to make it appear as if a further advance on the plain was to be made. Bridgeheads were to be established at the bridge on the main road, the the village of Sheikh Muannis and at the ford on the beach, and were to be taken over by infantry of the 54th Division. Accordingly on the 24th November the N.Z. Brigade was ordered to cross the river and to clear the enemy for a space of two miles northward. A very pretty little action followed. The Canterbury Mounted Rifles crossing the ford on the beach at a gallop quickly seized the hills that commanded the ford and then seized the village of Sheikh Muannis, but the enemy garrison, who were cavalry, got away. Then the Wellington Regiment, moving through the Canterburys, advanced eastward and captured Khurbet Hadrah which commanded the bridge on the main road. In Muannis, four prisoners were captured and at Khurbet Hadrah, 25 prisoners, one machine gun, one British Lewis gun and some ammunition.

The 161st Brigade (54th Division) then took over the line held by the New Zealand Brigade and asked that mounted men be left at the bridge and at the village of Muannis to patrol in front of the posts established at these places by them. Accordingly two squadrons of the Auckland Regiment (the 4th and 11th) and one squadron of the Wellington Regiment (the 2nd) were placed in position in advance of the infantry posts. In front of the ford on the sea beach the Canterburys placed the 1st Squadron. To each squadron were allotted two machine guns.

The enemy lost no time in accepting the challenge given by our crossing the river, and he brought up large reinforcements.

At a quarter to 3 on the morning of the 25th a Turkish mounted patrol appeared near the Khurbet Hadrah posts. At a quarter-past 3 the same post, which was held by a troop of the 3rd Squadron, was fired upon from the left flank, and under heavy fire it withdrew to a prearranged line of defence where the squadron was posted. Half an hour later another post held by a troop of this squadron was becoming surrounded, and also withdrew to the squadron line.

The enemy's fire now increased greatly and all horses were sent back to shelter and the squadron withdrew to the positions held by the machine guns. The 11th Squadron was also being heavily attacked, but was occupying a more favourable position and held its ground. The enemy were using guns well and accurately served, and about 8 o'clock the infantry received orders to withdraw to the south bank of the river. This was an operation of extreme difficulty, as the bridge was now swept by enemy fire and was being continuously shelled by enemy guns. Some men got across by swimming, though many of the infantry encumbered with equipment were drowned; and some men withdrew across the bridge. To cover this withdrawal the 11th Squadron, having already sent back their horses, took up a position close to the bridge on the north bank, where they remained until all the infantry and the 3rd Squadron were across. The 11th Squadron then took up a position on the south bank of the river covering the bridge.

The machine guns had remained to the last to cover the withdrawal, and they had put up a magnificent stand. Captain Robin Harper (Machine Gun Squadron Commander), who had come upon the scene as soon as the firing was heard, was wounded in three places during the withdrawal. Sergeant Emerson, the only unwounded N.C.O. remaining, managed to keep the enemy off by working one gun himself to the last moment, and then, with the help of a horse-holder he carried Captain Harper down to the river, and the two swam across with him and got him to a safe place.

Many of our wounded were brought across the river in this manner with the assistance of Sergeant T. Ronaldson and Troopers Oberhuber and O. Anderson, who performed this day deeds ranking with the finest done in any theatre of the war.

The Action at Khurbet Hadrah

While this was going on the attack upon the 2nd Squadron at Muannis was developing. At about 8.30 a force of some 2000 Turks, covered by a very accurate shell fire, made a very determined attack. This was gallantly held off for some time, the machine guns of the squadron giving great help; one gun in particular, fought by Trooper Kelland, made a great stand. But as at Khurbet Hadrah, the troops holding the post had no support at all from our artillery, and it was not until Khurbet Hadrah and the bridge post had been evacuated that the Somerset battery came into action, assisted in so far as their shooting upon Khurbet Hadrah was concerned by the guns of the 161st Brigade. Their support came too late, however, to influence the battle, and the infantry at Muannis were ordered to retire, which they also did under the greatest of difficulties. Before the pressure became too great to be held off, the 2nd Squadron had sent their horses down the river to the ford at the beach and they remained holding the post on foot. Also, before the attack upon Muannis had fully developed, Colonel Findlay, with the Canterbury Regiment, had crossed the river at the ford on the beach and had taken up a position on the hills to the north of the ford, and had sent the 10th Squadron to the help of the 2nd Squadron in Muannis. The horses of the 10th Squadron also were sent back by the ford.

The Wellington Regiment was ordered to reinforce at Khurbet Hadrah, but arrived just as the evacuation was taking place, and being heavily shelled, took up a position south of the bridge.

The evacuation of Sheikh Muannis was skilfully carried out with the help of the Somerset battery firing from a position 1400 yards south of the village on the south side of the river. This battery remained in action until after the village was occupied by the enemy, and the O.C. Battery (Major Clowes), who was in the village observing, had to swim the river.

Two troops of the 10th Squadron retired slowly towards the ford, and the remainder, with the 2nd Squadron and the infantry, crossed the river by means of a boat and over the weir-head at the mill.

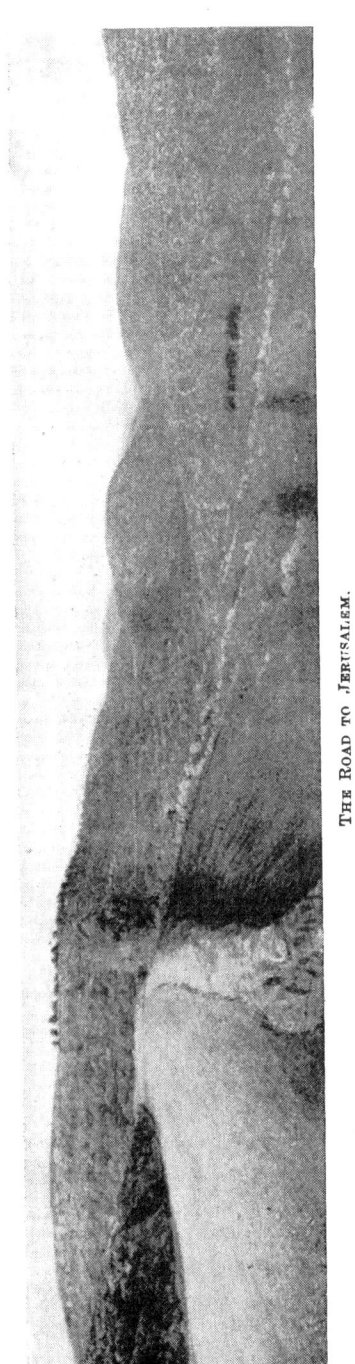

THE ROAD TO JERUSALEM.

RICHON LE ZION (AYUN KARA). ONE OF THE GARDEN-CITIES OF THE JEWS.

The Turkish attack fell now upon the Canterbury Regiment, who were covering the ford, but the 1st Squadron, under Major H. C. Hurst, held them off until the remainder of the regiment and the troops from Muannis had gone across the ford. Then the squadron fell back, covered to the last by the fire of the machine guns, splendidly fought by Lieutenant Eldridge.

Lieutenant Livingstone, who commanded the rear troop and who had behaved with the greatest coolness and skill throughout, was killed. His troop had held a commanding position to the last possible moment, and he himself, when all others were over, came across with the last party, and fell, just as his work was done.

The Brigade remained in support close up to the outpost line held by the infantry until December 1st, when it was withdrawn a little to the German village of Sarona.

On the 5th it relieved the Camel Brigade in the front line about half-way to the foot of the Judean hills. Here sniping with the enemy and endeavouring to dig trenches in the sodden ground—for the wet season had now set in—took up the next few days.

The fighting in the mountains for the possession of Jerusalem had gone steadily on. Bad weather, absence of roads, want of pack transport (though some 2000 Egyptian donkeys were used), delayed and hampered the troops.

Three infantry divisions, the 60th, 74th, and 10th, were at this time within a few miles of Jerusalem on the western side, with their right resting on the railway in the Wadi Surar. On their right flank was the 10th Light Horse, under Lieut.-Colonel Todd, and this regiment had the honour of being among the first British troops to enter Jerusalem.

About this time, while progress towards the taking of Jerusalem seemed at a standstill, the Corps Headquarters heard of the presence in Beit Jibrin of a notorious Turkish Intelligence Agent. Beit Jibrin was in no man's land, though frequently patrolled by our troops. So the A.P.M. set off to investigate in a Ford patrol car accompanied by one other Ford car. Each car carried a machine gun and a crew of three men. In the first car with the A.P.M. was Lieut. MacKenzie who commanded the Light Car Patrol from which the two cars came. MacKenzie was a New Zealander who upon the outbreak of war had enlisted in a Home unit.

The two cars reached Beit Jibrin only to find the Intelligence Officer had gone, and information obtained showed that he had gone to Beit Netief. Now Beit Netief is on the old Roman road which leads from Ascalon to Jerusalem, and is just through the narrow part at Tel Zakariya (the ancient Azekah).

Away the two cars went and found the Roman road in excellent condition, having just been re-built by the Turks. On running out the far end of the pass into the Wadi es Sunt the cars ran into a Turkish company of infantry marching into the pass. Boldness being the essence of the game both cars opened out with their machine guns and pushed on at full speed. The astonished Turks scrambled out of the way and in a moment the cars were clear and racing up the valley road, in the windings of which all sight of the Turks was soon lost. Beit Netief was reached and the inhabitants said that the wanted man had just gone up to El Khudr on the top of the plateau.

A consultation was held and MacKenzie decided that as they had evidently come right through the Turkish lines at Zakariya, unwittingly coming upon the enemy post on the road as a "change over" was in progress, and that as it would be impossible now to go back that way they might as well go on. So up the mountains went the cars and by dusk reached El Khudr, a small village just off the Hebron–Jerusalem road and overlooking King Solomon's Pools. Here was a Greek Monastery and the priests lodged the little party for the night. The machine guns were mounted upon the flat roof and an anxious night spent. However, no disturbance took place and it was decided, as no further trace could be found of the Intelligence Officer, that all speed should be made back to the British lines; and on the old hunter's rule, "never go back by the way you came," the two little cars headed down the Hebron–Beersheba road.

Hebron was reached without incident, but almost the first person encountered there was a Turkish Officer. After a breathless moment of suspense whilst the interpreter asked questions, it was found that he was a doctor and the only

Turkish Officer left in the town. All the troops he said had yesterday fallen back upon Jerusalem and he was left with his ambulance.

The journey was continued and eventually the British lines were reached a few miles further south in the shape of an infantry post. The astonishment of the Divisional Headquarters, met a few miles further on, can better be imagined than described. It is sufficient to say, however, that the party found a very cold reception when they told of the enemy's retirement; and they thought discretion the better part of valour and made off through Beersheba back to Corps Headquarters, where a full report was handed in.

There is no record of what the C. in C. said to the Divisional Commander concerned, but the fact remains that the next day the infantry advanced through Hebron close up to Jerusalem.

On December 8th began the last great act in which the Holy City was to pass from the hand of the Moslem who had held it since the days of the Crusades. At dawn, in the midst of rain and wind, the 60th Division (London Territorial), with the 74th Division (Dismounted Yeomanry) on its left, stormed the formidable hills to the east of the Wadi Surar; and by nightfall all the strong positions to the west of the city so laboriously and so skilfully dug out of the solid rock were in our hands.

During the night the 53rd Division pushed up the Hebron road and occupied Bethlehem.

General Allenby's report goes on to say—"Towards dusk the British troops were reported to have passed Lifta, and to be within sight of the city. On this news being received, a sudden panic fell on the Turks west and south-west of the town, and at 5 o'clock civilians were surprised to see a Turkish transport column galloping furiously cityward along the Jaffa road. In passing they alarmed all units within sight or hearing, and the wearied infantry arose and fled, bootless and without rifles, never pausing to think or to fight.

"After four centuries of conquest the Turk was ridding the land of his presence in the bitterness of defeat, and a great enthusiasm arose among the Jews. There was a running to and fro; daughters called to their fathers and brothers concealed in outhouses, cellars and attics, from the police who sought them for arrest and deportation. 'The Turks are running,' they called; 'the day of deliverance is come.' The nightmare was fast passing away, but the Turk still lingered. In the evening he fired his guns continuously, perhaps heartening himself with the loud noise that comforts the soul of a

VON FALKENHAYN AND DJEMAL PASHA AT JERUSALEM.

barbarian; perhaps to cover the sound of his own retreat. Whatever the intention was, the roar of the gun fire persuaded most citizens to remain indoors, and there were few to witness the last act of Osmanli authority.

"At 2 o'clock in the morning of Sunday, December 9th, tired Turks began to troop through the Jaffa gate from the west and south-west, and anxious watchers, peering out through the windows to learn the meaning of the tramping were cheered by the sullen remark of an officer, 'Gitmaya mejburuz' (We've got to go), and from 2 to 7 that morning the Turks streamed through and out of the city, which echoed for the last time their shuffling tramp. On this same day, 2082 years before, another race of conquerors, equally detested, were looking their last on the city which they could

THE MODERN JAFFA GATE, JERUSALEM.

ON THE TOP OF THE MOUNT OF OLIVES.

not hold, and inasmuch as the liberation of Jerusalem in 1917 will probably ameliorate the lot of the Jews more than that of any other community in Palestine, it was fitting that the flight of the Turks should have coincided with the national festival of the Hanukah, which commemorates the recapture of the Temple from the heathen Seleucivs by Judas Maccabæus in 165 B.C."

On December 11th the Commander-in-Chief, followed by representatives of the Allies, made his formal entry into Jerusalem. The historic Jaffa gate was opened after years of disuse for the purpose, and he was thus enabled to pass into the Holy City without making use of the gap in the wall made for the Emperor William in 1898. The General entered the city on foot—and left it on foot.

For this occasion the Brigade sent a troop as a bodyguard to General Sir E. Allenby. The troop was commanded by 2nd Lieutenant C. J. Harris, Canterbury Regiment, and was composed of 1 sergeant and 10 men from the Auckland Regiment, 9 men from the Canterbury Regiment, and 9 men from the Wellington Regiment, with 3 men from the Machine Gun Squadron and 1 from the Signal Troop—a total of 1 officer and 33 other ranks.

On this day the Brigade was relieved in the front line by the 162nd Brigade (infantry), and marched to bivouacs in the vicinity of Ayun Kara; but the Auckland Regiment was sent into Jaffa, where it came under the orders of the 52nd Division; and on the 12th the Wellington Regiment was sent to the village of Beit Dejan, on the Jaffa-Ramleh road, where it came under orders of the 54th Division.

Owing to the difficulty of supplies, for the whole plain was now almost a morass, the Brigade was ordered back to the vicinity of Ashdod, to which place the railway had now reached. Here there was plenty of good water in the Wadi Sukereir and an excellent camping ground among the sand dunes.

The Canterbury Regiment reached Ashdod first, and without very much trouble, but the Auckland and the Wellington Regiments spent Christmas Day on the march, and the Divisional Headquarters and other units of the Division started on Boxing Day.

Transport took over 24 hours to do the 12 miles, and it is to the lasting credit of the New Zealand horse and its driver that they got through at all.

It is interesting to note that King Richard with his army had attempted this same march from Ramleh to Ashdod. His chronicler says:—

"At dawn of day the men with the tents were sent forward and the rest of the army followed; the sufferings of the day before were nothing to those which they now endured from fatigue, rain, hail and floods. The ground, too, was muddy and soft beneath them, and the horses and men had the greatest difficulty to maintain their footing; some of them sunk never to rise again. Who can tell the calamities of that day? The bravest of the soldiers shed tears like rain, and were wearied even of their very existence for the severity of their sufferings. When the beasts of burden fell, the provisions which they carried were either spoiled by the mud or dissolved in the water. This day was the 20th January, in the year 1192, and they encamped for the night every man as well as he was able."

Many other units who were being sent back to railhead were in the same predicament as these Crusaders of old. Here and there upon mounds like islands in a sea of mud were Yeomanry with their horses, "camping, every man as well as he was able," while all around lay bogged wagons, jettisoned cargoes, and exhausted animals. The black soil seemed bottomless, and the streams and rivers unfordable to any but those of stout hearts and hardy bodies, and resolute and resourceful brains.

The rest of the month was spent in steady training—musketry, bombing, Hotchkiss gun, signalling and mounted drill. The work was much interfered with by the heavy rains, but as men and horses were camped upon the sand, all were fairly comfortable.

On January 12th the Brigade moved to its old bivouac near Ayun Kara (Rishon le Zion). Here for a few days no work was done owing to the wet weather.

On the 20th the Canterbury Regiment went into the line to relieve the Light Horse, who were holding a position connecting up the XX and XXI Corps in the vicinity of the village of Nalin. This village is in the foot hills (the Shepelah) of the Judean mountains and to reach it the regiment rode past the ancient town of Ludd (called Lod in the Old Testament and Lydda in the New Testament) where St. George of England is buried, and also past Nebi Daniel (the tomb of the prophet Daniel) which lies close to Jimzu

LUDD SHOWING THE TOMB OF ST. GEORGE IN THE BACKGROUND.

(the ancient Gimzo). Here the regiment remained making roads through rocky hills and building sangers and strong points until the 4th February when it rejoined the Brigade at Rishon.

How the Brigade went down to Jericho.

Though the British Forces had occupied Jerusalem on December 9th, the Turk remained occupying the "Wilderness"—that tract of rough, barren, rocky country which lies between Jerusalem and the Jordan. He also maintained control of the Dead Sea, and brought large portions of his grain supplies this way from Kerak and the country east of the Dead Sea. These supplies were landed by motor boats near the mouth of the Jordan and thence distributed northwards by motor lorry. It was decided, therefore, that Jericho must be occupied, and for this purpose the Anzac Mounted Division was ordered to move to the vicinity of Jerusalem, in readiness for a descent into the valley of the Jordan.

The troops for the operations were the 60th Division (London), with one Brigade of the 74th Division, the 53rd Division (all these were infantry), and the Anzac Mounted Division. The infantry formations were in position covering Jerusalem. On this occasion the Anzacs were without the 2nd L.H. Brigade, which was left on the plain holding a portion of the line there.

The role of the Division was to concentrate on the 19th in the vicinity of El Muntar, upon which rested the enemy's left; and to move before dawn on the following day for the purpose of assisting the infantry in their attack upon the

"THE WILDERNESS" NEAR JERICHO.

enemy force which held the Jerusalem–Jericho road, by threatening the retreat of the enemy through Jericho. In addition, as many as possible of the retreating enemy and their guns were to be captured, and the remainder driven east across the Jordan. And finally, all launches and dhows on the Dead Sea at Rujm-el-Bahr (the Turkish landing place) were to be seized and sent to Ras Feshkah, on the west side of the sea.

The enemy occupied a very strong line in exceedingly rough and waterless country, and the operations to drive him out were to be in two stages. The first stage was to consist of forcing him back upon his stronghold of Jebel Ektief on the main Jerusalem-Jericho road, and from El Muntar, a high hill between Bethlehem and Jericho, and over which was to lie the route of the mounted troops. The second phase was to be the storming by the infantry of the stronghold of Jebel Ektief, which blocked the road to Jericho; while the role of the mounted troops was to reach the Dead Sea by the shortest route and then to proceed up the Jordan, cutting off the garrison of Jericho.

On February 9th the Wellington Regiment left its bivouac at Richon and marched by the Jerusalem road to Bethlehem, camping for two days on account of the rain at Latron, a round hill surmounted by the ruins of a fort which commands the gorge at the foot of the hill through which the road to Jerusalem lies. In the days of the Romans this hill was occupied by a notorious robber, who levied toll upon all passers-by until a special expedition was sent against him. He was seized and hanged on the summit of the hill, which has been called since that time Latron (latro—a robber).

As it was not desired that the presence of the Division near Jerusalem should be known, the movement into the hills from Richon took place over the ancient Roman road which led from Ascalon to Jerusalem.

To reach this road the Division rode across the plain through the garden colony of Deiran (Rechoboth), past Akir, the ancient Ekron of the Old Testament and one of the capital cities of the Philistines, and into the foothills by following the Wadi Surar—the Valley of Sorek of the Bible—for some miles, and then striking across a beautiful flower-bespangled piece of low, rocky hill country, the Roman road was reached as it enters the Wadi es Sunt—the Valley of Elah. Right through the old Philistine country the route lay; past Tidnah (the ancient Timnath, the native place of Samson's wife), and past Tell Zakariya, the ancient Azekah, where, in the time of Joshua, the Philistines were utterly routed by the Israelites, who fell upon them in the midst of a hailstorm.

Beyond the narrow pass at Zakariya the wadi opens out into a level valley bisected by the steep bed of a stream. Here it was that David slew Goliath. Soon after passing the village of Zakariya the road rises rapidly, following the bed of the wadi, and there are many stretches of bare rock cut into huge steps by the old Romans as the road rises rapidly into the mountains of Judea.

On the top of the Judean plateau a little south of Bethlehem, the Jerusalem–Hebron road was reached close by King Solomon's Pools. These three vast rock reservoirs were found to be full of water, and were used for the watering of the Division.

These pools were originally made by King Solomon for the water supply of Jerusalem. They were rebuilt and the water

CHRISTIAN SYRIAN GIRLS.

scheme greatly extended by Pontius Pilate; and the pools still show large areas of wall covered with Roman plaster in an excellent state of preservation.

The remainder of the New Zealand Brigade reached Bethlehem on the 17th, and General Meldrum established his headquarters in a Greek monastery there. On the same day the Wellington Regiment, with a section of machine guns moved to Ibn Obeid, about six miles due east of Bethlehem on the

Wadi en Nar, which, taking its rise at Jerusalem as the brooks Kedron and Hinnom, falls rapidly through the wilderness into the Dead Sea. Regimental Headquarters were established in the monastery there and reconnaissances were made towards Jericho.

The weather on the plains had been wet, but the change to the heights of Judea was felt very much. Here the weather was cold, even in daytime, and very cold at night. Opportunity was taken to send parties to Jerusalem, and the padres proved invaluable as guides, for they were all enthusiastic students of the Holy Land and were well conversant with Jerusalem and its site from constant study.

Operations began on February 19th, and by nightfall the first phase had been successfully carried out. Daylight on the 20th found the Division strung out in single file extending over some eight miles of rough mountain track. The head of this singularly narrow column had reached about a mile east of the great El Muntar hill, and had run into a Turkish outpost. The infantry on the left away on the main road were attacking Jebel Ektief, where the Turk was putting up a very strong resistance.

During the night the Wellington Regiment had proceeded down the Wadi en Nar and had reached a valley to the east of the great El Muntar hill (the hill of the Scapegoat of the Old Testament), and now formed the advanced guard to the New Zealand Brigade, behind which came the 1st Light Horse Brigade. All night the men had been clambering over the rocky tracks leading their horses. The route followed was practically a goat track only, though marked on the map "Ancient Road"; no wheels were taken; no supplies but such as could be carried by man and horse; and the only ammunition taken was a small camel train of light active camels, each carrying two boxes of S.A.A. No guns accompanied the Division, but they had been sent down the main road to Jericho to follow the infantry advance.

To deploy for the attack a column in single file of eight miles in length cannot be done in a few minutes; and it was some hours before the New Zealanders thoroughly got to work.

THE ATTACK UPON JERICHO

El Muntar, the great hill which the Division crossed, is 1723 feet above sea level and 1250 feet above this flat-bottomed valley in which the head of the column had been held up by the Turkish positions on the hills on the far side of it. This descent of 1250 feet is all within a space of three miles, down which the track zig-zagged in full view of the enemy, and the sight of eight miles of horses slowly defiling down this hill must have had a great part in the ultimate abandonment of a very strong position which the Turks held with superior numbers and armament.

This position lay across the Ancient Road, with its left on the high hill Point 306 (Tubk-el Kaneiterah) and its right on the hill 288 (Jebel el Kulimum). Between these the road runs, and to get at the enemy our troops had to descend into a flat, open valley.

It must be remembered that in addition to holding these hills strongly with infantry and machine guns the enemy had five well-placed guns in position farther back at Neby Musa

NEBY MUSA—THE ALLEGED TOMB OF MOSES.

(Moses' Tomb), and from there shelled the valley in front of his position.

This had been boldly and skilfully reconnoitred by Sergeant W. M. Fitzgerald and Corporal G. H. Patton, of the Wellington Regiment, who, leaving the regiment on the evening of the 18th, had penetrated the enemy lines and had reached Neby Musa. They rejoined at daylight on the 20th, reporting the enemy in strength at Points 306 and 288, and three guns in position at Neby Musa.

By 6 o'clock all the New Zealand Brigade were in the valley, and the 1st L.H. Brigade began to descend from El Muntar, still in single file.

The Wellington Regiment attacked Hill 306, and the Canterbury Regiment, and afterwards the Aucklanders, Hill 288.

The advance was slow owing to the rough nature of the country and owing to the strength of the enemy position and the want of artillery support. At 10 o'clock the infantry were reported to have captured Jebel Ektief—the dominating position on the Jericho road—but they were driven off by a strong counter-attack, and it was not until half-past 12 that they finally obtained a footing there, after heavy artillery preparation and much desperate fighting.

Attempts were made by the Wellington Regiment and the 1st L.H. Brigade leading troops to force a way down the Wadi Kumran towards the Dead Sea so as to get behind the Turks' left. But the wadi was found to be too strongly held.

However, the New Zealand attack was progressing slowly and shortly after noon, assisted by a mounted advance of an Auckland Squadron, hill 288 was taken and the Brigade was soon in possession of hill 306 as well.

Attempts were made to get through the pass through which the road ran, but it was well covered by the fire of machine guns and artillery from the Neby Musa position, which lay on the far side of a great impassable chasm.

An outpost line was taken up on the south side of this gorge and as soon as darkness came on the 1st L.H. Brigade began the descent of the Wadi Kumran. The bottom of the valley from which the New Zealanders had attacked the enemy was about at sea level, and as the Dead Sea is 1300 feet below sea level the 1st L.H. Brigade had to follow a goat track with a fall of 1300 feet in a little over two miles, an operation of extraordinary difficulty on a dark night.

However, by midnight the Brigade had reached the bottom and turned north along a very rough track and by daylight had reached just east of Neby Musa.

During the night the New Zealand horses which had had no water during the day were sent back to the slopes of El Muntar where there were some cisterns; but the water was hard to get at and the tracks difficult in the dark, so the whole night was taken up in this work.

At daylight the New Zealanders were moving and the Canterbury Regiment occupied Nebi Musa, crossing the gorge on foot and finding that the enemy had evacuated the position and got away with his guns.

By 8 o'clock the leading troop of the 1st L.H. Brigade had reached Jericho to find that the enemy there had also flown.

An object lesson in the superior range of the Turkish guns was forcibly shown to the Divisional Staff about this time. Headquarters had reached Jericho and had set up its report centre about one mile short of the town and between the town and the Judean hills, and the Staff after a strenuous night's work sat down to a morning cup of tea.

At that moment the two Corps Commanders appeared on horseback—Generals Chetwode and Chauvel—having ridden down from the hills by the Roman road to confer with General Chaytor and to take a look at Jericho. Hardly had they dismounted when a shell landed close beside, coming from the direction of the Jordan river. Almost immediately afterwards another shell arrived and bursting beside the improvised breakfast table on the ground covered it and the Staff with earth. General Chaytor was sitting on the step of his car and had a very narrow escape, the front of the car being blown in, and he himself covered with glass from the wind screen and half stifled with the fumes of the shell. Needless to say a hurried move to continue breakfast a little further off was made.

For the rest of the morning this gun continued shelling the cross roads at a range of over 10,000 yards. Our 13 pounders under the most favourable conditions could get no farther than 6,000 yards.

The 9th Squadron of the Wellington Regiment went down to the Dead Sea to seize the Turkish boats and to report on the buildings there and as to any stores of grain. Later the Brigade took up a line along the Jordan facing the enemy, who

EARLY BREAKFAST ON THE MORNING OF THE CAPTURE OF JERICHO.
General Chaytor with Generals Chauvel and Chetwode.

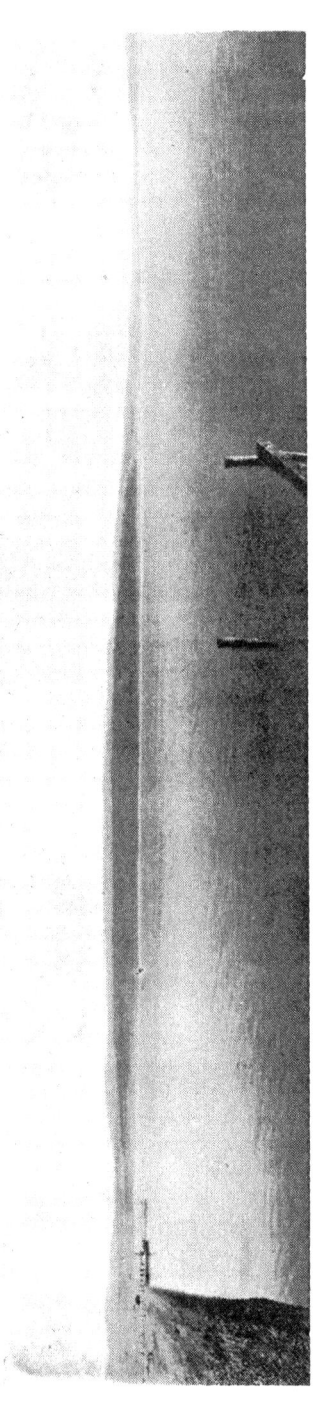

THE DEAD SEA.

was in a very strong position on the further bank, from which he intermittently shelled the Division throughout the day.

By 11 o'clock the Brigade was concentrated at the Wadi Kelt, just where the Roman road from Jerusalem descends to the plain, and good running water was found there for the horses.

The Auckland Regiment took over the town of Jericho, of which Major Munro was appointed Military Commandant.

Thus fell modern Jericho, a degenerate city full of loathsome disease.

Of all the cities of the east that our men had passed through, Jericho easily led the way as the filthiest and most evil smelling of them all. It is inhabited by a poor class of Bedouin numbering perhaps 500. It is extremely unhealthy and no white man lives there in the summer time. There are three small hotels, a Russian hospice, a Greek church and a

JERICHO.
An aqueduct in the foreground and the mountains of Moab in the background.

small block of Government buildings and a mass of mud huts. All the principal buildings were found by our advanced troops to be filled with dead and dying Turks, the dreaded typhus being the cause. The dying appeared to have been abandoned for some time. Immediate steps were taken to clean up these buildings by our Medical Officers, and volunteers to handle the typhus patients were called for, from the Field Ambulances. It is worthy of record that there were no lack of volunteers. Gloves were not worn much by our officers in those days, but a debt of gratitude is due to those who did. For after much searching throughout the Division six pairs of leather gloves were found with which to arm the six volunteers selected, and with these gloves these men safely handled the dead and dying.

These devoted fellows tended the sick and buried the dead and cleaned and fumigated all the buildings, turning the Russian hospice into a hospital, and happily not one contracted the dread disease.

The volunteers were specially thanked by the Commander-in-Chief for their splendid work.

The 21st was spent in reconnoitring the valley which on every hand showed signs of a former glory. Close to modern Jericho there can be counted some 13 or 14 "tels," obviously the ruins of ancient cities or fortresses. The greatest of them is Tel es Sultan, the Jericho of Joshua, showing great rents and fissures in its sides made by archæologists in their exploration of this most ancient city in the World. And many times this day did these same excavations among the old walls of Jericho prove places of refuge, sheltering our men from Turkish shrapnel and high explosive shells. Perchance even the walls of the house of Rahab the Harlot again gave shelter to an invader.

Across the plain in many places lie the remains of great Roman aqueducts, and there are several burkets, as the Arab calls them—great square reservoirs now covered with pasture.

Jericho is fed by a beautiful perennial spring called Ain es Sultan, which comes from out the rock immediately by Joshua's Jericho. It is the spring of the prophet Elisha, who purified its waters by throwing in a handful of salt, as told in the Second Book of Kings.

This procedure was easily understood by our men who had been daily witnesses of the medical orderly "chlorinating water" by throwing in a handful of bleaching powder.

The spring fills a modern stone reservoir with pure water for modern Jericho; and the over-flow is used to irrigate the gardens and a small area of corn land.

But though little use is made of irrigation, what little is done shows that great possibilities lie in this once fertile valley. There are banana trees 20 feet in height, vines nine inches at the base and covering 200 superficial feet of horizontal trellis work, all from one root.

But apart from a little cultivation at Jericho itself, and patches here and there where springs gush forth, as at Ain es Duk where the Brigade was afterwards camped, the western side of the valley of the Jordan is a barren wilderness. A few thorn bushes—the Dead Sea apple—and a little scanty herbage in the winter time, is all there is to relieve the appalling desolation.

The Brigade was afterwards to feel to the full the heat "down by Jericho," but at this time fresh from the cold and rain of the Judean Plateau the warmth of the valley was acceptable.

All day great masses of cloud hung over Judea and to the east the great mountain wall of Moab towered black and threatening. Heavy rain, thunder and lightning raged there; yet down in this weird narrow valley was peace and warmth and sunshine. Now and again a great mass of cloud would break off from the mountains of Judea and hurl itself across the sunlit valley upon Moab. Looking southwards down the Dead sea, brought to mind our New Zealand sounds with a westerly gale blowing, Judea on the one side and Moab on the other were shrouded in mist and great trailing clouds swept across the sunlit crack from mountain wall to mountain wall.

That first night down by Jericho was an eerie one.

Echoes of the gale in the mountains above occasionally were heard; a weird long-drawn sigh would go echoing down the valley, followed by a rush of wind, and then all would be still again. And above all hung Jebel Kuruntul, the Mount of Temptation, with its monastery tucked away half-way up its steep sides.

The air was mild and all ranks slept the sleep of tired men made comfortable after two nights spent in riding and combating the cold air in the mountains; and it was easy to realise how popular as a winter resort was this City of the Palms in the days of the Romans.

The 22nd was spent in more patrolling and feeling for the enemy who was found to be strongly posted at the Ghoraniyeh bridge and the fords at Makhadet Hajlah; and he successfully resisted all attempts of our men to reach the river; and it was not until 3 in the afternoon that a patrol of the Canterburys actually saw the running water.

The Political and Intelligence Officers finished their work by noon, and as there was no grain to be removed from the store houses on the Dead Sea, orders were given for the withdrawal.

At 6 in the evening, just as darkness was falling, the Brigade began its march back through the Wilderness, but

JEBEL KURUNTUL, THE MOUNT OF TEMPTATION, FROM JERICHO

this time by the old Roman road; leaving the Auckland Regiment and a sub-section of machine guns in a secure position just where the road falls into the plain.

This regiment with a battery was to keep the Jericho plain clear of the enemy and to prevent a resumption of the boat traffic on the Dead Sea.

Half-way to Jerusalem a halt was made and men and horses absorbed much needed supplies in the shape of bully beef, biscuits and grain, that had been brought down by camel transport. Bethlehem was reached at 5 o'clock on the morning of the 23rd, the latter part of the march proving bitterly cold.

The view of Jerusalem seen from the Bethlehem road is very fine. One sees the "old" City and it is not overshadowed by the "new," which clusters against the western wall and completely spoils the approach from Jaffa.

But of all the different points of view our men came in time to look upon the Holy City, not one appeals to the imagination so strongly as that seen from the Jericho road. Right through the Wilderness the road winds, up and ever up from Jericho's 1200 feet below sea level to Jerusalem's 2500 feet above. And when half-way up this truly awful piece of country, the traveller breasts the rise of the Inn of the Good Samaritan, and sees up against the sky-line far above him the trees and towers of the Mount of Olives; expectation rises and he eagerly looks for more. Then the road plunges into a great gorge to rise in sharp zig-zags to the village of Bethany, and on, round the shoulder of Olivet, there bursts upon view, with her long battlemented walls and her towers and domes silhouetted against the sky, the City of Jerusalem seated upon her hills. This was the view at the clear dawn of a winter day that our men saw and will ever remember.

Jerusalem, excluding the modern suburbs, is roughly a square and is walled on all sides with high stone walls in a perfect state of preservation. These walls are built upon approximately the same lines followed by the walls of King Herod. On the east side and between Jerusalem and the

THE EGYPTIAN TRANSPORT CORPS ON THE MARCH CARRYING RATIONS FOR THE BRIGADE.

Mount of Olives is the Valley of the Kedron, and on the west side is the Valley of Hinnom. These two valleys meet on the south side of the city and through the centre of the city runs the Tyropean Valley (now scarcely visible) joining the Kedron and Hinnom valleys at their confluence.

So it will be seen that Jerusalem was built on the ends of two spurs, that to the east being Mount Moriah, upon which

The Mosque of Omar on the site of King Solomon's Temple. Mt. of Olives in the distance.

Jerusalem from the Mount of Olives.

the Temple stood and where now stands the Mosque of Omar; and that to the west being Mount Zion.

The course of the ages and the results of Jerusalem's many sieges has almost filled up the Tyropean valley and raised the level of the valleys on either side of her, but the topography of the Bible is easily followed and all important places readily recognised.

We had been wandering for the past year in the lands of the Old Testament and had been imbibing the Old Testament stories from the "Land" and were now to have the greater pleasure in living in the New Testament.

No doubt many of the "traditional sites" owe their origin to the fraud or ignorant piety of the early pilgrims, but the "Land" is still the same. There can be no doubt as to Mount Moriah and to Mount Zion and to the Mount of Olives. There are also innumerable other places which can be seen

THE DAMASCUS GATE, JERUSALEM.

and identified from the Mount of Olives, from which is to be seen the most wonderful and the most moving panorama in the world.

On the 24th the Brigade remained in bivouac at Bethlehem and as many officers and men as possible were sent into Jerusalem in small parties. Luckily the skies cleared for the day and a bright sun tempered the bitter wind. The greatest of interest was shown by all ranks in seeing the Holy Places and full use was made of the permission to use a camera.

The show places of Jerusalem are innumerable and all the "traditional sites" were visited by our men, and the padres proved invaluable both in lecturing and as guides.

The Church of the Holy Sepulchre, a Christian Church in a city conquered by Christians, was still guarded by a Mohamedan guard. That its congregation in days gone by had misbehaved itself we all knew from our books; and we knew that the Turkish Governor had placed a guard just within the porch to keep the peace; but why that Moslem guard should remain there now passed the understanding of the man from the dominions beyond the seas.

On the 25th the Brigade took its way back down the mountains by the Roman road and stayed the night at Zakariya reaching its old bivouac at Rishon on the 26th.

A CONFERENCE OVER MEN AND HORSES IN RICHON.
Major Hercus, D.A.D.M.S., talking to Major Stafford, chief veterinary officer N.Z.M.R. Brigade, at D.H.Q., Richon le Zion.

Here horses were rested, shoes overhauled, after the spell of mountain climbing; and dismounted training for all units was again the order of the day.

Rishon le Zion, "the first in Zion," is a garden city of some 1500 souls. It was founded some 30 years ago and is the centre of the Palestine wine industry. Here is the most capacious wine cellar in the world, containing 104 vats each holding 60,000 pints. It also has extensive orange orchards and the mulberry trees exceed 20,000 in number. Almonds and olives are also cultivated.

The oranges were now at their best and a daily ration of an orange per man helped greatly to drive out the effects of a prolonged hard diet under a hot sun.

Our medical officers had rather an interesting time in teaching (or perhaps "re-teaching" would be better), the Jews of the colony among which we dwelt, the art of modern sanitation.

That greatest of generals, Moses, had taught his people a system of sanitation upon which modern civilisation lives, and it was with a feeling of hesitation rather, that our thoughtful and ever sympathetic D.A.D.M.S., called together the leading householders and gave them an address. However, his labours were not in vain, and to the other triumphs of our Medical Branch can be added the re-starting of these colonies on the lines laid down by Moses.

CHAPTER VII.

How the Brigade crossed the Jordan and entered the Land of Moab.

By the middle of March the Anzac Mounted Division was again called upon. This time, in conjunction with the famous 60th Division (with whom the Jericho operations had been carried out), a raid into the Land of Moab was to be undertaken.

The object of this raid was to cut the enemy lines of communication, along which he was feeding his forces that were operating against the Sherifian troops in the Hedjaz on the east and south-east of the Dead Sea.

In addition to the 60th Division and the Anzac Mounted Division, the I.C.C. Brigade was to take part and was again attached to the latter; and, as the undertaking included the crossing of the Jordan, an army bridging train was added to the Anzac Bridging Train, a small and efficient Australian unit that had so expeditiously built the wharf at El Arish.

THE BRONZE STATUE OF THE KAISER IN THE GERMAN HOSTEL ON THE MOUNT OF OLIVES.

On March 13th the Brigade left Rishon and marched to Junction Station (at the entrance of the railway to the Judean Hills), and reached Zakariya on the 16th, having remained on the 14th and 15th at Junction Station, owing to the heavy rains making the cross-country track impassable.

On the 17th Bethlehem was reached by way of the Roman road. Heavy rain had been falling on the Judean Hills for some days, and a good bivouac site was most difficult to find.

Eventually the Brigade was accommodated in the olive groves between Bethlehem and the village of Beit Jala, where shelter from the cold wet winds was obtained.

Here the Brigade remained until the 20th, again making use of every available hour by sending into Bethlehem and Jerusalem parties sight seeing.

But Jerusalem in winter, with rain, sleet and wind, is not the city of our books or of our dreams, and much more enjoy-

The Kaiser and the Kaiserin, surrounded by the Kings of Israel, in the Mosaic Roof of the Chapel in the German Hostel on the Mount of Olives.

able visits were paid in after days during the sojourn of the Brigade in the Jordan Valley.

On the 20th the Brigade marched down the main Jericho road after dark and bivouacked in the Wilderness close to Talaat ed Dumm—the Good Samaritan's Inn.

Here, among the rocky hills, which gave much discomfort to the horses, the next three days were passed, owing to the heavy rains interfering with the crossing of the Jordan. Every effort was made to study the country on the opposite side of the valley by observation from the tops of convenient hills, and many a glass was directed upon the great wall of the mountains of Moab. From the Jordan Valley up these mountains to the plateau on the top, which forms the great agricultural lands of Moab and of Gilead, there were said to be many roads, and these were marked on the map. From our Intelligence Agents, information about each route was summarised and made known to all, and each road was given a number, beginning with the southernmost, which went away south-east to Maan. In all there were six—the sixth leading from a ford north of the Ghoraniyeh bridge straight up to Es Salt, which is the largest town east of the Jordan and is some 20 miles, as the crow flies, north-east of Jericho, and 3940 feet above it.

The Moabite plateau averages some 3000 feet above sea level—a little higher than the plateau of Judea—and as the valley of the Jordan opposite Jericho is some 1200 feet below sea level, the scaling of these heights looked no easy task.

To an observer from the Judean Hills, Moab presents one great wall of rock, yet the edge of the plateau in reality in falling into the Jordan Valley is seamed with great wadis— huge gulches cut down by the heavy winter rains of countless centuries.

It is a rich limestone country and was once well wooded. The broken ground carries a splendid pasture, and on the top is one of the finest grain-growing lands in the world.

The plan of operations provided for the attack upon Es Salt to be made by way of the motor road from the Ghoraniyeh bridge. This was to be done by the 60th Division, to which was attached the 6th Squadron Wellington Regiment. The 1st L.H. Brigade was ordered to proceed up the Jordan valley on the east side to protect the northern flank of the 60th Division and to co-operate with that division in the attack upon Es Salt.

The remainder of the Mounted Division with the Camel Brigade was to make all despatch in scaling the mountains by several roads, then to get behind Es Salt so as to intercept the garrison, and finally to concentrate in an attack upon Amman with the object of destroying a portion of the Hedjaz railway.

Es Salt is to-day a city of some 18,000 inhabitants, and is famous for its raisins. It was in early Christian times an important town.

Amman goes back into the dim ages of the Old Testament It was Rabbath Ammon, the capital city of the Ammonites. Later, as Philadelphia, it was one of the cities of the Decapolis, and is now the finest ruined city east of the Jordan. There is still the Roman Citadel and also a great theatre, both in excellent preservation. The theatre is cut out of the hillside, and with its 35 tiers of seats held 4000 spectators. Its acoustic

Lt.Col. J. H. Whyte, D.S.O., in the Jordan Valley.

properties are so good that words spoken on the stage are distinctly heard on the highest tier of seats. As to the Citadel, it is still a strong place, and was to resist all our attacks for four days and nights.

Since the capture of Jerusalem the Auckland Regiment had remained in the Jordan Valley engaged in watching the enemy and in gaining information about the crossing over the river. It had found that the Jordan at this time of the year was unfordable at any available point, and that the only practicable places for throwing bridges across were Makhadet Hajlah and Ghoraniyeh. At the latter place the Turkish bridge had stood. This was of wood and had been burnt by the Turk after his evacuation of Jericho.

It was decided that the cavalry and camels should cross by a pontoon bridge to be thrown across at Makhadet Hajlah (Joshua's Crossing), and that the 60th Division should cross at Ghoraniyeh, where a pontoon bridge and a heavy barrel-pier bridge were to be built.

The enemy strength in Moab was estimated to be about 4850 infantry, 650 cavalry, 102 machine guns, and 30 to 40 field guns. Of the artillery the 11th Division was said to be at Amman with 16 guns.

The role of the Division, less the 1st L.H. Brigade, was to:
(a) Secure the right flank of the 60th Division
(b) To prevent any advance of the enemy from the south.
(c) To endeavour constantly to work up to the plateau and to secure the road junction near the Circassian village of Naaur.
(d) To work round the flank of the enemy opposing the advance of the 60th Division moving on Es Salt.
(e) To endeavour to create an opening for a raid to destroy the railway.

On March 21st the enemy reinforced his positions at the Ghoraniyeh crossing with 600 infantry, and sent two squadrons of cavalry to Makhadet Hajlah.

That night the 60th Division made the first attempt to cross the river by swimming; but there was so much flood water in the river that the swimmers of the 2/17 Londons were unable to make headway against the current. Repeated attempts were made to cross in punts and rafts; but these attempts were also unsuccessful, alarming the enemy and causing him to open fire.

Meanwhile the 2/19 Londons had been more fortunate at Makhadet Hajlah. Their swimmers had crossed unobserved; and at twenty minutes past one on the morning of March 22nd, the first raft, holding 27 men, was ferried across. By noon two battalions of the London Regiment were over and efforts were made to enlarge the bridgehead; but, owing to enemy machine gun fire and the density of the jungle on the eastern bank of the river, little could be effected.

The second pontoon bridge at Hajla was finished by half-past 1, a remarkably fine performance by the Anzac Bridging Train. But owing to enemy opposition little more was done that day.

At 4 o'clock on the morning of the 23rd the Auckland Mounted Rifles began to cross, in order to clear the enemy out of the country on the eastern bank as far north as Ghoraniyeh, to enable the crossing to be made there. This

THE JORDAN.

the regiment did in a most efficient and gallant style, galloping down detachments of the enemy and capturing 68 prisoners and four machine guns.

This was a fine example of mounted rifles fearlessly and successfully attacking cavalry.

For in addition to galloping into infantry in position with machine guns, Colonel McCarroll's men charged, killed and captured Turkish Cavalry.

Once up the bank of the river there is an immense plain stretching north for miles and to the eastward to the foot of the hills. One squadron was sent to the east while the other two advanced up the river to clear the Ghoraniyeh bridge; all pack horses and spares were left behind.

It was a beautiful morning, the horses were in great form, and the men eager for a ride. The pace soon increased to a gallop. Post after post along the bank of the river was ridden down and the Turks immediately surrendered. Away out to the east the detached squadron had a merry time. They charged some enemy cavalry and a long running fight ensued resulting in numerous casualties to the enemy, the superior weight and pace of our horses proving too much for the Turks. Lieut. K. J. Tait, the leader of the foremost troop was killed in a duel with the Turkish cavalry leader. This young officer's dash and determination were the feature of the morning's operations. The main body of the regiment found the Ghoraniyeh crossing strongly held, but the sight of the lines of galloping horsemen was too much for the enemy. Some of the Turks stood their ground and a troop of the 3rd Squadron galloped right into them, seized their machine guns, and turned them on to the fleeing enemy with good effect.

This bold move of the Auckland Regiment unlocked the Ghoraniyeh crossing and the infantry were soon hard at work on their pontoon bridge and by night-fall were beginning to cross.

At midnight the Anzac Mounted Division concentrated in the vicinity of Kasr Hajlah; and the 1st L.H. Brigade began to cross at 1 o'clock on the morning of the 24th, by the pontoon bridges at Makhadet Hajlah. The New Zealand Brigade followed.

By 5 a.m. the dispositions of the force known as "Shea's Group" (from Major-General Shea the commander of the famous 60th Division), were as follows:—The three brigades of the 60th Division were between Ghoraniyeh and Shunet Nimrin, with the leading brigade about two miles up the Es Salt road; the 1st L.H. Brigade was covering the northern flank of the 60th Division about one mile north of El Mandesi ford; and the rest of the Anzac Mounted Division was to the east of Hajlah, all safely across the Jordan.

For the next eight days this force was in the mountains, and the New Zealand Brigade went through the most trying times it had experienced since it left Gallipoli. The weather was bitterly cold, with constant showers of rain, sleet and a cutting wind. The mountain roads were mere pack tracks over bare slippery rocks upon which the horses stumbled and the camels fell, often never to rise again. The enemy were fresh troops, well fed and well equipped, and were fighting in well dug trenches supported by artillery; yet our wonderful men, short of sleep, short of rations, wet through, fighting in a strange country which was filled with hostile inhabitants, overcame almost insurmountable obstacles, captured impregnable positions in the darkness of night, and carried out their wounded for miles over mountain tracks.

Following the plan of operations, the New Zealand Brigade, in conjunction with the 60th Division, advanced upon the enemy who held the foot hills at Shunet Nimrin covering the Es Salt carriage road. With the Wellington and Canterbury Regiments in the lead, the Brigade soon drove the Turks from their positions, capturing a few prisoners, and with the infantry captured three mountain guns. This operation unlocked the number four road which led up to the plateau, past the Circassian village of Es Sir at the head of the Wadi Sir.

The Brigade, leaving the 6th Squadron (Wellington Regiment) with the infantry, headed into the mountains up this "road," beginning its climb of 4000 feet to the plateau of Moab. Heavy rain now came on, the "road" dwindled away to a mere track and all wheels had to be left. Though it was anticipated that the roads into the mountains would not be good, and though rations and forage were brought on camels, yet regiments were allowed to take their reserve ammunition upon half limbers, and it was intended that all the Divisional Artillery should be taken. The Brigade's half limbers had now to be left at the foot of the hills and a little reserve ammunition was taken on some camels together with the explosives for demolition purposes.

The remainder of the Division, comprising the 2nd L.H. Brigade and the I.C.C. Brigade, together with Divisional Headquarters and the Divisional Artillery and Ammunition Column, took the number three road which reaches the plateau at the Circassian village of Naaur.

This road also gave out and all wheels including the artillery and ammunition column were left on the plain. Not a gun could be taken except four small pack mountain guns with the Camel Brigade. All rations and forage were left, the men taking with them nothing but what they could carry on their horses. The best of the light-burden camels were taken from the Supply Train and given a load of two boxes each of S.A.A. The special explosives which were being taken on half-limbers for the purpose of blowing up the Hedjaz railway were placed on improvised pack-horses and light-burden camels.

So darkness found the men on each track walking on foot and leading their horses in blinding rain over muddy tracks and clambering up slippery rocks, hour after hour. The Camel Brigade were the greatest sufferers, for the one thing a camel hates is slippery mud; "and when he comes to greasy ground he splits himself in two." All night it rained, and all night the weary columns climbed and slipped and fell. Daylight found them far from the top, and the weather if anything became worse. By noon the New Zealand advanced guard had reached the village of Es Sir, where two Turkish Officers and 48 other ranks were captured, and at half-past 1 the Brigade concentrated at the cross roads on the plateau just above the village and which was to be the concentration point for the Division. But it was half-past seven in the evening before the remainder of the Division with the Camel Brigade reached the village of Naaur some eight miles south along the plateau. Without pause the march was continued and the head of the column reached the New Zealanders at 5 o'clock on the morning of the 26th; but it was nightfall before the last of the unfortunate Camel Brigade were in.

The force had now been marching under the worst possible conditions for three days and three nights and once again the weird hallucinations that beset the sleepless brain were experienced.

Hundreds of wet cold and tired men saw houses, tall houses brilliantly lit up and always on the windward side of the road, and many a man murmered to himself; "As soon as I get under the lee of that house I shall be warm again." It was so cold that one literally had to keep moving to keep alive. Gippy camel drivers, who laid down upon the wet ground, having given up the struggle with the Oriental's fatalism, died where they lay.

At daylight when the head of the Divisional Column, which had come by number two road, had reached the first of the New Zealand outposts, the question was asked immediately;

Concentration on the Plateau

"Where are your Headquarters?" and the answerer pointed along the rain and wind-swept track. The two leading officers who had asked the question saw a row of tall trees looming through the mist, on the windward side, and looking at each other remarked that the New Zealand Brigade Headquarters always "did itself well." They rode on joyfully but no trees came in sight, nothing but mud and rain and wind. Orders had been given for a concentration of the Division in the vicinity of the cross roads immediately east of Es Sir and in a shallow basin just north of this a halt was made. Some hours afterwards when a gleam of sunshine warmed the body and cheered the heart, these two officers rode back to see the New Zealand Brigade Headquarters. Not a tree was to be seen, for there was not a tree there, the Brigade Headquarters being on the edge of the plateau with a great sweep of mountain falling sheer down some 4000 feet to the Jordan; and up that great slope whistled the icy cold wind. This was a curious case of two men not only seeing the same hallucination at the same time, but of speaking about it at the time it was seen.

The plan of operations provided for the concentration of the Division on the plateau, for the interception of the garrison of Es Salt (who were being attacked by the 60th Division), and finally for the capture of Amman and the cutting of the Hedjaz railway.

The concentration had been successfully accomplished, and news was here received that Es Salt had been occupied by the 60th Division, with which was the 6th Wellington Squadron.

But General Chaytor, taking into consideration that the men had been three days and three nights without sleep and had been on their feet for the greater part of that time, and that there was not a camel in the Camel Brigade fit to move, decided to postpone the attack upon Amman until the next morning. So the troops settled down to get what rest they could, keeping patrols moving towards the east and north.

Shortly after the New Zealanders had arrived on the plateau an enemy patrol of six German infantry were captured, and during the night another German was shot who was approaching the lines. Later a cavalry patrol of three men were met and accounted for.

The 2nd L.H. Brigade, pushing north across the Es Salt–Amman road, captured prisoners in the village of Suweileh and found there 30 German lorries and a motor car bogged on the road, having been left by the Es Salt garrison, who had abandoned the town to the 60th Division.

As soon as it was dark a special patrol of a troop under Lieutenant R. Sutherland, of the Wellington Regiment, set out to cut the railway line to the south of Amman. They had a ride of about 10 miles there and 10 miles back, in darkness and in pouring rain across a country almost a morass and totally unknown. This fine effort was successful and the rails were blown up with gun cotton.

A similar party from the 2nd L.H. Brigade had attempted to wreck the line north of Amman, but were unsuccessful.

Daylight on the 27th saw the Division moving. The ground was found to be so wet and boggy (it was all ploughed, and the newly-sown crop was just showing above the ground) that any movement off the roads and tracks was almost impossible. The country was undulating and dotted with hills, and here and there an outcrop of rock and patches of scrub. In many places the stones from the fields were piled up in heaps or laid out in lines, and these gave good cover to concealed riflemen and machine guns. The wadis were very steep-banked, and the Wadi Amman was uncrossable except in one or two places in single file. A strong cold wind was blowing with heavy showers of rain.

The attack was to be made by the New Zealand Brigade from the south, with its right on the railway and its left on the wadi; the I.C.C. were to attack on the left of the New Zealanders and astride the Es Sir–Amman road, with the 2nd Light Horse on their left. By 11 o'clock all brigades were engaged, but it was not until after midday that the leading regiment (the Aucklanders) reached the railway line near Kissir station, about three miles south of the town. The brigade had been held up by the extremely boggy ground and by the crossing of the Wadi Amman.

A little later those in the vicinity were startled to see a train steam into the station from the south, and fire was immediately opened upon it by the nearest troops, the W.M.R. Headquarters on an adjacent hill.

After a momentary pause to disembark a garrison for the station the train disappeared into the hills immediately hiding Amman. The station was at once attacked, and in this attack a force of friendly Arabs took part. The result was the capture of 6 officers and 42 other ranks. The prisoners stated that the train contained 300 reinforcements for the Amman garrison.

By 3 o'clock the general attack was progressing well. A demolition party, under escort of the 4th Battalion I.C.C., with which was the New Zealand Company (No. 16), did

SOME OF THE HEDJAZ ARMY.

excellent work blowing up some five miles of railway and many culverts. On the completion of the work the 4th Battalion I.C.C. came under the orders of General Meldrum and was put into the attack on the extreme right of the New Zealand Brigade.

About 6 in the evening the enemy made a strong attack on a high ridge between the 1st and 8th Squadrons of the Canterburys, but Colonel Findlay sent in the 10th Squadron, which, by a fine counter-attack, drove the enemy out.

Darkness came on, and with it the troops dug in on the lines they held.

During the night a patrol of the 2nd L.H. Brigade reached the railway line about seven miles north of Amman, where it blew up a two-arch bridge spanning a steep wadi, causing a break of 25 feet and isolating Amman from the north.

Soon after daylight on the 28th the Turkish guns became very active, and the only reply that we could give was that of the four 12-pounder mountain guns of the Hong Kong and Singapore Mountain Battery of the I.C.C. Brigade. There was not another gun with the Division, and during the night the Turks had greatly strengthened their line. Therefore, much satisfaction was felt when a wireless message came through saying that the 181st Brigade of the 60th Division was on its way from Es Salt and would bring with it two batteries of mountain guns. The leading battalion arrived at half-past 10, and was put into the line on the immediate left of the camels and between them and the 2nd Light Horse.

A general attack was ordered for half-past 1, but before it began a heavy enemy counter-attack fell upon the junction between the New Zealanders and the Camels. The Turk got within bombing distance, but was driven off.

Our attack began at half-past one, and was met by a very heavy machine-gun fire on all sides. The ground in front of the I.C.C. and the infantry was convex, with no cover and no forward observation points. The enemy, with well-placed machine guns and supported by several field batteries, swept the ground from front and flank.

The New Zealanders were held up by the great dominating hill of 3039, and could make no headway.

On the northern flank the enemy counter-attacked the 2nd Light Horse with great determination, and no progress could be made there.

The Canterburys, who were on the sides of the wadi, made several attempts to get forward, but the enemy on Hill 3039 covered the ground in front of our men, who could make no progress. The Brigade asked for artillery assistance, as the enemy was being constantly reinforced. Two guns from the Hong Kong and Singapore Mountain Battery were ordered to report to the Brigade, but they did not arrive until 2 o'clock. One of the guns had defective sights and could not be used, so the single gun, short of ammunition, did not help matters much.

At 11 o'clock the enemy heavily attacked the 4th Camel Battalion, reaching bombing distance, but they were driven back.

During the general attack, which began at half-past 1, the 4th Camel Battalion, on the right of the New Zealand Brigade, suffered very heavy casualties and were assisted by Nos. 2 and 4 subsections of the New Zealand Machine Gun Squadron with enfilade fire at 800 yards, which caused the enemy great loss. By 4 o'clock in the afternoon the Auckland Regiment and the 4th Camel Battalion had advanced their line for a distance of 500 yards, reaching the low ridges at the foot of 3039.

Rain still fell and the weather was bitterly cold, and the supply of rations and forage caused much anxiety; and darkness found the troops in much the same positions.

Morning broke on the 29th March with the same cold rain and cutting wind. The enemy began heavy shelling soon after dawn, but there was little movement as far as our troops were concerned during the day. Several counter-attacks by the Turk were driven off, especially on the northern flank and between the infantry and the 2nd L.H. Brigade.

During the afternoon officers' patrols from the Auckland Regiment reconnoitred the enemy's position on 3039, and all units along the line made themselves as familiar with the ground in front of them as circumstances would permit with a view to a night attack.

The two remaining battalions of the 181st Brigade and two battalions of the 180th Brigade arrived during the day, and with them the two mountain batteries so eagerly looked for.

General Chaytor now decided to attack by night. The plan was that the New Zealand Brigade, with the 4th Battalion I.C.C., were to take Hill 3039; the I.C.C. Brigade, less the 4th Battalion, were to advance straight upon the town, with their right on the wadi; the infantry also straight on Amman, with their right on the Roman Citadel; while the 2nd L.H. were to attract as much attention to themselves as possible and to cover the left of the main attack.

Many were the anxious eyes turned towards Amman that day, but little could they see either of Amman or of the Turks. The town lay in a hollow, the approaches to which from the south-west, west, and north-west were convex and without a particle of cover. The enemy occupied well-protected positions on lower ground and out of sight of our troops, so that any advance upon him brought the attackers on to a sky-line facing a field of fire devoid of cover.

His guns were sited away back across the wadi, near the railway line.

On the south and east Amman is dominated by the great Hill 3039, against which the New Zealanders were striving. All one saw from the west was the great Roman amphitheatre on the far side of the town and carved out of the lower slopes of 3039. In the foreground and on the near side of the town the old Roman Citadel showed up; and it was against this old keep—conquered once by King David—that the I.C.C. and the infantry hurled themselves again and again.

The town itself was entirely hidden from all troops but the New Zealanders on 3039.

Away out beyond Amman in the far distance the great Arabian desert lay bright and shimmering in its leagues of sand under a burning sun, while the fertile land of Moab was being deluged with rain.

The many attacks against 3039 made by the New Zealanders and the many careful reconnaissances had disclosed fully the enemy dispositions and strength on the hills. He held a very strong position, somewhat in the shape of a shamrock, with the ridge leading to the main and highest position representing the stem of the leaf. This main position, marked "A" on the sketch, was of great strength, and consisted of two lines of trenches or sangers in tiers dominating the approach along the ridge; with a third trench "D" on higher ground behind; and a further position 300 yards further back on the northern point of the hill.

On either flank as one approached "A" were subsidiary positions marked "B" and "C," covering the advance along the ridge.

To capture this formidable position without any artillery support (as there were no guns available) the following plan

THE ATTACK UPON AMMAN

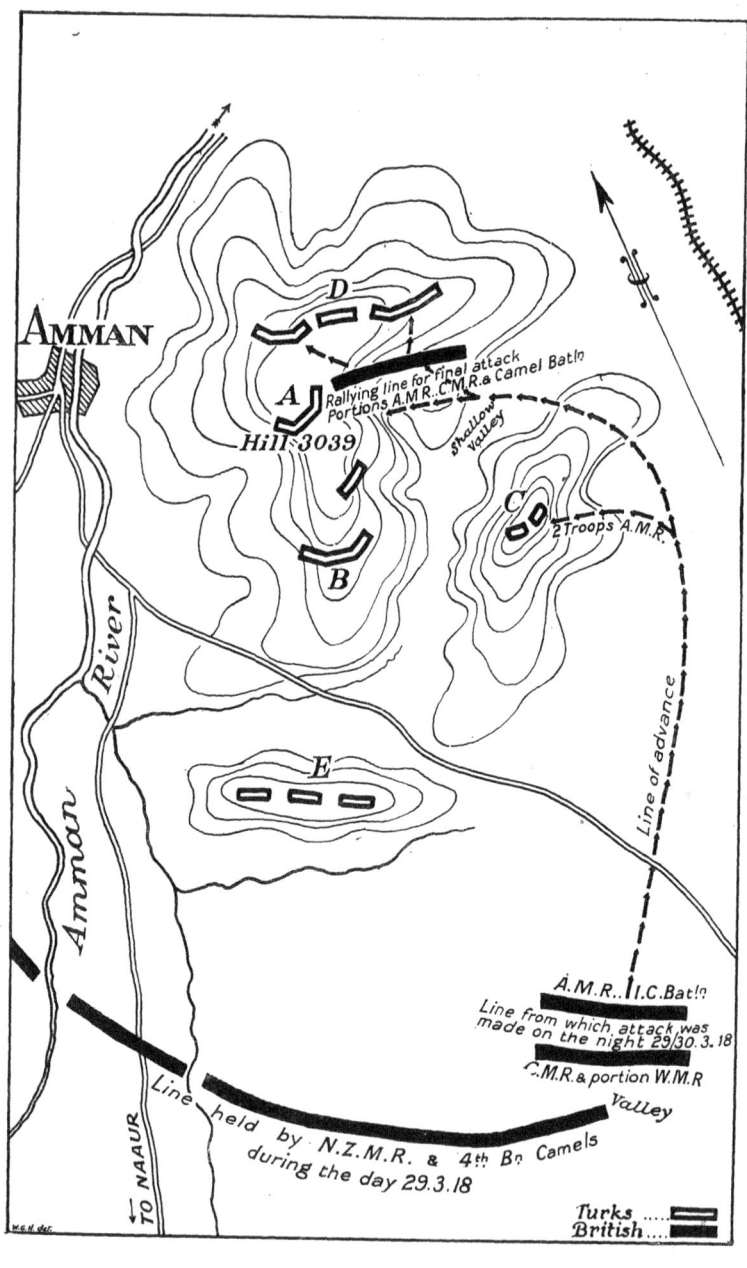

was adopted: The position "A" was to be the main objective, and was to be swiftly and silently approached by a force passing along the ridge between "B" and "C," which were merely to be contained by small parties in case they became active. "A" having been captured, it was considered "B" and "C" would be compelled to surrender.

This was the plan, simple yet daring, but requiring the most skilful leading in the dark, and the utmost resolution on the part of every officer, N.C.O., and man.

The Brigade's War Diary states: "This worked out according to plan."

It is a short phrase and often loosely used this "Worked out according to plan," yet containing in it unseen and untold agonies of hours. Think of that bitter winter night in the mountains. The men had been fighting day and night against nature's irresistible powers and against a stubborn enemy; without sleep or a hot meal or a hot drink for days; wet through, numbed with cold and weighted down by sodden clothes, yet these wonderful men cheerfully started out to face an almost impregnable fortress, garrisoned by a stubborn enemy, and in the midst of a dark night. But though underfoot was greasy mud or slippery rock and overhead a black, impenetrable sky, and though they were constantly lashed by the rain, yet these heroic hearts went forward, and, true to the record of the Mounted Brigade, what they undertook to do, that they carried out.

At half-past 1 on the morning of March 30th the Brigade, less the troops required for flank positions, concentrated dismounted at the line of deployment in the wadi at the foot of Hill 3039. All horses were left at Brigade Headquarters, the proportion of horse-holders being one man to eight horses.

The advance took place in two lines punctually at 2 a.m. In the first line were the Aucklanders and the 4th Battalion I.C.C., under the command of Lieutenant-Colonel McCarroll, and in the second line the Canterbury Regiment (less one squadron) and two troops of the Wellingtons. This line was under the command of Lieutenant-Colonel Acton-Adams.

The two lines advanced over an open flat for a distance of 800 yards, and then the course of a small wadi was followed until the ascent of the ridge forming the stalk of the shamrock was reached.

All machine guns were under the command of the O.C. Machine Gun Squadron, and two subsections went forward with the attacking force, leaving three subsections in position in some ruins to cover a retirement if necessary. These latter guns were in telephone communication with the O.C. Squadron.

When the ridge was reached the Aucklanders and Camel men, quickly following along it, attacked and captured the first enemy trenches, bayonetting the garrison with the exception of 23 Turks who surrendered with five machine guns. The trenches and sangers were immediately altered to face the other way; and the Canterburys and Wellingtons came through and went for the second position. They had about 300 yards to go, and when half-way across, the now alarmed enemy opened fire with rifle and machine guns.

This sudden burst of fire momentarily steadied the advance of our men, but inspired by the coolness and determination of Lieutenant Murray the line surged forward and captured the position, with 14 live Turks and a machine gun.

After this position had been consolidated, the 16th Company I.C.C. (the New Zealand Company of the 4th Battalion) joined the second line, and they, with the 8th Squadron Canterbury Regiment, went on again to the next objective overlooking Amman and from which the Turks retired.

Upon the capture of "A" the Turks in "B"—one officer and 28 other ranks and four machine guns—were taken, and in "C" 12 other ranks and one machine gun surrendered without firing a shot.

Every effort was made to strengthen the positions won before daybreak. The ground was almost solid rock, so trenches could not be dug, but sangers were built up as high as possible.

The Camels occupied the third position taken, but after daybreak, owing to its exposed nature, they were withdrawn, all but a post of 10 men with two Lewis guns, and were put into the right of the line.

This line ran across the top of the hill from east to west as follows: 4th Battalion I.C.C., Wellington Regiment, Canterbury Regiment, and Auckland Regiment.

The attacks by the other brigades were fairly successful. The I.C.C. took two lines of trenches and 12 prisoners. The infantry captured 135 prisoners and four machine guns. But after 4 o'clock scarcely any progress was made. On the left the 2nd Light Horse were hard put to it to hold their line.

So the situation was that at daylight the advance was everywhere held up, owing chiefly to the want of artillery support.

Away up on 3039 the New Zealanders were having an anxious time. Counter-attack after counter-attack was flung upon them during the day and between the attacks the hill was deluged with shells from Turkish guns situated to the east of Amman and out of range of the few guns our force possessed.

At 5 o'clock the first shelling began and the want of trenches was at once felt. The stone sangers, effective enough against rifle and machine gun fire, simply intensified the shell fire. Shrapnel ricochetted in all directions and high explosives hurled the rocky material broadcast. This bombardment lasted an hour and caused many casualties and as soon as it was over the surviving camel men left in the forward position were withdrawn and sent to join their battalion on the right.

About 9 o'clock a large number of the enemy could be seen from Divisional Headquarters (immediately west of the town) massing on the northern slopes. News of this was immediately sent to General Meldrum. But no artillery support could be given though the massing enemy presented a splendid target. The section H.K. & S. Mountain Battery with the New Zealand Brigade was at this time in possession of four rounds only.

At half-past 9 the attack came and was well met by the fire of machine guns. Nos. 1 and 3 sub-sections were in position on the right front of the Canterbury Regiment in sangers with a good field of fire covering the centre of the position. No. 5 was on the right flank of the Canterburys protecting the front of the camels. No. 2 was on the left flank of the Auckland Regiment and No. 6 on its right flank crossing the fire of Nos. 1 and 3. Five captured machine guns were also in action in the line.

The Turks pressed their attack with great determination and an unauthorised order to retire having been passed along the line held by the Camels, that battalion with the Canterburys and Wellingtons commenced to withdraw. The enemy succeeded in reaching the crest, but were held up by rifle and machine gun fire from the Auckland Regiment where Lieut. Harris handled his guns in a masterly manner.

The officers on the right quickly realised the position and rallied their men. It was a moment of extreme difficulty and nothing but the greatest determination could succeed, and the men to succeed were instantly forthcoming. Captain Hinson (Adjutant Canterbury Regiment) and Lieutenants Thorby and Crawford of the 16th (N.Z.) Camel Company, by their inspiring example each in his own part of the line, swept back their men in a magnificent charge.

The sight on that bare mountain top as seen from Divisional Headquarters opposite was a most stirring one. Our men surged up on to the crest and there seemed to be a short pause as the opposing lines faced each other at a bare 15 yards; and then our grand fellows hurled them back.

It was estimated that from 400 to 500 Turks assembled on the northern slopes of the hill for this attack and went up to the top. But no more than 50 were seen to come back.

During the morning the extreme left of the old New Zealand line held by a Canterbury Squadron got into the town, but the I.C.C. line on their left not being able to move they were forced to retire to their former position.

During the morning also the Somerset Battery, the battery that was always attached to the New Zealand Brigade and who now considered themselves almost New Zealanders, arrived having made a wonderful effort in overcoming all difficulties in climbing the mountains; and it was a welcome and a cheering sight to see their shells falling among the Turks. But the battery's arrival was too late to influence the tide of battle.

The Aucklanders on the extreme left of the line on the top of 3039 by machine gun fire silenced a forward battery of the enemy, which was in position near the Citadel in front of the Camel Brigade, and caused its withdrawal. This was the only battery belonging to the enemy put out of action during the operations.

14

At 2 o'clock in the afternoon three enemy batteries opened a heavy fire upon 3039 and continued for the rest of the day, causing many casualties; and great difficulty was experienced in getting away the wounded, owing to the exposed position and the impossibility of digging communication trenches.

AMMAN
Hill 3039 in the background.

At 4 o'clock another very heavy counter-attack was made upon the New Zealand line and this time the brunt of it fell upon the Camel Battalion causing them heavy casualties. The attack was beaten off by the help of a troop from the New Zealand Brigade reserve, prolonging the Camel right and thus outflanking the enemy.

At 5 o'clock the Turk made another bitter attack under cover of an intense bombardment, but he was driven back.

Throughout the day Lieut. Thorby of the 16th Company Camel Brigade was most conspicuous and his fine example and cheerful courage inspired his men to hold on under the most trying ordeal this fine Company had ever been under. He was killed in leading an attack against a body of Turks who were lodged in a position on the extreme right and from which they were enfilading the Camel line.

The difficulty of feeding the force was now becoming acute. The motor lorry service from Jerusalem to Jericho was taxed to the utmost. The supplies were brought from Jericho to the foot of the mountain by the Divisional Train and the horses were doing 24 miles per day. From the foot of the mountains to the troops investing Amman the camel transport did the work and the severe weather and slippery mountain tracks had caused fearful casualties to camels and drivers. And to crown all the Jordan overflowed its banks and swept all but one bridge away, to cross which the teams had to haul their loads through flooded roads. The total distance covered from rail head on the maritime plains to the men in the firing line in the mountains by lorry, horse and camel was 86 miles.

So it came about that soon after dark orders were received that the whole force would be withdrawn owing to the difficulty of supplies and because it had already performed the chief part of its mission in interrupting the communications of the Turkish Force operating in the vicinity of Maan against the King of the Hedjaz.

The principal objective given the Division by the Commander-in-Chief had been a large viaduct at Amman. This we had been unable to destroy, but owing to the extraordinary tenacity of purpose so characteristic of our Divisional General aided by the magnificent work of the men, our pressure at Amman had been so severely felt that the Turk had evacuated Kerak, the great grain centre east of the Dead Sea; and the troops of the King of the Hedjaz were enabled to make a substantial advance and to join hands with our forces.

In a letter of thanks to the Division the XX Corps Commander, Sir P. Chetwode, said that the Commander-in-Chief was more than satisfied with the result of the operations, and had stated that "what the Anzac Mounted Division and the 60th Division could not do no other troops could possibly undertake."

Then began that most difficult of military operations, a withdrawal when in contact with the enemy.

The first thing to be done was to move back the New Zealand Brigade from hill 3039 across the Wadi Amman.

At 6 o'clock in the evening the New Zealand Brigade received their orders to withdraw to the cross road at the western end of the plateau just above the village of Es Sir. The greatest difficulty the Brigade had to face was the evacuation of the wounded. These unfortunate men had to be carried from the battle field in blankets to the dressing station, a distance of one-and-a-half miles down rocky hills. From the dressing station to the nearest clearing station on the Es Salt–Amman road was a distance of 10 miles over country so boggy and slippery that the cacolet camels, the only means of ambulance transport, could not be used. Therefore each sufferer had to be strapped upon his horse and so taken over the 10 miles to the clearing station. Here he was placed upon a horse ambulance and taken to the Jordan valley where he had a 50 mile ride in a motor ambulance over the mountains of Judea to the hospital railway train, and then 200 miles to hospital in Cairo, though some of the very worst cases were accommodated in the hospitals in Jerusalem.

Among those who worked so devotedly and so untiringly in aiding the wounded was Captain J. G. Gow, the popular Medical Officer of the Wellington Regiment; and it was largely owing to his splendid work that the wounded were all collected and dressed and sent away by 11 o'clock that night and the Brigade commenced to re-cross the Wadi Amman at midnight, reaching the cross road above Es Sir at 4 o'clock on the morning of March 31st.

An outpost line was thrown by the Brigade across the country between Es Sir and Amman and the whole day was spent in concentrating the Force—mounted troops, infantry, camels and camel transport; and in getting all camels, both camel brigade and camel transport down the mountains.

The 2nd L.H. Brigade and the Somerset Battery took the Es Salt road; and the remainder of the force, including the infantry, withdrew by way of the Wadi Es Sir track, up which the New Zealand Brigade had come.

This track had been used continuously by the transport camels while the investment of Amman had been going on, and it was now in an appalling state of mud and slippery rock. So all day long and all the next night a long line of weary camels, horses and men, slowly stumbled, slipped and fell, down this mountain track which descends some 4000 feet in eight miles. It was well after daylight on the morning of April 1st before the rear guard could move.

The New Zealand Brigade had been selected for this difficult task and were kept fully occupied in holding off the enemy.

The Wellington Regiment which had now regained the 6th Squadron, detached throughout the operations with the

60th Division, was detailed to take up a position to cover the rear of the Brigade.

All night the long line of camels, infantry and horses, had been filing down the narrow gorge and it was not until 7 on the morning of April 1st that the New Zealand Brigade began to leave the plateau.

At a quarter to eight the enemy attacked the Wellington Regiment's rear guard; but were successfully held off until the regiment filed down through the village of Ain Es Sir.

AIN ES SIR.

The last to move was the 2nd Squadron and as they rode through the last of the village, the inhabitants, Circassians, suddenly opened fire from a mill and from adjacent caves, at very close range.

This treacherous attack was at once dealt with and the mill rushed and its occupants killed, but not before the squadron had suffered 18 casualties. Among these fell the popular commander of the 2nd Squadron, Major Charlie Sommerville (a veteran of South Africa), and Lieut. R. Hall, the capable signalling officer of the regiment.

About 1 o'clock a saddle was reached which looked down upon the Jordan valley. A halt was made here for the purpose of distributing rations and forage that had been brought up to meet the Brigade; and the sun came out and the wind died away; and an hour afterwards we were riding down through flowers up to the horses' knees—cornflowers, anemonies, ranunculi, poppies in the greatest profusion, acres of lilies, miles of colour—and all was peace and warmth and quietness; and one could scarcely realise that but a few short hours before the winds were raging, rain falling, and a bitter battle not yet finished.

Shortly after dark the Jordan valley was reached without further incident, and all ranks settled down to the sound sleep of worn-out men.

It has already been told how all wheels had to be left behind in the valley. The only guns to follow the Division were those of the Somerset Battery, and they were double-horsed, and experienced tremendous difficulties in climbing the mountains. The remaining batteries and Ammunition Column

General Chaytor receiving a decoration from the Duke of Connaught in the Old Citadel, Jerusalem.

had a very painful experience while the fighting was raging up above at Amman. The enemy planes, failing to find targets in the rain and mist above, came down repeatedly into the valley and mercilessly bombed the gun teams and the camels.

The quality of the Turkish troops was exceptionally good. They appeared to be fresh troops and were of good physique, and very well clothed and equipped. To guard against the cold, all ranks wore a well-made cotton-quilted long waistcoat.

Prisoners taken by the force were 20 officers, 595 other ranks; and the material taken included 10 machine guns, 2 automatic rifles, 207 rifles, and 248,000 rounds of S.A.A. The enemy abandoned on the Amman road two travelling field cookers, 26 motor lorries and 5 motor cars, besides many horse wagons. On the Hedjaz railway the New Zealanders captured an enemy aeroplane.

The expenditure of small arms ammunition by the force was 587,338 rounds.

CHAPTER VIII.

DOWN BY JERICHO.

Watch how the young exultant sun climbs high
O'er Moab's drear and desolate waste.
On lonely Nebo's rugged peaks descry
His first red beams, thence onward chased
To sacred Pisgah's craggy precipice;
And ere the depths of dead Bahr Lut
Have coldly answered his fierce ardent kiss
The weird fantastic figures cut
Across the plain on Quarantana's crest,
Till e'en Mar Saba's dismal towers
Seem less foreboding while by him caressed;
Though soon the whole wide valley cowers
And trembles 'neath his keen relentless gaze,
Each narrow wadi shadeless as
Its steep hillsides all shimmering in the haze;
Rejoicing in his strength he says
"This is my day, I'll have my way
     Down by Jericho."*

Mark how the Khamsin casts his baneful spell
O'er all life, and the very dust,
Foul breathing of the Desert, hot as hell,
More deadly than the dragon's thrust.
He chokes and smothers with his noxious stench
Like some foul reptile, men, whose throats
Too dry to curse find naught their thirst to quench
Whose rattle death's approach denotes.
See how his fiery tongue licks up the dust
And spues it at the tight closed eyes,
Blasting the sight and with each scorching gust
Stifling the birds and e'en the flies.
How his hot fury slacks not day nor night
But dries the marrow in the bones,
Bleeds energy and stunts life with its blight;
He says in no uncertain tones
"This is my day, all own my sway
     Down by Jericho."*

    —C. C. in the "*Palestine News.*"

On April 2nd the Division moved back across the Jordan by the Ghoraniyeh bridge and bivouacked "down by Jericho" and began the long sojourn there which was to last right through the sweltering summer.

The New Zealand Brigade bivouacked on the plain between Jericho and the Jordan river, almost upon the site of Gilgal of the Israelites.

The warmth after the cold mountain top was very pleasant for a few days, but the warmth rapidly increased to a heat as the Khamsin season came on. The first of these hot winds of the season, bringing from the deserts of Arabia a stifling air from which all ozone is excluded, began to blow on the 17th and lasted for 48 hours. There is a great deal of lime and a great deal of sulphur in the soil, and the combination formed the greatest dust plague yet experienced. It was a dust of a most penetrating and irritating quality.

JORDAN VALLEY DUST.

With the lessons of Salonica before them, our medical officers immediately began an anti-malarial campaign. Swamps were drained, all running water canalised and water that could not be made to run or otherwise drained off was treated with crude oil, which, floating upon the surface, prevents the Anopheles mosquito (the malaria-carrier) from breeding. This work was a great one and it entailed much labour, and to reinforce the efforts of the mounted troops who were holding the line a number of Sikh pioneers were brought down to the valley.

Owing to the foresight in taking in hand the latest anti-malarial methods, and to these efforts being kept up throughout the whole of the summer, the malarial casualties to the mounted troops in the valley were astonishingly small. And a clear proof that these efforts were on right lines and most efficacious was given towards the end of the campaign when our men left their own areas and advanced into the ground which had been occupied all the summer by the Turks. Malaria immediately attacked all ranks, and the casualties from this disease were exceptionally heavy.

Another proof that these anti-malarial measures were good was given by the fact that the few malarial casualties that the Division did suffer occurred invariably among the troops holding the front line on the west side of the Jordan north of Jericho. Here there was a large area of swampy ground, which on our side of No Man's Land was thoroughly drained and canalised, while on the other side of No Man's Land the Turk did nothing. The prevailing wind at night blew from the Turkish lines to ours, and it was here that the only malarial cases occurred.

Following their precedent of cleaning up the towns which we had occupied, our medical officers turned their attention to Jericho, and very nearly met their Waterloo. The officer in command of the Divisional Sanitary Section was an Australian Rhodes' Scholar and a most enthusiastic worker, and a man who had the knack of working the native races. The head man of the town was ordered to turn out every able-bodied man he had to clean up the town under the supervision of the O.C. Sanitary Section and his men. The work began with much enthusiasm, but the working party rapidly dwindled away. The head man was again lined up and told to muster the inhabitants, and a fresh start was made, with the same result, and the Sanitary Officer was in despair. Eventually a guard was put over the workers, and after much trouble and many days the village was cleared of its worst rubbish heaps and its most evil smells.

When the force which had raided Amman returned across the Jordan a "bridgehead" was formed covering the Ghoraniyeh bridge. Trenches were dug, wire put out, and the position was well covered by guns from the western bank. The line was held by the 1st L.H. Brigade, and on April 11th was heavily attacked by a large force of Turks. The attack began at 4 o'clock in the morning, and at the same time the enemy heavily shelled our lines on the Wadi Aujah, north of Jericho, which were held by the Camel Brigade. The attack at Ghoraniyeh was a most determined one, and parties of the enemy pushed forward to within 100 yards of the line. They were heavily shelled by our artillery, and at half-past 12· a regiment of Light Horse rode out and attacked them in the flank.

The attacks on the Aujah were also beaten off. After nightfall patrols found that the enemy had retired in front of the Ghoraniyeh bridge to his old line at the foot of the hills. In these attacks he lost very heavily, a rough estimate giving his casualties at 2500; the only casualties to the Division being 26 killed and 65 wounded, and horses, 28 killed and 62 wounded.

On April 18th the Brigade moved across the river to the Ghoraniyeh bridgehead, and on the 19th took part in an attack upon the Turks in the foothills.

The object of this attack was to ascertain the strength of the enemy and to make him think that another advance

A CONFERENCE AT THE JORDAN.
From left to right: Gen. Meldrum (N.Z.M.R.); Gen. Ryrie (2nd L.H.); Gen Chauvel (Corps Commander); Gen. Chaytor (Anzac Division); Gen. Cox (1st L.H.).

towards the Hedjaz railway was intended. The operations fulfilled their object and the enemy greatly strengthened his positions and brought up a number of fresh troops. That night the Brigade returned to its old bivouac west of the Jordan and took up its duty of guarding the fords on the Jordan between the Ghoraniyeh bridge and the Dead Sea.

On the 23rd the Brigade moved to a new bivouac near the foothills, close to old Roman Jericho. This was the city which, with its district, Anthony had given to Cleopatra. She sold it to King Herod, who embellished it with palaces and made it his winter residence. And here it was that he died. Close to the camp also was the Birket Musa, or Pool of Moses. It was a great pool built by Herod to conserve water from the Wadi Kelt to irrigate the gardens which were the beauty of Jericho, and in which grew the balsam which made Jericho noted.

The city was also famous for its palms, and history states that for many generations there existed a vast grove of majestic palms nearly three miles broad and eight miles long. Scarcely a solitary palm now remains as a remembrance of "Jericho the City of Palms." Close by the Brigade bivouac the Wadi Kelt, a small stream of running water, debouches on to the plain from out of a mighty gorge. In this great cleft, many hundreds of feet deep, the Monastery of St. George is built into a series of caves high up on the face of one of its cliffs. Along the face of this cliff are many other caves which are rented by the monks to pious Pilgrims who have come to bathe in the Jordan and who include in their Pilgrimage a period of hermitage.

On April 29th began the second raid into the Land of Moab. This was the raid upon Es Salt, the object of which was to cut off and destroy the enemy forces at Shunet Nimrin; to take Es Salt and if possible to hold it until the Arab forces could take it over; and finally generally to help the Arab forces. The Beni Sakr tribe who had helped the Amman raid stated that they had 7,000 men concentrated at Madeba.

The Desert Mounted Corps were given this operation to carry out and the troops at General Chauvel's disposal were the Anzac Mounted Division, the Australian Mounted Division, the Imperial Camel Corps Brigade and some Yeomanry and Indian Cavalry together with the 60th Division and an Indian Brigade of infantry.

The plan provided that the attack upon the enemy's strongly entrenched position was to be made by the 60th Division while the cavalry scaled the mountains at night and took Es Salt and then threw their weight upon the rear of the Turks in front of the 60th Division.

For this latter purpose the Australian Division with the assistance of two brigades from the Anzacs crossed the Ghoraniyeh bridge before daylight on the morning of April 30th and galloped up the plain on the east of the river through the line of enemy posts. Then leaving the 4th L.H. Brigade to watch the bridge over the Jordan at Ed Damieh, rapidly climbed the mountain track and late in the afternoon had taken Es Salt.

In the meantime the 60th Division with the aid of the New Zealand Brigade attacked the Shunet Nimrin position. This was of great strength and no headway was made that day during which the Canterbury Regiment had been attached to the 60th Division and were in action on its right against a very strong position well backed up by guns.

After dusk the Brigade withdrew into reserve by the bridge leaving the Wellington Regiment with the 180th Brigade of the 60th Division.

The next day May 1st the attack was continued and the Canterbury Regiment was sent to reinforce the 179th Infantry Brigade.

Meanwhile the 4th L.H. Brigade watching the bridge at Ed Damieh had been heavily attacked and were driven back some miles, losing their guns. At about noon General Chaytor received orders to take all the troops he could and to go to their assistance for there was a great danger, if the 4th L.H. Brigade were forced to retire any further, that the communications with the force at Es Salt would be broken.

The New Zealand Brigade, therefore, less two regiments, and with a Yeomanry Regiment and some machine guns were hurriedly sent up the east bank. Soon afterwards the Canterbury Regiment rejoined and a line was established by General Chaytor covering the foot of the only track remaining open to the Australian Division on the mountains at Es Salt.

This Division finding opposition stiffen after the capture of the town, had been unable to attack the Turks holding up the 60th Division, for they were occupied in keeping what they had gained.

During the next two days the attack on the Turkish position continued and though the 60th Division had been reinforced no progress was made.

Though their main road through Es Salt was in the occupation of our cavalry, the Turks had a road open through Es Sir and were being steadily reinforced. The Commander-in-Chief therefore ordered a withdrawal which was successfully carried out during the night of the 3rd.

The bringing of five Mounted Brigades down a single mountain track was a very difficult operation and to assist in this the Canterbury Regiment occupied (dismounted) the lower slopes of the hills down which the track from Es Salt came.

As soon as all the troops were down from the mountains and the 60th Division had withdrawn within the Ghoraniyeh bridgehead the New Zealand Brigade withdrew and recrossed the river, reaching their bivouac by 4 o'clock on the morning of May 5th, leaving the Wellington and Auckland Regiments temporarily at the bridgehead.

Though this raid had been unsuccessful and the Amman raid had not resulted in the capture of that town, yet the two raids were invaluable to General Allenby in that the Turkish High Command were now fully convinced that he would not advance on the coastal plain until he had secured his right flank by the capture of Amman. This induced them to keep a whole army facing our troops in the Jordan valley leaving the extreme right of their line comparatively weakly held, thus giving General Allenby an opportunity of which he was not slow to avail himself, when the time was ripe.

The question of the occupation of the Jordan valley throughout the summer was now considered. Local authorities stated that it was impossible for Europeans to live there after May 1st, on account of malaria; and that even the Arabs evacuated Jericho during the summer months, the only inhabitants who remained being a hybrid race descended from African slaves which had been imported by the Arabs in the days of their prosperity. There were three reasons why the valley should be held. The first reason was that the road from the Turkish railway at Amman, crossing the Jordan at Ghoraniyeh, was always a serious menace to our right flank; the second because it would be necessary to re-take the valley before the advance in the spring and this was considered more costly in lives than holding it; and the third and perhaps most important reason was that it was desired to hoodwink the enemy by the display of a large mounted force and constant activity upon that flank. The Turkish High Command had already paid our mounted troops the compliment in several "appreciations" which had come into our hands, of assuming that in whatever part of our line they were in evidence, it was from there we might be expected to strike. In the wilderness overlooking the Jericho plain, which was the only alternative position to hold, there was neither space nor water for a large body of cavalry. It therefore was decided to hold the Jordan valley and do the best that could be done to combat disease.

Though our losses from malaria were considerable, the heat intense, and the dust worse than our troops had hitherto experienced, the ultimate results more than justified this decision.

General Allenby was a strong forceful man and as such was beloved by our men. He was impulsive but just and was known far and wide as the "Bull." He was a frequent visitor to the valley and much interested himself in the fight that the cavalry were making against the climate. Naturally everyone tried to appear at his best when the Commander-in-Chief came round, and the news of his appearance in the valley was always promptly passed round. One day during a Turkish attack upon our outposts he appeared and went forward with the Divisional Commander to see what was going on. Immediately in front of him was one of a series of posts of Light Horsemen. While the C.-in-C. was standing there he noticed a man at the post waving his arms frantically and persistently. After a while he asked what this man was doing and was told that he was only signalling to the next post. But the man kept on and at length the C.-in-C. sent an officer across to enquire what the urgent message was. The answer was given after much hedging, "B.B.L.," and the embarrased officer had to explain to the C.-in-C. that "B.B.L." meant "Bull broken loose."

In order to shorten as much as possible the tour of duty of each brigade in the valley and hold it with as few troops as was compatible with safety the line was divided into two sectors in each of which there was the equivalent of three brigades. After the necessary reserves were provided for, three brigades were available for a rest out of the valley.

In accordance with this scheme the New Zealanders left the valley "down by Jericho" and reached Talaat ed Dumm (by the Good Samaritan's Inn) half way to Jerusalem, on the evening of May 16th, and remained there for some days. Situated in the heart of the wilderness, among rocky hills composed of a limestone that produced perpetual clouds of dust, this was a very uncomfortable place in which to be camped. The water for men and horses was pumped up some 600 feet from the gorge of the Wadi Kelt, and when the pumps failed the horses were led down rocky goat tracks to be watered.

However on the 29th after an all night march, the Brigade, passing through Jerusalem and Bethlehem, reached a fine ground some five miles south of King Solomon's Pools and about half-way from Jerusalem to Hebron. Here ample water was obtained in the Wadi Arrub (the valley of Beracah of the Old Testament) and the men and horses enjoyed a well earned rest in the cool mountain air of Judea.

There is much of historical interest in this old Judean plateau and not the least were the pools of King Solomon with their huge ramifications of contributory conduits.

The occupation of the country by Rome was in evidence everywhere in the land, and curiously enough was shown always by her industry in the conserving and the distributing of water, or by her love of games, *i.e.*, by aqueducts or amphitheatres.

Here in the Wadi Arrub our army engineers, old friends who had brought the Nile to Palestine, were busily re-creating the water supply of Jerusalem.

Herod had re-built the system of King Solomon, and Pontius Pilate had greatly extended it, by tapping the numerous springs of the Wadi Arrub, and had conveyed the water thus collected in the great masonry reservoir (now called the Birket el Arrub) by an aqueduct of some 25 miles to King Solomon's Pools and from there it reached the city, by the upper and lower aqueducts which still exist. Now Pontius Pilate's scheme was a very ambitious one and cost a huge sum of money; and the story is told that the people of Jerusalem

The King's Birthday in Bethlehem

refused to pay and complained to Rome. The consequence of this was that ultimately Pontius Pilate was recalled.

However that may be, our engineers traced out the old Roman conduits that were blocked with an accumulation which can literally be described as "the dust of ages," including the remains of several individuals who may have belonged to almost any period. They then repaired the ancient reservoir. Then, in our modern way, instead of leading the newly-found water along its miles of aqueducts, they put in pumps—oil-driven—and pumped the water to the top of an adjacent hill, where it flowed through two lines of steel pipes by gravity to Jerusalem. This work was begun on April 15th, and nine weeks later, on June 18th, water was delivered to the inhabitants. So in a short six months after our occupation the city of Jerusalem was in possession of a

THE WOMEN ON THE HOUSE TOPS AT BETHLEHEM.

water supply of 280,000 gallons per day. Not since the days of the Romans has running water been so plentiful in the Holy City.

On June 3rd, the King's Birthday, was held a parade in Bethlehem.

The Commander-in-Chief had expressed a wish that on this occasion, His Majesty's first birthday anniversary since the capture of the Holy Land, the ceremony should be made a public one and that the inhabitants of Bethlehem be invited to attend.

The townspeople, in their happy and cheerful way, took up the idea with enthusiasm, and erected at the entrance to the square, in front of the Church of the Nativity, a triumphal arch decorated with flowers and flags and with this inscription: "Bethlehem Municipality Greeting on the Occasion of the Birthday of His Majesty King George V."

The square is an awkward shape for a mounted parade, so half the men paraded on foot. They were chosen from the two Brigades in the vicinity—the N.Z.M.R. Brigade and the 1st L.H. Brigade.

The ceremony was a great success and a most picturesque sight with its backing of hoary old buildings crowned with crowds of gaily-dressed women. In the old, old way the

KINGS BIRTHDAY PARADE BETHLEHEM, 1918.
Little girls presenting General Chaytor with a bouquet.

women stood upon the housetops, and as the General rode in, welcomed him with their quaint lu-luing.

After the Royal salute had been given the townspeople presented the General with a loyal address, and a little girl, the representative of a large orphan school that was present, gave him a bouquet.

The General was accompanied by his Staff and by General Cox, commanding the 1st L.H. Brigade, and by Colonel Findlay, commanding the N.Z.M.R. Brigade; and there were present the Governor of Bethlehem (an English officer) and two French Army officers, representing France.

The people were greatly impressed by the little ceremony, and especially so by the magnificent physique of our men. A 6-foot man on a 16-hand horse was to them a vision of the giants of old. And the French officers present were enthusiastic in their praise of the physique and bearing and quiet steadfast purpose shown by our men.

Bethlehem is a Christian city and the people are open, frank and vivacious, very different from the Moslem Arabs. It was a pleasure to ride through the streets. The people were always pleased to see our men, and took no pains to disguise their feelings, as the gloomy Mahomedans do. And it was a clean city, free from that appalling "Eastern smell" one had found everywhere.

Early in the 19th century Kinglake travelled through Palestine and found Bethlehem an oasis in the Mahomedan desert—just as now. He says: "You know what a sad and sombre decorum it is that outwardly reigns through the lands oppressed by Moslem sway. The Mahometans make beauty their prisoner, and enforce such a stern and gloomy morality, or at all events such a frightfully close semblance of it, that far and long the wearied traveller may go without catching one glimpse of outward happiness. By a strange chance in these latter days, it happened that, alone of all the places in the land, this Bethlehem, the native village of our Lord, escaped the moral yoke of the Mussulmans and heard again, after ages of dull oppression, the cheering clatter of social freedom and the voices of laughing girls."

The people declare that they are not Arabs, but that they are descendants of the Crusaders. They certainly are not generally so dark and swarthy as the Arabs. All the women have colour in their cheeks and many have blue eyes, and their dress is interesting and picturesque. Apart from its attractive colouring—a sky-blue robe with red girdle and embroidered jacket—they wear a head-dress extraordinarily like that of the ladies of the Crusaders of old.

The Crusader's lady wore a head-dress not unlike a giant extinguisher, from which flowed white drapery. The women of Bethlehem wear a snowy white cloth covering the head and borne aloft upon an erection closely resembling that of the Crusader's lady, and from which it flows down the back.

WOMEN OF BETHLEHEM.

Certain indeed it is that Bethlehem is to-day as it was then, the one place in all that Mahomedan world where one hears the "cheering clatter of social freedom and the voices of laughing girls."

About this time a letter was received from the Mayor of Richon le Zion asking when the Division was to come back again as the billets they had occupied were being kept for them. And when the time came for leaving Bethlehem a general cry of regret went up from the whole town, a regret not only at losing our men, but at the knowledge that as soon as our men moved off, their places would be taken by other troops; and other troops were never welcomed a second time as were our men no matter wherever they went.

On June 13th the Brigade moved out to return to its work "down by Jericho" reaching bivouac areas in the vicinity of the Ain es Duk on the 16th. This remarkable spring gushes from out a mass of stones in an arid valley, and in a few yards is a full flowing stream of delightfully cool and clear water, giving a flow of some 200,000 gallons per day. A portion of this stream is still conveyed across a small valley by a beautiful arched aqueduct of three tiers of Roman arches in a perfect state of preservation.

The weather was now at its full summer heat, and the thermometer in the ambulance tents registered a daily shade temperature of 109 to 110 degrees and often as high as 120 degrees. Naked iron was so hot that one literally dared not handle it. The manner in which the horses stood this great heat was remarkable and impressed upon the mind the fact that a hot country must have been the original habitat of the horse. To put one's hand upon his back at midday was positively painful. Yet on the whole they throve amazingly in spite of the dust the heat and the many diseases in which the Jordan Valley abounded. The chief among these, Surra fever, was an illness communicated by the Surra fly, and it simply decimated the Turkish transport in 1917; as many as 42,000 camels are said to have died in the Jordan Valley. Judging from the acres of bones lying about, this enormous number cannot have been far from correct.

The water was plentiful and good and the forage all that could be desired and above all they were attended to by past masters in the art of horse mastership.

For the rest of the month the Brigade was kept busy holding the left sector of the defences in the Jordan Valley, trench digging and patrolling taking up the time, varied by encounters with enemy patrols.

The men talked a little and the officers grumbled and higher authority tried to find out why all these fine men and horses, the greatest cavalry command united under one man since the days of Darius, should be kept cooped up in this stifling valley. English speaking people in Jerusalem and any local inhabitants spoken to, had most emphatically declared that no white man could live through the summer there, and that no white man had attempted to live at Jericho in the summer time since the days of the Romans.

There was no rest for anyone. A vigorous campaign was carried out perpetually against the mosquitos. There were always new trenches to be dug, and as it was too hot for trench digging by day, all such laborious work was carried out by night. The conditions were such in the valley that no one ever slept in the day time. It was too hot, the flies were to troublesome and a hot wind full of dust blew from 11 a.m to 11 p.m. From that hour until dawn were th four least hot hours of the twenty-four, and the was the only possible time for sleep. But these preciou

A HALT IN THE JORDAN VALLEY.

hours were usually taken up in the front line in trench digging and in the back areas in anti-malarial work. So sleep was not a plentiful commodity down by Jericho.

Mounted patrols were constantly on the move leading to skirmishes and minor actions. In the bridge heads there was always some fighting going on and a small fleet of armed launches had to be maintained and guarded on the Dead Sea, for patrolling the eastern shore and for keeping up a precarious communication with the Arab forces of the Sherif Feisal.

No engagement of any importance took place after the Es Salt raid until July 14th, when the enemy made an attempt to cut off the mounted troops on the Jordan by penetrating between them and the right of the infantry away up on the highlands of Judea.

The attack commenced before dawn upon the 1st L.H. Brigade who were astride the old Roman road which ran from Jericho up the western side of the Jordan Valley close against the foot of the hills. The line held by the 1st L.H. consisted of a series of strong posts in two lines. By daylight the attack had become general along the whole line in the valley, and a German Battalion had penetrated the first line under cover of a heavy artillery barrage, and were held up against the second line, where they established themselves for some time.

The 1st Light Horse, with a magnificent counter-attack, assisted by the Wellington Regiment, soon drove off the enemy, capturing 448 prisoners, of which 377 were Germans. The remainder of the New Zealand Brigade then cleared the country for a distance of 1000 yards in front of the line held by the 1st L.H. Brigade.

It was interesting to note the great use made of machine guns and automatic rifles made by the Germans in this action. One party of 100 was captured, and they were in possession of no less than 42 automatic rifles. No doubt some of the party had been killed, but even so the proportion is most striking compared to our own one Hotchkiss gun to 35 men.

On the evening of July 19th the Brigade moved up into the Wilderness and bivouacked at Talaat ed Dumm for its second spell out of the valley, and reached King Solomon's Pools at daylight on the 27th, where a well-earned rest was enjoyed.

The return to the valley took place in two stages, beginning on August 16th, and the Brigade came into Divisional reserve just north of Jericho, in the vicinity of its old bivouac. The rest of the month of August was spent in regimental training, and on the 28th the Commander-in-Chief presented a number of decorations to members of the Brigade.

On September 5th the New Zealand Brigade went into the left sector of the Jordan valley defences and active patrolling became the order of the day, and on the same day General Chaytor took over the command of the whole Jordan valley defences, and the last great phase of the campaign began.

Early in April, 1918, the urgent call for reinforcements, owing to the general break through in France, had led to the despatch of large numbers of British troops from Palestine, their places being taken by Indian troops. The Desert Mounted Corps lost eight Yeomanry Regiments, which were dismounted and turned into machine gun battalions. In place of these the 5th Cavalry Division (less its British regiments and Royal Horse Artillery) was sent from France with five extra Regular Indian cavalry regiments. The Indian Imperial Service Brigade, consisting of two regiments which had been throughout the war in the E.E.F., was added, so that in exchange for the eight regiments of Yeomanry the Corps Commander had acquired 13 Indian cavalry regiments. It therefore was decided to expand the Corps into four Divisions. The Anzac Mounted Division was not altered, but the Yeomanry Brigade in the Australian Division was withdrawn and its place taken by a new Australian Brigade—the 5th Light Horse Brigade. This new Brigade was to have been composed of the I.C.C. Brigade reorganised, and to consist of two Light Horse regiments and one New Zealand, the Yeomanry companies being kept intact as camel men for service in the desert. However, the New Zealand Government did not see its way to consent to a new mounted rifles regiment being formed or of the Otago Mounted Rifles being reorganised. So in the end the third regiment was composed of French Spahis and Chasseurs d'Afrique, and New Zealand found the machine gun squadron to the new Brigade. The Cavalry Corps therefore now consisted of four Divisions, of which the Anzac was the only one unchanged and the only purely white Cavalry Division in the Force. The Australian Mounted Division was Australian all but one regiment and the New Zealand machine gun squadron (known as the 2nd N.Z. Machine Gun Squadron), while the remaining Divisions were three-fourths Indian troops.

The general situation early in September was as follows:—The Turkish IV Army was facing our troops in the Jordan valley with the great bulk of its strength east of the Jordan. The remainder of the Turkish line running westwards, was held by the VII Army on the Judean hills, and by the VIII Army on the plain of Sharon. General Liman von Sanders with the Yilderim Headquarters was at Nazareth. The IV Army was based on Damascus via Amman and the Hedjaz railway.

The lines of communications for the VII and VIII Army crossed the plain of Esdraelon (or Armageddon), the great battlefield of the ancient world. The only lateral road between the IV Army and the two Armies west of the Jordan crossed the river at Jisr ed Damieh.

The plain of Esdraelon with the plain of Jezreel, intersects northern Palestine, forming an easy communication from the sea to the river Jordan at Beisan. There were no defensive works of any kind on the plain of Esdraelon or covering the approaches to it, though there were some German troops at Nazareth which lies in the mountains to the north.

It is obvious that, with a large force of cavalry let loose on the plain of Armageddon, with the IV. Turkish Army pinned down to its position east of the Jordan, and with the front of the VII and VIII Armies attacked by the two Infantry Corps, the fate of the VII and VIII Armies would be sealed. The IV Army would then have to retire on Damascus with a possibility of being cut off before it reached that refuge, either by our cavalry or by the Arabs who were assembling in the Hauran. The way up the coast through the Plain of Sharon north of the Turkish right was good going for cavalry, and there were two passes from it through the mountains of Samaria on to the plain of Esdraelon. It remained only to get the cavalry through the enemy's line.

General Allenby's plan was to break the Turkish line on our extreme left on the Plain of Sharon, where a gap was to be made for the cavalry to pass through. While this was being done it was necessary to leave sufficient forces in the Jordan Valley, to pin down the Turkish IV Army; to seize the bridge at Ed Damieh breaking the communications between the forces east and west of the Jordan; and to attack the IV Army, should the main operations be successful. This difficult and important task was allotted to Sir Edward Chaytor, who was given a composite force with which to carry out the operation. The remainder of the Desert Mounted Corps (three cavalry Divisions), were moved at night during the fortnight before the great blow was to be struck; and marching across the Judean hills, they were hidden in the orange groves near Jaffa. In front of them and immediately behind the line, were concentrated the five Infantry Divisions and the necessary artillery, selected to make the gap.

The way in which this preliminary concentration was carried out and concealed from the enemy was one of the most remarkable achievements of the whole operation. A hostile air reconnaissance on September 15th after our concentration was complete reported as follows:—"Some regrouping of cavalry units apparently in progress behind the enemy's flank; otherwise nothing unusual to report"; and this at a time when three cavalry Divisions, five Infantry Divisions, and the majority of the heavy artillery of the force were concentrated between Ramleh and the front line of the coastal sector, there being no less than 301 guns in place of the normal number of 70. On the same date enemy intelligence reports showed an *increase* of cavalry in the Jordan valley.

Such briefly was the situation and the plan. The preliminary movements and preparations for the execution of the plan began an intensely interesting period "down by Jericho." Movement was in the air, and the stimulus of coming operations once again upon their horses encouraged the fit and braced up those who were tired and worn, and the sick rate went down. This was always a remarkable proof of the thoroughness and steadfastness of purpose of our men. With "nothing doing" the regimental doctor had a long queue of men waiting at his tent door every morning— cuts, abrasions, colds, debility and fevers; but as soon as a whisper of operations got abroad the queue dwindled until the last two or three days before the "move" it was with the greatest difficulty that even a seriously sick man could be persuaded to parade sick for fear of missing the "stunt."

Every effort was made to deceive the enemy and to make him believe that the next blow would fall in the Jordan valley.

To confuse the enemy airmen, several dummy bridges were erected across the Jordan, with wide roads leading to them. New camps filled with empty tents were made, and as the cavalry were moved under the cover of darkness from the valley to the olive groves around Jaffa, their vacated lines were filled with empty tents and dummy horses, with real horse-rugs upon them and real nose-bags upon their dummy heads. Fires were kept alight in these camps; and to convince the people of Jerusalem (through whom the Turks were bound to get some information), the Hotel Fast, the principal hotel in the European suburb, was cleared of all guests; and the information was given out that it was to be General Allenby's Headquarters. This was substantiated by the erection of notices at the hotel door with the legend "G.H.Q."

A CAMOUFLAGED BRIDGE OVER THE JORDAN TO DECEIVE THE AIRMEN.

Another factor in the success of our secrecy was the activity of our air force, who made it almost impossible for an enemy aircraft to obtain reliable information.

These preliminary preparations and movements took up the fortnight immediately preceding the break through, and as the other mounted Divisions were removed from the valley, increased responsibility and work were thrown upon all units of the Anzac Mounted Division.

In the sector held by the New Zealand Brigade General Meldrum had under his command additional troops—two Battalions of the British West Indies Regiment and two Battalions of Jewish volunteers, under the command of Colonel Patterson, the writer of "The Man Eaters of Tsavo." There was also a field artillery battery and an Indian mountain battery.

Although the valley force had been reduced to a minimum, every effort was made to indicate to the enemy the continued pressure of a large force. Patrols were kept always on the move and the Turk was constantly engaged and given no rest.

On September 16th the troops remaining in the valley were consolidated under the command of Major General Chaytor and designated "Chaytor's Force" consisting of the following units:—

Anzac Mounted Division.
A/263 Battery R.F.A.
195th Heavy Battery R.G.A.
29th and 32nd Indian Mountain Batteries.
No. 6 (Medium) Trench Mortar Battery.
3 anti-aircraft sections R.A.
Detachment No. 35 A.T. Company R.E.
38th Battalion Royal Fusiliers (Jewish Volunteers).
39th Battalion Royal Fusiliers (Jewish Volunteers).
20th Indian Brigade.
1st Battalion British West Indies Regiment.
2nd Battalion British West Indies Regiment.

This new force was immediately taken in hand by the Divisional Staff and arrangements made as far as possible to make it mobile, for its services would likely be required in the first place to capture the Ed Damieh bridge, cutting the VII Army's retreat to the Hedjaz railway; and secondly if the great break through on the plains was successful to pursue and capture the IV Army in the mountains east of the Jordan; and finally if the Turks right was not broken it would fall to Chaytor's Force to turn the enemy's left by advancing north along the Hedjaz railway, cutting off the troops in Palestine.

Though our men had lived all the summer almost immune from malaria it was well known that the Turks made little effort to check this dread disease; and so mosquito nets were issued to be worn by all, as soon as new country was reached.

The extremes of heat in the Jordan Valley are in direct contrast to the intense cold and heavy rain of the mountains of Moab, as experienced during the first operations against Amman. For this reason it was difficult to decide upon a kit suitable to both. A blanket or a great coat with a water-proof sheet are however always useful; it was decided to carry the great coat and water-proof sheet for the pending operations. Supplies were to consist of two days' rations and one emergency ration for the man and two days for the horse.

NIMRIN NELLY

On these last days the enemy shelled the Division with his long range gun at Shunet Nimrin, known to our troops as "Nimrin Nelly." This gun fired right across the Jordan valley bursting shrapnel at a range of 10 miles; and together with "Jericho Jane," who sat upon the mountains north of Jerusalem, was fond of putting their great shells into Jericho causing many casualties among the inhabitants there.

CHAPTER IX.

How the Brigade Crossed the Jordan for the Last Time.

On the early morning of September 19th Allenby's blow fell upon the enemy's extreme right and broke clean through his defences with scarcely a pause. The advance continued all day with hardly any opposition after the first barrier had been broken down; and by daylight on the 20th the leading mounted troops had reached Nazareth on the far side of the plain of Esdraelon. Here Liman von Sanders' Staff was captured with all his records and papers and the General himself only just got away.

On the 20th the XX Corps began its attack; and captured Nablus (the ancient Shechem) on the 21st, driving immense numbers of the broken VII Army eastwards towards the Jordan. These were pursued by the 5th L.H. Brigade with whom was the New Zealand 2nd Machine Gun Squadron.

The experiences of this squadron in the great drive north to Damascus are told in the "Kai Courier," the journal of the transport "*Kaikoura*," by Sergeant M. Kirkpatrick. He says:—"Had General von Sanders known prior to September 19th what was going on in that quiet sector on the plain of Sharon, he might have been able to prevent a defeat becoming one of the most complete and terrible disasters in history.

"Our powerful raids towards Amman and what appeared to the enemy to be tremendous activity in the Jordan valley, had led him to believe that beyond the Jordan, and not on the coastal plain, our main attack would be directed, and, accordingly, his great energies were consumed in making extensive preparations to meet us in that quarter. While he was busy shifting his best troops towards the threatened area in the east, General Allenby, secretly and mainly by night, was collecting a powerful striking force in the west, and hiding it away among the trees round Jaffa and Ludd. In this area everything during the day appeared to be quite normal, but at night all the roads leading northward were crammed full of organised military traffic, to be planted during the daylight hours in the grateful shade of many groves. The sword had been added to the equipment of the Australian Light Horse

Division, and, although the training in the use of this new weapon was in some cases not long, yet the men were wonderfully keen and confident, and great was the satisfaction at the prospect of charging down on the old enemy and cutting him to pieces.

"Our airmen had not been idle, for the enemy's aerial eye had been knocked out on this side, while in the Jordan valley he was allowed to see just what was thought good for him.

"The night of September 18th witnessed the final marshalling of our forces close up to the enemy line for the supreme manoeuvre. Our many guns were ready in a half hour's bombardment to overwhelm and smash the enemy's artillery and confuse his infantry. Our own infantry were eagerly awaiting the signal to go over the top and breach the battered line, while beyond the cavalry, conscious of a great impending event, were impatient to pour like a torrent through the gap, sweep up the coastal plain and then down Esdraelon (the ancient plain of Armageddon) and the valley of Jezreel to the Jordan, thus encircling on two sides the enemy's position on the central range, cutting all his communications and closing every avenue of escape from the Mediterranean to the Jordan valley. This Napoleonic plan, grand and bold, was worked out beautifully in every detail, and, as we saw it unfold in its successive stages, every man felt that proud confidence and exhilaration of spirits that it felt only when fighting under a great commander. We, of the 2nd New Zealand Machine Gun Squadron attached to the 5th A.L.H. Brigade, were the only New Zealanders on this spectacular stunt, which ultimately reached Damascus and far beyond. The New Zealand Brigade was in the Jordan valley in readiness to assist, as soon as the enemy right and centre began to retreat, in the race up the Jordan valley to close the fords, thus completing the net round the VII and VIII Turkish Armies. Completing the 5th A.L.H. Brigade was a Regiment of French Colonial Cavalry regulars. These wiry men, dressed in attractive and almost fantastic uniforms, were mounted on hardy, cleanlegged stallions, as diverse in colour as their masters were in blood. The combination produced a most picturesque sight, especially in a charge. Before we reached Damascus, the Turks were fully confirmed in this opinion.

"Our waiting guns awoke the morn in thunder, hailing Victory. The infantry broke the dazed enemy's battered line, and through the gap we poured, while the hot-throated horse artillery limbered up to press the pursuit, with the magnificent transport following quickly behind. No one engaged in that wild ride will ever forget it. The pace was terrific. Our horses were very fit. They had need to be. We rode light, but still each horse carried three days' rations and bore about twenty stone in weight.

"The blow was so sudden and swift that resistance was slight. Those who opposed were galloped down, machine guns were blanketed, there was neither halt nor check. Most of the fleeing enemy made for the hills, or the Tul Keram road, leading to Nablus. For a time the Indian Lancers and Yeomanry Cavalry, who had broken through nearer the coast, were galloping on our left. With swords and lances flashing in the sunlight, this great host thundered over the rolling ridges. It was a wonderful and inspiring spectacle.

"As our Brigade swerved to the right in order to deal with Tul Keram, we lost sight of them, they had a "through ticket." Crossing the railway above the village, which is set on a hill, we captured a number of guns, much transport, and about two thousand prisoners. The fleeing foe, heading up the narrow gorge that leads from Tul Keram by Anebta to Nablus, were caught by our airmen, who flying very low, raked the unfortunate column with machine guns and bombs. The destruction was frightful. Those who escaped death and wounds soon abandoned their wagons, guns, and lorries, and took to the hills, only to be captured a little later on. In their impetuosity, the leading French and Australians, who were pursuing the enemy, came under fire from our own 'planes, and many narrow escapes were recorded. Seeing that all was lost, Tul Keram surrendered. Halting only to water, reform, and feed, under cover of darkness, we struck across country to cut another life line behind Nablus and Samaria. This stroke was as successful as it was bold. The country was very rough and broken, but the long thin column clambering along goat tracks and up boulder-strewn torrent beds, reached the line, destroyed a portion, captured some prisoners and machine guns, and, as the evening shadows darkened into night, camped before Tul Keram. But the halt was not for long. Rations and horse feed, a few hours' precious sleep, daylight, and we were off again, this time to assist in the capture of Nablus. We threaded our way through the wreckage that was strewn nearly all the way. Dead men and animals, torn about with ruthless bombs, swollen and distorted, stank fearfully. Many of the animals still lived in speechless agony, and some of the wretched wounded were in many cases pinned down by carrion, but there was no time to stop and help them. That was for others who came behind. War is hell, and looks well only in a picture show.

"As we approached Nablus, the road was nearly a foot deep in limestone dust, that blinded our eyes and parched our throats. Any kind of water was drained up greedily by horse and man. The enemy, stubbornly resisting, were pushed back from about Mounts Gerizim and Ebal, and soon, to the accompaniment of thundering guns and circling 'planes, we rode in triumph through the streets of ancient Shechem, and encamped on the little plain beyond. The interior of Shechem, is very like Jerusalem, but it is far better supplied with water, to which it mainly owes its existence. It has been the scene of many battles, perhaps the most awful being in 67 A.D., when Vespasian slew 11,000 of its inhabitants. The batteries sang us to sleep with "hymns of hate." Next morning we doubled back, and turned up the Samaria road leading to Jenin. Among the many scenes of death and devastation one remains firmly rooted in my mind. Near old tumbled down Samaria, reclining against a bank on the roadside, was a young German lad, aged about 16. Tall, fair-headed, blue eyed, and a complexion fresh as a girl's, he struggled hard twixt pain and pride. Poor beggar! he was badly wounded, and had just put up a fight worthy of a better cause. There was no time to turn "Good Samaritan"; there was but one order, "ride on." We reached Jenin and its fertile fields, and, as darkness came down, we camped a little beyond the village. Here our 'planes had smashed the railway station, and here the Third Brigade, swooping in from the Haifa side, had secured a great haul of prisoners, who had intended to escape across the Esdraelon Plain. The Turks surrendered readily, and indeed, after the first few days, it was the

Germans who did nearly all the fighting. Across the hills, hidden from our view, the Anzac Division, in the difficult but familiar ground of Gilead and Moab, were closing round the IV Turkish Army. At Jenin we rested most of the following day (September 25th), and in the evening pushed on to the valley Jezreel, and bivouacked by the railway near Zerin, having Mount Gilboa on our right. Here a beautiful fountain of extraordinary volume bursts from the foot of a great rock, and the next day we bathed our horses there, and drank deeply of its living waters. Saul would have wondered, Jehu would have glowed had he seen our cavalry sweep down this grand old battlefield.

"Cleaned and refreshed, we sped away as eve closed down on the grey hills and brown valleys. Passing through the big railway junction of El Fuleh, where thousands of infantry (British and Indian) had already gathered, we struck along the Nazareth road.

"On the second 'night out,' the Yeomanry had captured Nazareth and its garrison of three thousand men, most of whom were asleep. This job was performed at the expense of only 18 casualties.

"It was 'lights out' when we passed through Nazareth, but the old place looked well in the moonlight. At Kefr Kenna, which is, according to tradition, the ancient Cana, we halted for water and forty winks, but were quickly on the move again on our way to Tiberias. As we approached that place, the soil became more fertile, and the rank grass grew more thickly among the numberless boulders. The shadows were lengthening as we wended our way down the steep road leading to the quiet old city that reposes by the beautiful waters of Galilee, where our thirsty horses drank their fill. The inhabitants of the town, seven-eighths of whom are Jews, gave us a right royal welcome. They knew that deliverance came with the British. It may be of interest to note that they were, also, the cleanest people we had met with in the East.

"That night we bivouacked on the hillside beside the grand old ruined walls, and, throwing ourselves on the rich warm volcanic soil, we took no thought of the morrow. Astir before the earliest lark, we passed quickly through the town and up the west side of the lake. The 4th Brigade of

Australians, swinging round by Beisan, had encountered very stiff opposition at Semak, where the Germans, drunk, desperate, and under orders to fight to a finish, obeyed as becometh good soldiers. The 3rd Brigade had come down from Nazareth and occupied Tiberias before us, and now, with our Brigade leading, the Division set out for Damascus.

"At the Jordan crossing a little before Lake Hulch (Waters of Moram), German Machine gunners put up a fine resistance, delaying the Division for several hours. Curving to the right, part of our Brigade forded the turbulent and treacherous torrent, and, clambering up the steep banks to the tune of a brisk machine gun fire, began to envelop the enemy's position. Darkness fell and left us among the endless boulders, where, with the reins over our arms, we reclined against these substantial pillars and slept the sleep of the just. A direct attack, delivered during the night, took the position, and the engineers worked so quickly and well that soon the damaged bridge was repaired sufficiently to allow transport to pass.

"This treeless region, that now supports only a few sheep and goats with their wild and woolly owners, had once a teeming population and many strong cities. We reached El Kuneitra in the evening (September 29th), where a big concentration of British and Indian Cavalry began, and an advanced aeroplane base was established for operations against Damascus. Here we secured some hay for our horses, and here many a cock, that in the pride and vanity of youth crowed lustily that morn, was heard to crow no more. In the evening of the following day we left the main Circassian village, heading for the city beautiful. Belts and girths were getting slack with the long hard ride, but the spirit of victory animated all. Toward the morning sharp opposition was encountered from a battery and some machine guns well posted in difficult ground, all strewn with Mount Hermon's apples. Deploying in the dark and over such ground was no easy matter, but finally the tenacious enemy was driven out and captured.

"The sun rose that morning in a blaze of glory. Few pens could well describe it. It was the sun of Austerlitz witnessing the 'Pearl of the East' passing from the hand of the Turk. Halting only for water and a hasty meal, we passed on at quickened pace on the last lap for Damascus. As we came in sight of the beautiful verdure that envelops the city, we thought that here, at last, was something worth fighting for. German machine gunners, defending the suburbs, were quickly rooted out by our active horse artillery, while we galloped between the cultivation and the arid hills. Suddenly encountering a sharp and well-directed fire, we swerved abruptly into these hills, where the enemy, picketing the heights, were as quickly dispersed. From these hills we obtained a magnificent view of the city which 'The Prophet' thought 'A Paradise,' fortunately for his belief, he went not down, neither did the wind blow his way. Away to the south-east we could see a great converging column of the enemy struggling on to reach the city. They were the 20,000 Turks from the Deraa Base. Most of the fugitives were bagged by our Division ere they reached what they had fondly hoped was their haven of refuge.

"And now occurred one of the most frightful tragedies of the campaign. On the west side of the city the Adana River ('the reason why' of Damascus) tumbles through a deep, narrow and particularly beautiful gorge. The road and railway leading to Beirout are also crowded into the ravine Through this narrow pass a great enemy column was seeking to make its escape. Part of our squadron, racing ahead of the screen and reaching the brink of the precipice, quickly took up positions almost invisible to the dense mass of enemy below. The head of the column was felled, and, as the unfortunates behind kept pressing forward, they were mown down as by some invisible scythe. Horses and men went down together in hundreds and died in one tangled bleeding mass. Many fell into the river and were drowned. The Germans fought desperately from the tops of lorries and from a train with their machine guns, but, seeing not where to fire, their shots were wild, and they too went down in the slaughter. The water in the M.G. jackets hissed, and bubbled, and steamed. The barrel in one of the guns was so hot that it bent like a crooked stick. Australian Hotchkiss guns and rifles joined in the work of destruction. Above the rattle of the machine guns and the roar of the river, the cries of anguish and despair swept up from this valley of death.

With every avenue of escape cut off, the stricken survivors surrendered to their unseen foes.

"Next morning the West Australians (Third Brigade), who were the first to enter the city, had to pile up the bodies of men and horses in order to get a bridle path through which to pass. As the night of this wild day (October 1st) closed round, the fine wireless station and huge ammunition dump were blown up by the enemy, and roaring explosions flung high in the air thousands of projectiles of all sizes. It was a magnificent spectacle, a fitting end for the great pile of artillery 'iron rations.'

"The most ancient of cities, fed and purified by the rushing Adana through which only its noblest features are seen by the distant spectator, waited that night with its twelve thousand soldiers for surrender on the morrow. Watching by the guns that night, I thought, what many others must have been thinking, that the blighting rule of the Turk was broken forever, that soon the soft flesh of verdure would cover the skeleton lands through which we had passed, restoring them to their former loveliness and glory, and that a smiling future would look back in admiration of this turbulent present when it recalled the Tenth Crusaders and their last great ride."

Meantime down by Jericho the N.Z.M.R. Brigade began to push north on the morning of the 20th. The Auckland Regiment worked along the old Roman road for some miles; and after dark the remainder of the Brigade with the B.W.I. battalions and the 29th Indian Mountain Battery and with the Ayrshire R.H.A., joined the Aucklanders at Kh. Fusail, about half-way to the Ed Damieh bridge and the main road from Nablus to Amman.

At Kh. Fusail one battalion of the B.W.I. were left to guard the rear and the column pressed on. The work entrusted to it was of the utmost importance. The road to the east was vitally necessary at this stage to the VII Army. The XX Corps had dealt it a staggering blow; and our cavalry had reached the plain of Esdraelon in its rear and its only way of escape was by access to the Jordan and so to the Hedjaz railway.

The responsibility of denying this advantage to the enemy therefore devolved upon General Meldrum's force.

The position was strongly held and presented many obstacles to an attacking force. In addition large bodies of the enemy were converging on the crossing. Swift and bold measures were essential to effect the capture of the objectives ordered or to gain close contact with the enemy before daylight appeared.

The general line of advance lay along the Roman road along a narrow plain shut in between the western hills and the Jordan and exposed to the enemy's artillery which was posted on the other side of the river. When within striking distance the Auckland Regiment was sent forward north-east to attack the bridge, and the Wellington Regiment straight ahead to cut the Nablus road and to seize El Makhruk the Headquarters of the 53rd Turkish Division.

These operations were carried out to the letter in spite of the darkness. The Auckland Regiment fought its way close up to the bridge and occupied a position astride the road and overlooking the bridge. The Wellingtons, by most skillful leading, at daylight had completely encircled El Makhruk, capturing some 400 Turks, a great mass of war material and the Divisional General and his complete Staff.

Soon after daylight the systematic attack on the bridge began.

At 7 o'clock an enemy force of about 500 with two mountain guns appeared advancing down the Wadi Farah facing the left of the Wellington line. This was the advanced guard of the broken VII. Army endeavouring to escape to the Hedjaz. The position of the Brigade at this time was precarious. In addition to the 500 Turks advancing against the left an enemy counter-attack of about 1200 men was developing on the right flank at Ed Damieh. On the right rear a body of Turks having crossed the river from the eastern bank had attacked the B.W.I. battalion (left at Talaat Amrah) in an endeavour to cut off the column; and one of the captured Staff Officers of the 53rd Division had divulged the fact that a force of two battalions of infantry was only three to four miles distant on the left rear.

General Meldrum reinforced the Wellingtons with the 10th Squadron of the Canterbury Regiment, and the 500 Turks were soon forced back into the hills, from which they intermittently shelled the Wellington Regiment for the rest of the day. The enemy's counter-attack from the bridgehead upon the Aucklanders was strongly pressed, and the 1st Squadron Canterbury Regiment and one company B.W.I. were sent to reinforce Colonel McCarroll. A general advance was made at 11 o'clock and by a splendid bayonet charge the enemy position was carried, our machine guns causing great casualties to the fleeing enemy. The bridge was soon taken and the 11th Squadron, crossing mounted, pursued the enemy for some distance and captured many prisoners.

THE BRIGADE CROSSING THE JORDAN AT JISR ED DAMIEH IN ITS ADVANCE UPON ES SALT.

The capture of El Makhruk and Ed Damieh was the result of a daring plan quickly and boldly carried out. Hesitation or delay during the night would have entailed heavy casualties. It was essential to penetrate the enemy's positions silently under cover of darkness. This was accomplished and when daylight came success was assured. The day's captures included 786 prisoners, six guns, nine machine guns and 200 tons of ammunition and quantities of stores, and among the guns were two 18 pounders which had belonged to the H.A.C.

lost by the 4th L.H. Brigade in the attack upon Es Salt at the end of April.

At noon on September 23rd, the New Zealand Brigade began its dash upon Es Salt from Ed Damieh, leaving the West Indians to guard the bridge. After crossing the eastern plain for a distance of about eight miles in intense heat, opposition was encountered on the edge of the foothills of the mountains of Moab. This was soon brushed aside, and with the Canterbury Regiment in the lead the advance up the Es Salt track (a climb of some 3000 feet) continued—no enemy opposition, no difficulties of track could stop our men.

One mile west of Es Salt a strong redoubt was located, completely commanding the road. Major Hurst who was in command, and to whose indomitable energy and skill the advance owed its wonderful success, immediately took steps to outflank this position, and it was rushed with but little delay

NEW ZEALAND MOUNTED RIFLES RIDING THROUGH ES SALT.

to the advance. In the redoubt were captured nine officers and 150 other ranks, and four machine guns, by a most brilliant little piece of work.

By half-past four in the afternoon Es Salt was enveloped and captured. After a thorough search of the town had been made for Turks and records the Brigade bivouacked there for the night.

Early next morning patrols were pushed out east and north and the enemy's rearguard located a few miles on the Amman road. The day was spent in the concentration of Chaytor's Force in the vicinity of Es Salt, with the New Zealand Brigade just east of Suweileh and the two other Brigades between this village and Es Salt. One battalion of the Jewish force was left behind exhausted by their marching and fighting in the heat, and one battalion of the B.W.I. was at Ed Damieh holding the bridge over the Jordan.

THE ROAD TO ES SALT, THROUGH THE MOUNTAINS OF MOAB.
(from a photograph taken by a German Officer.)

During the night a successful raid upon the railway north of Amman was made by a party of four officers and 100 men chosen from the Auckland Regiment. To ease the horses, saddles were stripped and nothing was carried but the necessary tools. These were just such as could be scraped up in a hurry and consisted of two picks, two shovels and four spanners. No explosives were available. Every man was fully armed and carried the maximum of ammunition. The party penetrated 12 miles into unknown enemy territory at night, took a section out of the Hedjaz line under the noses of the Turkish patrols and returned next morning without the loss of a man. By skilful leading in the darkness the little band reached the railway without mishap and found that the road that runs alongside the line was occupied by a great Turkish Transport Column, a part of the IV Army fleeing north. This caused delay and when the work of destruction began the party was several times interrupted, once by a train full of troops and several times by enemy patrols. But the work was completed without any alarm being raised and the party got away safely and rejoined their regiment next morning.

All eyes in the New Zealand Brigade were now turned towards Amman, and orders to attack the enemy there were eagerly awaited. It was felt that of all old scores yet to be wiped off against the Turks, this was the most important. The memory of those four days of bitter fighting in the rain and cold were yet fresh in everyone's memory.

General Chaytor's orders arrived in the evening. The advance was to commence at 6 o'clock in the morning of the 25th, the New Zealand Brigade attacking from the north-west with their right resting upon the Amman-Es Salt road; while the 2nd L.H. Brigade was to come in from the west following the road from Es Sir, by which they had come up from the plain. The 1st L.H. Brigade had orders to keep watch to the north and to be ready to support the attacks of the other brigades. The artillery which were coming up from the plains by the Jericho-Es Salt road were blocked by a broken bridge some miles down and could not be expected to assist, and the B.W.I. could not be expected until late in the day.

Strong opposition was expected, as the possession of Amman to the enemy was of vital importance to allow of the retirement of the Maan garrison and Turkish force operating to the south.

With the Wellington Regiment in the lead the New Zealand Brigade was soon within a few miles of the town. At a quarter to eight the first opposition was met with as the Wellington Regiment came under machine gun and artillery fire.

The regiment with one section of machine guns, one section 29th Indian Mountain Battery attached, was soon fully engaged and at 9 o'clock gained touch with the 2nd L.H. Brigade on the right.

THE CAPTURE OF AMMAN

At half-past 10 the Aucklanders were sent in on the right of Wellington and between the Wellington Regiment and the 2nd L.H. Brigade. The enemy's advanced posts were soon driven back upon his main line of defence which consisted of a series of machine gun nests.

At noon the Canterburys went forward under orders to test the main entrance to Amman with a view to galloping

THE HORSE-ARTILLERY NEGOTIATING A BLOCK ON THE ROAD.

through; but heavy fire from well-concealed machine guns held them up, a stone tower proving a great obstacle.

In the meantime the Auckland Regiment was steadily working forward and at 2.30 the Canterbury Regiment advanced its line.

A Canterbury troop got into a position from which they enfiladed the Turks in the Citadel, and a few minutes later the 10th Squadron and a troop of the 8th Squadron stormed the stone tower with the bayonet. By 3 o'clock the Canterburys held the town and in conjunction with the 5th L.H. Regiment were busily engaged in hunting out snipers and capturing prisoners.

In the stone tower were captured the Commander and Staff of the 146th Battalion and a total of 19 officers and 100 other ranks principally Germans. The advance of the rest of the New Zealand line was continued and the enemy in front of the Auckland and Wellington Regiments were driven into the wadi where they were attacked by the Canterburys coming in from the right through the town. 1700 prisoners here surrendered to the Auckland and Wellington Regiments. Amman railway station was captured at 4.30 with many prisoners, a complete wireless plant and much stores and war material.

The 2nd L.H. Brigade on the right of New Zealand occupied hill 3039 fraught with such bitter memories to the

ROMAN MASONRY IN AMMAN.

New Zealand Brigade; and the 1st L.H. on the left closed in upon the railway and captured many hundreds of prisoners who were endeavouring to get away.

So fell Amman, on September 25th, 1918, the Rabbath Ammon whose stout resistance made its seige and fall the crowning act of David's conquests.

Since the attack made by the Division in March the enemy had greatly strengthened his defences. He had built a series of redoubts in which were numerous machine guns. And the natural difficulties of the broken country made Amman a very hard nut to crack. But the systematic method of our men combined with quick outflanking of the machine gun nests overcame every obstacle. The ground was hard and favoured rapid movement on horseback whereas in the previous attack in March all work had to be done on foot.

The Surrender of the Turks

There remained now the remnants of the IV Army to be dealt with. These consisted of some 10,000 men including the garrison of Maan and some Arabs and Circassians. The movements of this force were doubtful. There was the probability that it would try to get down to the Jordan valley. But the difficulties in the way made this improbable; and there remained the Darb el Haj, the great route running north to Damascus and passing east of Amman. General Chaytor, therefore, sent the 2nd L.H. Brigade south to destroy the railway, as it was to our advantage to make the march of the enemy as long as possible and to increase his water difficulties.

If he chose the Darb el Haj, the nearest water to Kastal (where his advanced guard was reported to be), was (excluding Amman) at the Wadi el Hammam some 10 miles north of

4,000 Turkish prisoners at Amman.

Amman. Kastal is 15 miles south of Amman so the Turks would have a 25 mile march before them.

The 1st L.H. Brigade were sent early on the 26th to the Wadi el Hammam and captured there 105 prisoners and on the following day another 300.

On the 27th the 2nd L.H. Brigade captured prisoners at Leban station 12 miles south of Amman, who confirmed the intelligence as to the enemy's position, and at daybreak on the 28th the Turks were located near Kastal with three trains in the station.

A message was dropped upon the Turkish Headquarters by aeroplane, summoning the Commander to surrender and point-

THE ROMAN AMPHITHEATRE AT AMMAN.

ing out to him that all possible water north of him was held by us.

No answer was received to this and arrangements for the attack were made; but at 11.45 the Turkish Commander opened negotiations with the Commander of the 5th L.H. Regiment, sending to him a Staff Officer.

The situation was very difficult owing to large numbers of Arabs who surrounded the Turkish position intent upon looting. Any sign of a white flag was likely to precipitate matters, and the 2nd L.H. Brigade were despatched to Kastal. While they were coming up the Turkish Staff Officer formally agreed to a surrender of the whole force to General Chaytor; and Captain A. E. T. Rhodes, M.C., the Divisional Commander's A.D.C. pluckily penetrated the Turkish lines in a motor car and brought out the Turkish General, Kaimakam Ali Bey Whahaby, as a hostage.

Upon its arrival the 2nd L.H. Brigade put a cordon round the Turks; and the Arabs were told that any attempt to rush in on the Turks would be met by force. Even after our troops were in position the Arabs attempted to get at the hospital and had to be driven off.

This little episode presented an extraordinary spectacle, a British force guarding the enemy with whom it had been fighting for years, from the depredations of one of Britain's Allies. Next day the New Zealand Brigade arrived to relieve the 2nd L.H. and found the Turkish trenches manned by Light Horsemen and Turks with their guns jointly trained upon the Arabs.

The Brigade immediately set to work and cleared out all Arabs from a radius of 2000 yards and then mounting Hotchkiss guns fired at anything that appeared. This had the desired effect and the Arabs soon melted away. The Turks

GENERAL CHAYTOR AND THE COMMANDER OF THE TURKISH IV. ARMY WITH FRIENDLY BEDOUINS.

were then brought into Amman, and the Canterbury Regiment remained behind to guard the sick until transport arrangements could be made for them.

A squadron from the Auckland Regiment was sent to Madeba, the ancient Medba mentioned in the Book of Joshua. Here is the famous mosaic map, the oldest map existing of

MEN OF MOAB.

Palestine. It originally showed the whole of the then known world, and formed the floor of a Christian Chapel. In the town were captured a number of prisoners and a very large store of grain.

On October the 1st and 2nd the Brigade bivouaced at Amman on the old battlefield of March. On the 3rd began the march back to the valley. The night was spent at Es Sir and on the 4th the Brigade rode down the mountains to the Jordan valley, where the Canterbury Regiment rejoined and all vehicles which had gone by the Es Salt road.

The total captures by Chaytor's force since leaving the valley were as follows:—
Prisoners 10,332
Guns: 5.9 Gun 1; 5.9 How. 3; A.A. 1; 10 cm. 10; 77 mm. 32; 75 mm. 6; 3 Inch 2; 13 Pdr. (Bri). 2;
Total 57
Machine Guns 132; Automatic Riffes 13; Hotchkiss Rifles 1; Lewis Guns 1; Total 147

In addition there were two wireless sets, 11 railway engines, 106 railway trucks and carriages, 142 vehicles of all descriptions and an immense quantity of shell, S.A.A. and other material. A large number of motor lorries were abandoned by the enemy after being rendered useless.

Of these captures the New Zealand Brigade's share was:—
Prisoners 3,190
Guns: 4.2 3; 77 mm. 4; 75 How. 2; 75 mm. 4; 13
 Pdrs. 2; Total 15
Machine Guns 40; Automatic Rifles 8; Total .. 48
Wireless Sets 2
and large quantities of grain, ammunition wagons, horses, stores, etc.

In his report upon these operations General Chaytor lays particular stress upon the extraordinary vigilance of all ranks in the Jordan valley during those momentous days after General Allenby's attack had commenced on the left. Such

GERMAN OFFICERS TAKEN PRISONERS AT AMMAN.

was the excellence of the watch kept that not a movement of the enemy escaped notice. He also draws attention to the steadiness under fire of the B.W.I. battalions recruited from the natives of the West Indies. Another point he lays particular stress upon was the wonderful march of the New Zealand Brigade from the bridge at Ed Damieh to the mountain tops at Es Salt, and on that march the way in which the Canterbury Regiment quickly dealt with the opposition which they met. The attack upon Amman was pressed with the greatest of vigour. The method of defence by nests of machine guns made progress difficult and it was only by galloping to points of vantage and bringing fire to bear on the flanks of such machine gun nests that the opposition was finally broken down.

Whilst the Anzac Mounted Division was smashing the remnants of the Turkish IV. Army east of the Jordan, culminating in the surrender of the II. Corps at Kastal on Septembr 29th, the remainder of the Desert Mounted Corps had been closing in on Damascus.

Upon this city there had been retreating large bodies of Turks from the IV., VII. and VIII. Armies.

Early on the morning of October 1st the city was entered by our old friends the 10th Light Horse and all further retreat of any formed bodies of the enemy was cut off.

Large numbers who went further northward were without organisation, without transport—a mere mass of individuals

TURKISH PRISONERS AT ES SALT.

and were overtaken and captured in the push through to Aleppo, which was reached by the Desert Mounted Corps and the Arab Army on October 25th.

The Turkish Armies had now ceased to exist and the Armistice was arranged and came into force at noon on October 31st.

Though the casualties throughout these operations were remarkably small, as soon as the fighting was over the dreaded malaria broke out and in a few days the evacuations from this disease increased by leaps and bounds.

Our fight with malaria has been well described by Major C. Hercus, the Division's able D.A.D.M.S. He says:—

"During our progress across Sinai no indigenous malaria occurred in the Division. A few lapses amongst men previously infected were our only cases of malaria. It was not until at the end of April 1917 when we took up the line of the Wadi Ghuzzeh that the necessity for anti-mosquito operations along several miles of front on definite organised lines became apparent. It was early realised that in anti-malaria operations as in tactics, 'the best defence is a vigorous attack' and the direct limitation of mosquito activity by attacking them in their breeding places again proved itself to be the only practical method of controlling the incidence of malaria.

"Throughout the period, March 24th to October 31st, 1917, unceasing war was waged on the larvae of *anopheles turkhudi* which were found to be literally teeming in the pools and connecting streams of the wadi. Work was carried out by regimental parties working under the direction of the Sanitary Section. The work included weeding pools which were choked with green weeds in which the larvae swarmed, canalising connecting streams, oiling stagnant pools at five day intervals, and in filling in holes and shallow extensions of pools.

"This work was so successful that in September and October, Major Austen the British Museum Entomogolist to whose work and advice we owed so much, reported that he was unable to find a single larva in the Wadi Ghuzzeh. Our malarial incidence was correspondingly satisfactory. A few cases of *benign tertian* occurred in August and September, but the percentage was negligible. To prove that the enemy was only being held at arm's length Major Austen reports that a few days after we had moved forward to Beersheba active breeding was taking place from Tel el Jemmi to Shellal along the Wadi Ghuzzeh.

"After the capture of Beersheba we moved rapidly into Palestine, notorious as being a highly malarial zone. Fortunately it was the winter season and though infections occurred from mosquitoes hibernating in the wells around Jaffa, no epidemic occurred. It was realised, however, that if we were to spend the following summer in Palestine all our resources would be tested to the full. Steps were taken at once to organise more extensively than was necessary in the Wadi Ghuzzeh. Each unit, however small, was ordered to make available and to train malarial squads who were to be responsible for the anti-mosquito work in their immediate environments. The Anzac Field Laboratory was increased in size and malarial diagnosis units were formed in anticipation of the oncoming of the malarial season. The arrival of the warmer weather in April found the Division in the Jordan valley, that unique scorching valley some 1200 feet below the level of the Mediterranean, notorious for subtertian or malignant malaria, and in which with brief respite we were to spend the summer. The portion of the valley within our lines was crossed by several streams issuing from the hills and making their way down to the Jordan (the Auja, the Mellahah, the Nueiameh, the Kelt) and also contained the Jordan with several extensive marshes in the jungle which fringed its banks. The problem was a difficult one, the area involved was large, and the climatic conditions were trying. The Wadi el Mellahah was a particularly dangerous stream commencing in marshes in No Man's Land and running in a swampy valley choked with reeds across our line down to the Wadi Auja just before the latter entered the Jordan. Its whole valley was swarming with anopheles larvae. A working party of 1000 men was put on to the work and within a week the marshes in No Man's Land were drained as far as the enemy would permit; and the stream within our lines was canalised and cleared and the reeds cut or burnt out. No breeding could be demonstrated three days after the work was completed. The work in the other wadis consisted of canalising, cutting down jungle, filling in holes and oiling stagnant pools. The work when once carried out required constant attention and maintenance and the Sanitary Section with the unit malarial squads were continually employed on the maintenance work, special working parties being provided for the initial work. Two large swamps on the east bank of the Jordan, one at El Ghoraniyeh bridgehead, the other at El Henu ford, were found to be prolific breeding places and were drained and oiled. A large amount of this extensive work was carried out by the Indian Infantry Brigade. Breeding was also found to be rife at Ain es Sultan the source of Jericho's water supply, situated about one-and-a-half miles north of Jericho. Here there was an area of several acres in extent consisting of banana plantations and other cultivated land copiously irrigated by the over-flow from the Ain es Sultan spring. With the aid of a company of E.L.C. 600 strong working for two months breeding was supressed in this area.

"This in brief was the extent of the problem with which we were confronted. The measure of the success of the work carried out can be best estimated by the rise in the malarial incidence when we advanced into unprotected country. During the six months prior to the advance on September 21st the percentage of incidence of malaria in the Desert Mounted Corps was just over five and the majority of these cases were contracted in the front line where the evening breeze brought down hordes of mosquitoes from the Turkish positions and No Man's Land. In the reserve areas where the protective measures were fully operated the incidence of malaria was very low.

"On September 21st the N.Z.M.R. Brigade, the 1st L.H. Brigade, and the 1st and 2nd B.W.Is. moved forward into the Jisr ed Damieh area, swampy ground in which no attempt had been made to cope with the mosquito menace. The air was full of hordes of peculiarly aggressive and blood-thirsty mosquitoes, laden with as subsequent events proved the parasites of malignant malaria. It was here that a great deal of infection was incurred, for the 2nd B.W.I. Battalion which remained in this area when the rest of Chaytor's Force moved eastward into Moab, suffered severely. By October the 19th, seven officers, 719 other ranks of this unit (practically the whole strength), were evacuated with malignant malaria. Malaria began to appear in the mobile force in Moab on September 28th. The 1st L.H. Brigade were the first to experience the epidemic, evacuating 126 cases during the week. The N.Z.M.R. Brigade almost simultaneously commenced to evacuate large numbers of men acutely ill with the disease. The incidence reached a climax on October the 4th, when the 3rd L.H. Regiment evacuated 62, 1st L.H. Regiment 58 and the N.Z.M.R. Brigade 145. Many dramatic incidents occurred on the march back into Judea. There were cases of one man leading as many as eight horses, all his mates having been stricken down, and many men fell from their saddles in high fever. This exceptionally high rate of malignant malarial cases was experienced until October the 9th when the numbers fell abruptly. Additional proof that the Jisr ed Damieh area was responsible for the majority of the infections is supplied by the 2nd L.H. Brigade which moved directly from the protected area into the hills. Their evacuations from malaria during the period September 21st to October the 10th were 57 as compared with 239 cases in the 1st L.H. Brigade and 316 in the N.Z.M.R. Brigade for the same period. It has been truly said that the last phase of the Palestine Campaign was fought and won in the incubation period of malignant malaria which is 10 to 14 days.

"To people accustomed to ordinary benign tertian malaria the serious and dramatic nature of the malignant type was most alarming. The men attacked were suddenly prostrated in high fever, 105° and 106° F. being frequently reported, they were often delirious and occasionally maniacal. Unless treated immediately and efficiently with quinine the mortality was high. Once again it was amply proved that prevention is better than cure."

CHAPTER X.

Leaving the Jordan Valley for the Last Time.

The 5th, 6th and 7th of October were spent down by Jericho and on the 8th the Brigade began its last march out of the valley. The next few days were spent at Jerusalem and on the 14th October the Brigade arrived in its old camping ground at Richon-le-Zion.

Here equipment and clothing were overhauled and the men indulged in a good rest, though a certain amount of training was always carried on.

On October 13th the Canterbury Mounted Rifles left Ludd without their horses, for service overseas. The 7th L.H.

LEAVING THE JORDAN VALLEY FOR THE LAST TIME.
Jericho can be seen in the middle distance with the mountains of Moab in the background.

Regiment from the 2nd L.H. Brigade went also, the destination of both regiments being the Gallipoli Peninsula.

On the 27th of November with a strength of 25 officers, 464 other ranks and 81 horses the Regiment sailed from Kantara in the transport *Huntscastle* and disembarked at Chanak and camped at Camburnu near Kilid Bahr in an old Turkish hostel with the 10th Squadron at Maidos. Very bad weather was experienced on the voyage over, the transport was quite unsuitable, and many men were down with influenza.

The Regiment came under the orders of the 28th Division by whom they were treated as honoured guests. In conjunction with the 7th Light Horse Brigade the Regiment carried out a reconnaissance of the whole of the southern part of the

A Memorial erected by the people of Richon le Zion to the memory of the New Zealanders who fell at Ayun Kara on November 14th, 1917.

Peninsula to report as to how the Turks were carrying out the terms of the Armistice.

A great deal of time was spent in identifying the graves of those New Zealanders who had died on the Peninsula; and the studying of the Turkish position gave an immense amount of interest to the old hands who had been through those strenuous days at Anzac.

The sudden change from the heat of Palestine to the cold and wet weather of Gallipoli caused much sickness. Four officers and 106 other ranks were evacuated to hospital and one officer and 10 other ranks died and were buried in the English cemetery at Chanak.

The Regiment re-embarked on the *Norman* for the return to Egypt on the 19th January, 1919—strength 20 officers, 332 other ranks, leaving four officers, and 90 other ranks with all animals and transport to return by a later ship.

On November 14th a Memorial Service was held on the battlefield of Ayun Kara over the graves of those who fell in the action there on November 14th, 1917. The Jewish inhabitants of the colonies of Richon le Zion and Wadi Hanein, out of their gratitude to the New Zealand Brigade for their deliverance from the Turk on that day, provided the material for a Memorial Column and planted trees round the grave, undertaking to look after them in the years to come.

THE COMMANDER-IN-CHIEF AT THE RACE MEETING AT RICHON LE ZION.
Left. to right: Lieut.-Col. McCarroll, General Meldrum, Lieut.-Col. Whyte, General Allenby, General Chaytor.

The remainder of the month was taken up with regimental training varied by sports and rifle shooting competitions.

On the 11th December the Anzac Divisional Race Meeting was held and proved a great success.

While the Brigade was camped in the vicinity of Richon le Zion a disturbance occurred in the divisional area following on the murder of a New Zealander, during which a village and an Arab camp were burned and some 30 Arabs killed and injured.

For a very long time there had been a feeling of bitterness throughout the forces on account of the many acts of the natives and the manner in which they were protected against the troops. Claims for damage, alleged to have been done by our men were always supported and the men had to pay up. This began as far back as Sinai where regiments were made to pay for damage alleged to have been done to the date palms there. Later in Palestine our troops suffered very much from the thieving propensities of the Arab. Here again if any damage were done to crops or stock of a native the claim was upheld, but no redress was ever obtained against a native for theft. At Rafa some natives attacked two of our men severely wounding one and killing the other and also stealing his horse. Subsequently the dead on the Rafa battle-field were dug up and stripped. This happened again after the action at Ayun Kara which took place close by Surafend and there is not the slightest doubt that these villagers were responsible. All troops round Surafend had been suffering from the depredations of the Arabs and could get no redress. Many times our men suffered by being fired upon by the native inhabitants and it must be remembered also that the murder of this New Zealander was not the first that had been committed by the Arabs in this district. An Australian had been shot here only a short time before.

Many messages were received from Jewish settlers and senior officers of other formations that this disturbance would have a very good effect on the natives.

The result was that at the inquiry it was found impossible to get any evidence as to who took part in the disturbance. But such evidence as was obtained showed that parties from units outside the Division took part in the disturbance which was probably organised in the murdered man's unit. The evidence showed clearly that many small parties came over from Ramleh, Ludd and G.H.Q. at Bir Salim.

It appears that the murdered man's comrades feeling aggrieved that the murderer was not immediately brought to book went to the village and demanded his surrender. They were met by an insolent answer from the head man of the village so they determined to find him and the searching of the houses led to a collision with the natives which resulted in a riot.

As a result of this disturbance the Commander-in-Chief did not forward names of officers or men of Anzac Units which were camped at Surafend at the time and who had been recommended by the Divisional Commander for inclusion in the Peace Despatch; but subsequently he relented out of consideration for the good work of the Division and forwarded most of the names in a supplementary despatch.

At 9 o'clock on December 18th the Brigade began its march back to Egypt. The journey was carried out by easy stages bivouacking at Yebnah, Mejdel, Gaza, Belah, and arrived at Rafa at 3 o'clock in the afternoon of the 22nd. The next

ON THE SANDS AT RAFA—"FAITHFUL UNTO DEATH."

two or three days were spent in erecting tents and laying out camps. Now began training and lectures under the re-education scheme laid down for the New Zealand Expeditionary Force. The lectures covered a wide variety of subjects mostly of a commercial value and did much to keep up the interest and spirits of the men.

On the 22nd the Canterbury Mounted Rifles arrived at Port Said and reached the Brigade next day.

With rest, sports, and good food, the health of the Brigade soon showed much improvement. Malaria had almost gone, and the depleted ranks had been filled up again from reinforcements.

Regimental training and educational classes continued for the next few weeks. Disquieting news had been coming through for some time about the disturbances in Egypt. On Monday, March 10th, the rioting in Cairo had begun. Crowds paraded the streets breaking windows and looting, and were dispersed by police and troops armed with batons.

The rioting spread throughout the country and railways were torn up, telegraph lines cut, bridges damaged, and railway stations destroyed, and Europeans went in danger of their lives.

Wild rumours of these events had been coming through and they culminated on March 17th with the receipt of orders that the Brigade was to move to the Canal to re-equip.

Orders were received about noon to be ready to move at once to Kantara. The Brigade left Rafa by two special trains about 10 p.m. the same night with orders to draw horses, wagons, saddlery, ammunition, machine guns and full equipment on arrival at Kantara. But the procuring of these arms, equipment and horses proved to be slow, a good deal of the equipment required having to be obtained from Cairo and a very large number of the horses having to be shod. The work was pushed forward as fast as possible by detailing all regimental farriers for duty at the Remount Depot. On the 20th the Auckland Mounted Rifles moved off to Tanta a town in the Delta. They were quickly followed by the Canterbury Regiment and later by the Wellington Regiment and Brigade Headquarters.

The Auckland Mounted Rifles went to Damanhour by rail (about mid-way between Kantara and Alexandria), but after a few days were withdrawn and moved back to Tanta and from there to Mehallet Kebir and later to Mansura and then across the river to Talka where they remained until withdrawn for embarkation.

The Canterbury Mounted Rifles went to Benha and then to Tanta and later from Tanta to Kafr el Sheikh where they remained until withdrawn for embarkation.

The Wellington Mounted Rifles moved by road from Kantara to Benha by way of Salhia, Fagus and Zagazig. On arrival at Benha one squadron went to Cairo and the remainder of the Regiment moved to Quesla where they remained until withdrawn for embarkation.

Brigade Headquarters and Details from the Machine Gun squadron, signal troop, field troop, train, ambulance and mobile veterinary section were the last to move, and went to Tanta by road.

Each Regiment had its quota of machine guns, transport, A.S.C., field troop, signal troop, and ambulance.

THE RETURN OF THE NEW ZEALAND MOUNTED RIFLES TO THE DELTA.

The duty of each unit was to patrol the area allotted to it and to endeavour to trace the principal offenders who when caught were court-martialled and sentenced to various terms of imprisonment.

This duty imposed an enormous amount of patrolling upon our men. They were received with fear in the multitude of little villages with which the Delta is filled. Our men were tired of the war and exasperated at being retained in Egypt after the war was over and all other troops had returned, and so went about their work with a determination and thoroughness that soon brought peace and quietness to a turbulent community.

Though they were received in each village with fear, their departure was the signal for much regret and lamentation on the part of the head men and peaceable villagers, who found that though strict and stern to the evildoers, our men were generous and just to a degree.

Kafr el Sheikh was a typical disaffected area. The Canterbury Mounted Rifles reaching Tanta on the 22nd, Colonel Findlay was ordered to immediately proceed northwards. He had under his command his own regiment, four armoured cars and an armoured train. By a night march Kafr el Skeikh was surrounded at daylight and much amusement was given the men by the desperate efforts of disaffected individuals to escape. Among these was the Omda (or head man of the town). He was caught in a motor car. Later when peace and order were re-established the Omda was a firm friend of the Regiment and gave a dinner at which he made a speech and described his arrest. He said he was "in much fear of the men in the big hats and when a man came up to me after my arrest, told me to put my arms to my sides and to stand up and hold my head erect, at the same time placing his hand on his belt, I felt my last moment had come, and began trembling and to say my prayers and to consign myself to God, when he pulled out a camera and took my photograph, I could have kissed him."

A Court was set up and all rioters arrested and brought in. Some 30 to 40 a day were tried and sentenced to fines, imprisonment and the lash.

In a few weeks the whole district was patrolled and all disaffected people dealt with. The Gyppy went back to his usual industrious life a firm friend of the big men on the big horses. Those not actually friendly treated our men with civility and respect, and as one of our men says, "The whole district seemed very sorry when we at last moved off for demobilisation—we were not!"

The difficulties of keeping discipline in an army after the excitement of war is over is well known. For a while the work of keeping the Egyptian in order served to bury the grievances, fancied or real, of the delay in demobilisation. As the work became stereotyped other interests were brought in. Horse racing caused an immense amount of fun, and tennis proved a welcome recreation. Each unit improvised a race-course and tennis courts; and cricket pitches were to be seen wherever our men were camped.

Inter-squadron and inter-regimental tournaments were held and a cricket team journeyed to Cairo and played a strong team from the Gezireh Sporting Club.

But the events which undoubtedly gave the greatest pleasure were the horse races. The natives took an immense amount of interest and helped in the arrangements and provision of the various race-courses required. A totalisator run on New Zealand lines was established. No charge was made for admission and the inhabitants were invited to come and to bring their horses.

All Egyptians are great gamblers and a large amount of native money used to pass through the "tote."

The programme consisted usually of eight races of which two were open to the force in Egypt and two for native ponies.

The latter caused tremendous excitement and the native winners if at all favourites were greeted by the assembled natives with band and flagwaving and escorted in triumph back to the judge.

Race meetings were also held at Alexandria and at Cairo, at which regimental representatives won much prize money. Amongst the many races won, were the Victory Cup and Palestine Plate at Alexandria, the Birthday Plate at Quesna and the Farewell Cup at Cairo. A great race was one at Cairo for N.C.Os. and men and was won by Trooper Quigley's (C.M.R.) "Sunday," magnificently ridden by Trooper Wormald of the same regiment.

At Heliopolis, on May 24th, the Brigade won five out of the six horse events, including the Allenby Cup, won by "Gazelle," ridden by Capt. Black, W.M.R.

Sports—cricket, tennis, racing were all invaluable and kept the men interested and happy until the time at last came for demobilisation. They did more. They undoubtedly helped in the pacifying of the disturbed districts in which our men were. The brotherhood of "sport" is world-wide.

On June 17th orders were issued to all Brigade Units to send in their horses to the Remount Depot at Bel Beis.

The whole Brigade, minus horses, concentrated at Chevalier Island, Ismailia (Chevalier Island is near Ferry Post, it is bounded by Lake Timsah, the Suez Canal and the Sweet Water Canal).

After the great disappointment at Rafa, when the Brigade was re-equipped and went to its trying duties in the Delta

The New Zealand Mounted Rifles Football Team that won the celebrated Moascar Cup. Taken at Ismailia, 1919.

instead of being demobilised and sent home, the move to the Canal was welcomed with quiet thankfulness.

No story of the Mounted Brigade would be complete without a further reference to Aotea Home.

Quietly and unobtrusively there was opened in Heliopolis, the modern suburb of Cairo, on the 25th November, 1915, a small Convalescent Home of 25 beds for New Zealanders. By 1918 the Home had increased to 250 beds and was firmly established as the Home of the New Zealand Mounted Rifles Brigade. Its success was indeed great and as a Convalescent Home, founded and run by women and in which there was no enforced military discipline, it was a standing wonder to the Egyptian Expeditionary Force.

In 1915 three ladies of Wanganui, the Misses M. Macdonald, M. McDonnell and M. Duncan conceived the idea of forming a Convalescent Home and the idea was enthusiastically taken up in Wanganui, Rangitikei and Wairarapa.

A strong executive committee was formed and the Government accepted the offer with the proviso that the Home and all concerned were to be under the absolute control of the New Zealand Military Authorities, and that there should be on the staff of the Home a duly qualified Matron and two nurses.

The Military Authorities undertook to provide the necessary tents and buildings and rations and medicines, while the committee undertook to find the staff, the beds and bedding and comforts required.

On September 10th, 1915, six weeks after the proposal was mooted, the staff of "The Aotea Home for Convalescent N.Z. Soldiers" left New Zealand, arriving in Egypt on the 20th October. The personnel was as follows:—The Matron, Sister M. A. Early (Wellington Hospital), Sisters K. Booth and N. L. Hughes (Wellington Hospital), Misses E. and M. Macdonald (Mangamahu), R. Cameron (Wanganui), L. McLaren (Masterton), M. McDonnell (Wanganui) and Sergeant G. H. Sleight (Wanganui).

This devoted band carried on the Home with ever increasing success until the Mounted Brigade was disbanded in 1919.

In 1917 owing to the congestion at Aotea, an auxiliary home was opened at Port Said for the whole of the summer.

In October, 1918, a Convalescent Camp was established at Chevalier Island, as an adjunct to the N.Z. Training Depot, and was kept going (under the charge of the Misses Macdonald), until demobilisation took place.

An indication has been given in this book of the lack of home life for the men when on leave. Aotea provided a true home for all who passed out of hospital, and it went further, it was the home-centre for the whole of the Brigade. Though existing as a Convalescent Home for the N.C.Os. and men exclusively, yet all New Zealanders of whatever rank were welcome visitors there, and a table overflowing with good things from New Zealand was always open to any officer or man who chanced to be in Cairo.

The composition of the staff, a matron with two trained nurses and the promoters with their three helpers, proved to be exactly what was required. In Miss M. A. Early, the

AOTEA.
The New Zealanders home in Cairo, taken from the air.

matron, the Home possessed a head who combined with her thorough New Zealand Hospital training, a personality that endeared her to all who came in contact with her, and which insensibly enforced a code of conduct among the patients that was the admiration of the whole army. In this she was loyally and most ably supported by the voluntary section of the staff and the whole formed a band of women workers whose sustained efforts through a period of three and a half years is surely unique.

Apart from the advice of the medical officer who for the time being was attached to the Home, and apart from the ever-present good sense and ready help of Sergeant Sleight, the Home was entirely without military rule or regulations, and yet the discipline and good conduct of its inmates was unimpeachable.

Towards this high reputation the men themselves contributed no little part.

Aotea was a piece of New Zealand, a "home within a home," and every man felt in duty bound to treat the staff as his hostesses, and to his everlasting honour be it said the New Zealand Mounted Riflemen throughout the whole of the life of the Home "played the game."

Want of space draws this little story to its close, but one more reference to the voyage home must be made.

On June 30th, 1919, the N.Z.M.R. Brigade was disbanded and 75 officers and 1014 other ranks embarked on the transport *Ulimaroa* for New Zealand.

The final draft left on 23rd July, on the transport *Ellenga*, leaving an engineer officer, Captain Bale, and four men to hand over stores.

The officer commanding the Ismailia district came down to see the final draft away, saying that he could not let the men leave without letting them know his great appreciation of their good work and excellent behaviour during the trying times they had just been through.

This last draft of 1000 men eventually reached Australia and the transport put into Newcastle for coal. During the ship's stay here of several days they were treated with that great hospitality for which Australia is famous. Special trains were put on by the Commonwealth Government and the men taken to Sydney. Everything was done to make the visit of our men enjoyable and their bearing and behaviour after five years' strenuous warfare was the admiration of all those with whom they came into contact. As one of the Sydney papers said "They had a great time and Sydney loved them. In all our experience of the war we have known no finer and better behaved body of troops. They were everywhere. The theatres had them in hundreds, and (a fact that prohibition theorists may do well to notice) they kept resolutely sober, though all hotels were open and everybody was injudiciously keen as ever to offer them Australian hospitality."

A tribute also taken from a letter written to the officer commanding the troops on the ship, Lieut.-Col. E. J. Hulbert, is worth quoting. "It is my pleasure to convey to you the following resolution which we passed at last night's meeting of this Council, viz.—"That a letter be written to the officer commanding the New Zealand Forces congratulating him on the way the men have behaved themselves during their stay in Newcastle. In forwarding this resolution it was generally agreed by the Aldermen present, that the men under your care have during their stay in Newcastle, behaved in an exemplary manner. Their fine appearance combined with their general conduct has been the subject of much favourable comment by our citizens, and I have pleasure in conveying the decision of the Council to this effect to you. (Sgd.) Robert Gilison, Mayor, Newcastle."

And these men were returning after five years of war.

So ends our story—far far too short and too poor to do justice to these splendid men, who like Jason of old and his companions set forth with stout hearts and tireless bodies and rested not until the quest was won.

And some did not return.

> "*Blow out you bugles, over the rich Dead!*
> *There's none of these so lonely and poor of old,*
> *But, dying, has made us rarer gifts than gold.*
> *These laid the world away; poured out the red*
> *Sweet wine of youth; gave up the years to be*
> *Of work and joy and that unhoped serene,*
> *That men call age; and those who would have been*
> *Their sons, they gave, the immortality.*"
>
> RUPERT BROOKE.

ABBREVIATIONS.

G.O.C.	..	General Officer Commanding.
O.C.	..	Officer Commanding.
D.A.D.M.S.	..	Deputy Assistant Director Medical Services.
A.A. & Q.M.G.	..	Assistant Adjutant and Quartermaster General.
A.P.M.	..	Assistant Provost Marshal.
L.H.	..	Light Horse (The Mounted Rifles of Australia).
I.C.C.	..	Imperial Camel Corps.
N.Z.M.R.	..	New Zealand Mounted Rifles.
A.M.R.	..	Auckland Mounted Rifles.
W.M.R.	..	Wellington Mounted Rifles.
C.M.R.	..	Canterbury Mounted Rifles.
O.M.R.	..	Otago Mounted Rifles.
N.Z.M.C.	..	New Zealand Medical Corps.
M.G.S.	..	Machine Gun Squadron.
N.Z.V.C.	..	New Zealand Veterinary Corps.
N.Z.S.T.	..	New Zealand Signalling Troop.
N.Z.E.	..	New Zealand Engineers (Field or Signalling Troops).
N.Z.M.F.A.	..	New Zealand Mounted Field Ambulance.
E.E.F.	..	Egyptian Expeditionary Force.
R.H.A.	..	Royal Horse Artillery.
S.A.A.	..	Small Arms Ammuniiton.
A.G.H.	..	Australian General Hospital.
E.G.H.	..	Egyptian Government Hospital.
A.S.H.	..	Australian Stationary Hospital.
D.S.O.	..	Distinguished Service Order.
M.C.	..	Military Cross.
D.C.M.	..	Distinguished Conduct Medal.
M.M.	..	Military Medal

APPENDIX I.

GLOSSARY.

Descriptive terms which occur with place names, and the abbreviations used:

ABU	..	Father	KHAN	..	Inn
AIN	..	Spring	KHURBET	..	Ruin
BEIT	..	House	MAKHADET	.	Ford
BIRKET	..	Pool	NAHR	..	River
BIR	..	Well	NEBY	..	A Prophet
DEIR	..	Monastry	RAS	..	Head, cape, top
ED, EL, ER, ES, EZ	..	The definite article "The"	SHEIKH	..	Chief, Elder, Saint
JEBEL	..	Mountain	TEL	..	Mound (especially one covering ruins)
JISR	..	Bridge	WADI	..	A watercourse (normally dry)
KEFR	..	Village			

18A

APPENDIX II.

TABLE SHOWING COMMANDING OFFICERS
as at January 19th, 1916.

N.Z.M.R. BRIGADE—

Brigadier	Brig.-General E. W. C. Chaytor, C.B., N.Z.S.C.
Brigade Major	Major C. G. Powles, D.S.O., N.Z.S.C.
Staff Captain	Major G. A. King, D.S.O., N.Z.S.C.
AUCKLAND REGIMENT	Lieut.-Col. C. E. R. Mackesy
CANTERBURY REGIMENT	Major P. M. Acton-Adams (Temp.)
WELLINGTON REGIMENT	Major J. H. Whyte, D.S.O. (Temp.)
SIGNAL TROOP	Capt. E. J. Hulbert
FIELD TROOP	Capt. L. M. Shera
MOUNTED FIELD AMBULANCE	Lieut.-Col. C. T. H. Newton

N.Z.M.R. BRIGADE

NAME	DATE APPOINTED	DATE RELINQUISHED	REMARKS
Brig.-General E. W. C. Chaytor	20/12/15	22/ 4/17	In Command
Lieut.-Col. C. E. R. Mackesy	1/ 6/16	4/ 7/16	Temp. Command
,, ,, ,, ,,	13/ 8/16	19/12/16	Temp. Command
Lieut.-Col. W. Meldrum	23/ 4/17	30/ 6/19	In Command
Lieut.-Col. J. Findlay	2/ 9/17	1/10/17	Temp. Command
,, ,, ,,	16/ 5/18	28/ 6/18	Temp. Command
,, ,, ,,	2/ 3/19	10/ 3/19	Temp. Command

AUCKLAND MOUNTED RIFLES.

NAME	DATE APPOINTED	DATE RELINQUISHED	REMARKS
Lieut.-Col. C. E. R. Mackesy	29/12/15	23/ 4/17	In Command
Lieut.-Col. J. N. McCarroll	9/10/15	27/12/15	Temp. Command
,, ,, ,,	1/ 6/16	4/ 7/16	Temp. Command
,, ,, ,,	13/ 8/16	19/12/16	Temp. Command
,, ,, ,,	23/ 4/17	30/ 6/19	In Command
Major H. S. Whitehorn	14/11/17	25/11/17	Temp. Command
,, ,, ,,	16/12/17	15/ 1/18	Temp. Command
Major D. Monro	25/11/17	16/12/17	Temp. Command

APPENDIX II.—Continued.

CANTERBURY MOUNTED RIFLES.

Name	Date Appointed	Date Relinquished	Remarks
Lieut.-Col. J. Findlay	rejoined 18/ 2/16	30/ 6/19	In Command
Major P. M. Acton-Adams	28/ 6/16	17/ 7/16	Temp. Command
,, ,, ,,	3/10/16	18/11/16	Temp. Command
,, ,, ,,	2/ 6/17	8/ 6/17	Temp. Command
,, ,, ,,	12/ 9/17	1/10/17	Temp. Command
,, ,, ,,	22/ 1/18	4/ 4/18	Temp. Command
,, ,, ,,	16/ 5/18	28/ 6/18	Temp. Command
,, ,, ,,	7/ 2/19	12/ 2/19	Temp. Command
,, ,, ,,	27/ 2/19	1/ 3/19	Temp. Command
,, ,, ,,	26/ 6/19	30/ 6/19	Temp. Command
Major H. C. Hurst	20/ 8/17	27/ 8/17	Temp. Command
,, ,, ,,	7/ 9/17	12/ 9/17	Temp. Command
,, ,, ,,	7/ 7/18	21/ 7/18	Temp. Command
,, ,, ,,	19/ 9/18	9/10/18	Temp. Command
,, ,, ,,	10/ 1/19	19/ 1/19	Temp. Command
,, ,, ,,	2/ 3/19	10/ 3/19	Temp. Command
Major D. S. Murchison	2/ 9/17	7/ 9/17	Temp. Command

WELLINGTON MOUNTED RIFLES.

Name	Date Appointed	Date Relinquished	Remarks
Lieut.-Col. W. Meldrum	rejoined 20/12/15	23/ 4/17	In Command
Lieut.-Col. J. H. Whyte	4/11/16	8/12/16	Temp. Command
,, ,, ,,	23/ 4/17	29/12/18	In Command
Major A. F. Batchelor	31/10/16	1/11/16	Temp. Command
,, ,, ,,	2/ 7/18	9/ 7/18	Temp. Command
,, ,, ,,	29/12/18	30/ 6/19	In Command
Major C. Dick	23/ 4/17	12/ 6/17	Temp. Command
,, ,,	9/ 7/18	2/ 8/18	Temp. Command
,, ,,	11/ 8/18	28/ 9/18	Temp. Command

1st MACHINE GUN SQUADRON.

Name	Date Appointed	Date Relinquished	Remarks
Capt. R. P. Harper	15/ 7/16	15/ 2/18	In Command
Capt. A. C. Hinman	27/12/17	21/ 5/18	Temp. Command
,, ,, ,,	22/ 5/18	30/ 6/19	In Command
Capt. T. McCarroll	9/11/18	27/12/18	Temp. Command

APPENDIX II.—*Continued.*

2nd MACHINE GUN SQUADRON.

NAME	DATE APPOINTED	DATE RELINQUISHED	REMARKS
Capt. D. E. Batchelor	13/ 8/18	30/ 6/19	In Command

FIELD TROOP NEW ZEALAND ENGINEERS.

NAME	DATE APPOINTED	DATE RELINQUISHED	REMARKS
Lieut. H. A. Lockington	28/12/16	8/12/18	In Command
Lieut. Browne	14/ 1/17	28/ 9/17	Temp. Command
Lieut. H. G. Alexander	7/ 3/17		Temp. Command

SIGNALLING TROOP NEW ZEALAND ENGINEERS.

NAME	DATE APPOINTED	DATE RELINQUISHED	REMARKS
Capt. E. J. Hulbert	28/12/15	8/3/16	In Command
Lieut. Patrick, R. T. G.	8/ 3/16	7/12/18	
Lieut. T. G. Hinton	7/12/18	30/ 6/19	In Command

RARATONGAN COMPANY.

NAME	DATE APPOINTED	DATE RELINQUISHED	REMARKS
Capt. G. A. Bush	28/12/16	14/12/18	In Command

No. 15 CAMEL COMPANY.

NAME	DATE APPOINTED	DATE RELINQUISHED	REMARKS
Capt. J. G. McCallum	15/ 7/16	11/ 1/17	In Command
Capt. R. S. Priest	23/10/16	19/ 4/17	In Command
2/Lt. J. D. Stewart	5/ 2/17	20/ 3/17	Temp. Command
2/Lt. J. E. Jago	21/ 3/17	5/ 4/17	Temp. Command
Capt. J. B. Davis	16/ 7/17	30/ 7/18	In Command

No. 16 CAMEL COMPANY.

NAME	DATE APPOINTED	DATE RELINQUISHED	REMARKS
Capt. G. F. Yerex	16/ 7/17	31/ 7/18	In Command
Lieut. R. F. MacKenzie	7/ 1/18	27/ 2/18	Temp. Command
,, ,, ,,	22/ 4/18	12/ 5/18	Temp. Command
,, ,, ,,	12/ 7/18	31/ 7/18	Temp. Command

APPENDIX II.—Continued.

N.Z. MOUNTED FIELD AMBULANCE.

NAME	DATE APPOINTED	DATE RELINQUISHED	REMARKS
Lieut.-Col. C. T. H. Newton	16/ 2/16	17/12/17	In Command
Lieut.-Col. R. H. Walton	12/ 2/18	15/ 2/19	In Command
Major A. M. Trotter	17/12/17	12/ 2/18	Temp. Command

NO. 2 MOBILE VETERINARY SECTION.

NAME	DATE APPOINTED	DATE RELINQUISHED	REMARKS
Major J. Stafford	resumes command 24/12/16	4/ 9/18	In Command
Capt. E. E. Elphick	23/ 9/17	4/ 3/18	In Command
Capt. W. E. Barry	9/ 5/18	—	In Command

ANZAC MOUNTED DIVISIONAL TRAIN.

NAME	DATE APPOINTED	DATE RELINQUISHED	REMARKS
Major H. W. Smith	27/ 4/16	12/ 7/17	In Command

5th COMPANY N.Z.A.S.C.

NAME	DATE APPOINTED	DATE RELINQUISHED	REMARKS
Capt. S. H. Crump	1/ 8/17	2/12/17	In Command No. 5 Coy.
,, ,, ,,	18/ 5/18	17/ 3/19	In Command No. 4 Coy.
Lieut. E. N. Valpy	17/ 3/19	6/ 5/19	Temp. Command
Capt. G. R. Hutchison	3/12/17	17/ 3/19	In Command

A BRIGADE DIARY.

A Diary showing the more important moves taken by the N.Z.M.R. Brigade throughout the Sinai and Palestine Campaigns.

1915
Dec. 20 Left Gallipoli
 27 Arrival at Zeitoun (Cairo)

1916
Jan. 23 Marched out from Cairo for the Suez Canal
 29 Arrived at Serapeum
March 4 Took over portion of the Canal Defences at Ferry Post.
Apr. 1 Back to Serapeum
 7 Camped at Salhia
 24 Crossed the Canal (Turkish raid on Katia)
 25 Camped at Anzac Siding
May 11 Marched to Bir et Maler
June 20 Camped at Hill 70
Aug. 4-5 Battle of Romani
 6-12 Actions of Katia, Aogratina and Bir el Abd
 13 Camped at Hod el Amara
Sep. 16-17 Action at Mazar (M.G. Squadron only)
 18 Camped at Bir et Maler.
Oct. 27 Camped at Moseifig.
Nov. 13 Camped at Mazar.
 24 Camped at Mustagidda.
Dec. 20 Night march on El Arish.
 21 Occupation of El Arish.
 22 Night march to Magdhaba.
 23 Battle of Magdhaba.

1917
Jan. 1 Camped at Kilo 139.
 4 Camped on the beach at El Arish.
 8 Night March on Rafa.
 9 Battle of Rafa.
Feb. 23 Reconnaissance of Khan Yunus.
 23 Camped at Sheikh Zowaiid.
March 10 Camped at Rafa on the beach.
 25 Night march to Deir el Belah.
 26 First Battle of Gaza.
 27 Outposts at Deir el Belah.
April 17-18-19 Second Battle of Gaza.
 20-29 Outposts on Wadi Ghuzzeh.
 29 Camped at Tel el Fara.
May 23 Destruction of Asluj railway.
 28 Camped at Abasan el Kebir.
June 8 On the beach at Marakeb.
 18 Camped at Abasan el Kebir.
July 6 Camped at Tel el Fara.
Aug. 18 Camped at the Beach Marakeb.
Sept. 18 Returned to Abasan el Kebir.
Oct. 24 Night march to Bir el Esani.
 28 Moved to Khalasa.
 29 Night march to Asluj.
 30 Advance on Beersheba by all-night march.
 31 Action of Tel el Saba and Capture of Beersheba.

Nov.	1-6	Actions of Ras el Nagb and Tel Khuweilfeh.
	7-10	Advance through Philistia.
	14	Action of Ayun Kara.
	16	Occupation of Jaffa.
	24	Action of River Auja.
	25	Action of Khirbet Hadrah.
Nov.	26–Dec. 10.	Holding trenches North of Jaffa.
Dec.	26	Marched to Ashdod.

1918.

Jan.	12	Camped at Rishon le Zion.
Feb.	17	Marched to Bethlehem.
	19	Advance on Jericho.
	20	Action of El Muntar.
	21	Capture of Jericho.
	26	Returned to Richon le Zion.
Mar.	13-17	Marched to Bethlehem.
	20	Camped at Talaat ed Dumm.
	24	Crossed the Jordan.
	24	Action near Shunet Nimrin and began to climb the Mountains of Moab.
	25	Arrival on top of plateau at Ain es Sir.
	27-30	Battle of Amman.
March	31–April 1.	Withdrawal from the mountains.
April	2	Camped at Jericho.
April	9	Action on East Bank of Jordan.
May	1-6	Raid on Es Salt.
	16	Camped at Talaat ed Dumm.
	29	Camped near King Solomon's Pools.
June	3	King's Birthday Parade at Bethlehem.
	13	Camped at Talaat ed Dumm.
	15	Camped under Mt. of Temptation.
	16	At River Auja (Jordan Valley).
July	14	Action of Abu Tellul.
	19	Moved to Talaat ed Dumm.
	27	Marched to King Solomon's Pools.
Aug.	6	Camped at Talaat ed Dumm.
	7	Camped at Ain es Duk.
Sept.	5	Moved to River Auja.
	20	Night march up River Jordan.
	21	Actions at Jisr ed Damieh.
	23	Capture of Es Salt.
	24	Capture of Suweileh.
	25	Capture of Amman.
	27	Surrender of remainder of Turkish IV. Army at Ziza.
Oct.	4	Return to Jordan Valley.
	8	The Brigade leaves the Jordan Valley for the last time.
	14	March from Jerusalem to Richon le Zion.
Nov.	14	Memorial Service at Ayun Kara.
	27	Canterbury Mounted Rifles sail for Gallipoli.
Dec.	18	The Brigade marched to Yebna en route for Egypt.
	19	Marched to Mejdel.
	20	Marched to Gaza.
	21	Marched to Deir el Belah.
	22	Arrived at Rafa.

1919.

March	17	The Brigade received orders to proceed to Egypt to he quell the disturbances.
April–May–June.		On duty patrolling the Delta.
July	23	Final draft left Egypt for New Zealand.

NOTES.

The Authors' thanks are due to the many kind friends who assisted in the making of this book; and especially to Lt.-Col. W. J. Foster, Major Anderson, Lieut. Stevenson, Lieut. Dunning and Lieut. A. Murray (all of Headquarters A.I.F., Egypt); and also to Capt. Gotch (Survey of Egypt) for maps and to Corpl. Hogg (Cant. M.R.) for copying maps, and to M. Compton Smith, Esq. and W. G. Harding, Esq., of the New Zealand Lands and Survey Office, Wellington, for help in the preparation of maps.

Their thanks are due also to Lt.-Col. J. N. McCarroll, Capt. A. Rhodes, Capt. M. Johnson, Corpl. McKay, Padre Isaacson and Padre Macdonald and to those others who so generously lent their photographs; and the Authors regret that owing to limited space so many thus kindly lent were not reproduced.

www.ingramcontent.com/pod-product-compliance
Ingram Content Group UK Ltd.
Pitfield, Milton Keynes, MK11 3LW, UK
UKHW022121230426
12048UKWH00011BA/653